# EDUCATION
## AND THE FUTURE

Selected Articles on Education from
THE FUTURIST: A Journal of Forecasts, Trends, and Ideas About the Future
and The World Future Society BULLETIN

### Edited by Lane Jennings and Sally Cornish
**Introduction by Christopher J. Dede,**
Associate Professor, University of Houston at Clear Lake City,
and President, Education Section, World Future Society

**World Future Society**
4916 St. Elmo Avenue
Washington, D.C. 20014, U.S.A.

Published by
**The World Future Society**
4916 St. Elmo Avenue
Washington, D.C. 20014 USA

Copyright © 1980 by
The World Future Society

All rights reserved. No part of this book may be reproduced by any means nor transmitted, stored electronically, or translated into any language without the written permission of the publisher.

**Library of Congress Cataloging in Publication Data**

Main entry under title:

Education and the future.

    Bibliography: p.
    1. Educational research—Addresses, essays, lectures.
    2. Social prediction—Addresses, essays, lectures.
    I. Jennings, Lane.  II. Cornish, Sally.  III. Futurist.
    IV. World Future Society. World Future Society
      Bulletin.
LB1028.E275     370     80-13453
ISBN 0-930242-09-2

This volume is the second in a series, *The Futurist's Library*. Previously published in the same format is *1999: The World of Tomorrow* (160 pages, $4.95)

Series Editor: Edward Cornish
Production Manager: Peter Zuckerman
Editorial Coordinator: Hugh Myers
Design: Diane Smirnow
Cover Art: Diane Smirnow from a painting by Gerard C.
          Pilachowski for the December, 1976 cover of
          THE FUTURIST

# TABLE OF CONTENTS

## Introduction
**Educating for the Future**
by Christopher J. Dede .................................................. 5

## Selections from THE FUTURIST

**Population and Education**
by Joseph F. Coates ..................................................... 8
How demographic trends will shape tomorrow's schools

**An Educator Looks Back from 1996**
by Ronald E. Barnes ................................................... 15
A vision of individual-centered learning and its impact on traditional goals and methods of education

**Education for a Leisure Society**
by Robert Strom ....................................................... 19
How learning could replace job-status as the key to social worth and self esteem

**Beating Unemployment Through Education**
by William Abbott ..................................................... 24
Lifelong learning offers a way to fight worker obsolescence

**Is Going to College Worth the Investment?**
by Andrew Spekke ..................................................... 31
In the years ahead, the road to success may no longer lead through academia

**Illiterates with Doctorates**
by Peter H. Wagschal .................................................. 39
In an electronic age, the "three Rs" may no longer be the basics of education

**Robots in the Home and Classroom**
by Michael Freeman and Gary P. Mulkowsky .......................... 41
From science fiction to scientific fact, robots are coming to teach and entertain

**Educational Packagers: A Modest Proposal**
by Philip Kotler ....................................................... 46
New communications technology is opening many options to the traditional classroom

**The Case of the Vanishing Colleges**
by Samuel L. Dunn .................................................... 50
Before this century ends, the residential college may have vanished from the educational scene

**America's Educational Futures 1976-2001**
by Harold G. Shane .................................................... 58
A summary of how 50 leading thinkers view the future of education in the United States

**Education for Tomorrow's World**
by Harold G. Shane .................................................... 64
An analysis of 10 leading problems facing U.S. society, and their significance for education in the future

**The Pre-Schooler and the Future**
by Chester Pierce ..................................................... 68
The importance of nursery school experiences in shaping the attitudes and skills of the citizens of the 21st century

**Futurizing Education**
Six mini-articles by futurist educators presenting examples of how future studies techniques can be successfully applied in the classroom .............. 71

## Selections from the World Future Society Bulletin

### Educational Technology: The Next Ten Years
   by Christopher J. Dede .............................................. 84

Instead of resisting new technologies, teachers need to speak out forcefully to guide the development of machines that *help* teachers, and students, achieve the goals of education

### Images of the Future: Some Questions for Study
   by Gary D. Wooddell ................................................ 91

How the future shapes the present through the individual and collective expectations that motivate action

### Education and the Creation of the Future
   by Scott W. Erickson .............................................. 97

More than just preparing students for a changing world, future studies in the classroom can actually contribute to bringing change about

### Educational Predictions: Past, Present and Future
   by Betty Dillon and Ralph Wright .................................. 102

A look at predictions by educators in the years 1900 to 1940, and their implications for the accuracy of today's forecasts on the future of schools and schooling in the United States

### Looking at the Future of Education
   by Dwight W. Allen and Jake Plante ................................ 111

An inquiry into the reasons behind the popularity of futures studies among students and the problems they pose for teachers

### Educational Futures: A Reconstructionist Approach
   by Jim Bowman, Chris Dede, and Fred Kierstead ..................... 118

An assessment of today's educational process and how outmoded systems might be revamped to achieve the goal of participatory, life-long learning for all

## Suggestions for Further Reading
A Selective Bibliography of Books on Issues in Education and the Future ........... 120

 

    The World Future Society is a non-profit, non-partisan association of people interested in the future. The Society takes no position on what the future will be like or should be like, but serves as a neutral clearinghouse and forum for a wide variety of forecasts and opinions from scholars, government officials, planners, and others all over the world.

    Interested persons may join the Society by sending their name, address, and occupation plus $18 for their first year's dues to: Membership Committee, World Future Society, 4916 St. Elmo Avenue, Washington, D.C. 20014. Membership in the Society includes a subscription to the Society's bimonthly magazine *The Futurist;* subscription without membership may be obtained for the same price as membership. Persons joining the Society will receive information on other Society publications and programs.

# INTRODUCTION

by Christopher J. Dede
President, Education Section, WFS

Imagine the future as a tree. Its trunk represents the present; its branches, the alternative futures possible given the confines of today. As we move in time toward the future, we move up the trunk toward the branches. Each decision we make chops off a branch—destroys an alternative future. By the time we reach the future, only one branch remains: the unitary present; and again, a host of possible future alternatives spreads out before us.

The distinctions between theoretical and applied futures research can be explained within this metaphor. Theoretical work in futures centers on forecasting the number and nature of the major branches. Applied futures research is focused on delineating how we should make decisions so as to chop off the undesirable branches and direct the present into the best of our alternatives futures.

Some of the contributions to this volume lean toward the theoretical end of educational futures research; others, toward the applied. All the articles represent considerable achievements by their authors, for the task of forecasting alternative futures for education is extremely difficult. Education, being purely a social phenomenon, has futures far more confused and ill-defined than the futures of technology or global resources or population—which are all sharply limited by physical constraints in the present.

On the other hand, this very challenge of prediction makes educational futures research an exciting and crucial area. Using Peter Wagschal's definition of a futurist as one who makes other people's futures more real to them, an educational futurist can synthesize a viable, positive alternative future for education and then can interest others in making this scenario a reality. The technological futurist works with physical inventions, but the educational futurist works with social inventions, discoveries forged by the mind and based ultimately on human nature and on present value systems.

The heart of this process is to discover the full range of alternative futures for education and then to describe a series of decisions that avoids the undesirable branches. Of course, an understanding of the larger set of societal futures is crucial, for education is at present far more shaped by forces outside its institutions than by actions within them. Thus, education is in a paradoxical situation: its institutions are society's sole long-range mechanism for anticipating and controlling the future, and yet its current policies reflect the vagaries of hundreds of contemporary issues.

The most obviously futures-relevant educational institutions in our society are the schools; for teachers are trying to anticipate events by up to thirty years—to the time when their current students become the new generation of decision-makers. Yet the focus of educational futures should not be confined to this one area alone. Though to most people, the word "education" is synonymous with "schools," a broader definition of education— one that includes schools, on-the-job training, the media, and communications-oriented community action organizations—is far more useful. This shift in definitions is crucial in our rapidly changing, highly technological society, as the need for an education that is continuous, universal, life-long, and community-focused becomes increasingly clear. Much of the uncertainty in forecasting educational futures stems from how inefficient we now are at coordinating the efforts of these various institutions, and how radically different the future might be if we were to conceptualize education more broadly.

The need for such a reconceptualization of education has never been more crucial than now, when most serious forecasters see American society—and the entire world—entering a fifty-year period of crisis and turmoil. For a long time, a continuing debate has raged between optimists and pessimists in futures research: those who believe the majority of plausible future branches to be positive, and those who believe the majority to be negative. In the last decade, the pessimists have advanced a series of compelling arguments which have convinced most professionals in the field that we are entering a perilous period in human history. (Detailed discussion of this issue is impossible in the space of this brief introduction. For a more thorough treatment, see "The Future of Technology," in *Handbook of Futures Research* (Jib Fowles, ed.), Westport, Connecticut: Greenwood Press, 1978.)

Whether one believes the optimists or the pessimists, education emerges as playing a crucial role during the next two generations. Ironically, both sides agree that education is extremely important in arriving at a positive future, but disagree on what role education should play. Optimists, such as Daniel Bell, Herman Kahn, and Buckminster Fuller, visualize a "post-industrial" society with information as the key resource, educational institutions as a central component of societal decision-making, and educational advancement as a key to power. Accordingly, optimists call for education oriented primarily toward training, toward the production of a scientific elite, and toward managing a technocracy.

Pessimists, such as Willis Harman, Robert Theobald, Jim Bowman, and Fred Kierstead, see education playing a very different role in the next fifty-odd years. These futurists cite reconstructionist philosophies as the theoretical basis for education re-directing American society toward alternative goals and values appropriate to the difficult futures our reliance on technology has created. Such an alternative society would still have communications-based technologies as a central resource, but would move toward a more democratic, less bureaucratic form of government based on conservation, low-complexity technology, and non-accumulative lifestyles. Pessimists, then, call for new types of educational centers oriented toward instilling creativity, community-building, and group problem-solving skills.

The central issue is not which group is more correct, but that *both* groups see education as the crucial component in a bright future for humankind. For better or for worse, our generation of educators lives in a time fraught with choices whose outcome will alter the course of civilization. We have a tremendous responsibility; we are the individuals whose actions—in schools, media, workplaces, communities—will shape the decisionmakers in this period.

Without forward-looking education, our positive futures will vanish. To remain embroiled in a crisis-oriented, present-oriented approach to education is to decide—by default—to abdicate our responsibilities. This volume, and the overall work of the World Future Society's Education Section, both represent expressions of commitment to better education and to a brighter future.

006# SELECTIONS FROM THE
# THE FUTURIST

# Population and Education: How Demographic Trends Will Shape the U.S.

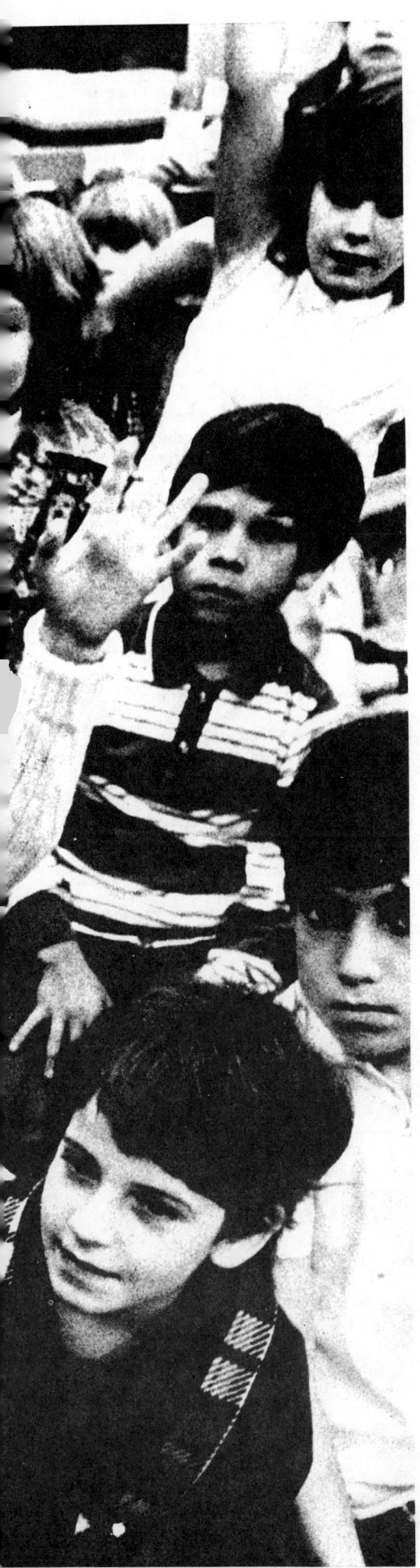

by Joseph F. Coates

**Changing life-styles are transforming U.S. schools. More women are entering the work force and marrying later, and fewer babies are being born. Unless population trends are better understood, education planners may be increasingly baffled by changes in school enrollment.**

Birthrates in the United States have declined significantly over the past 18 years, with 28% fewer children being born now than were born in 1959. This "baby bust," which has followed the post-war baby boom, has already reduced the number of children enrolled in elementary school by about 10%, and a drop of another 7 or 8% by the mid-1980s is certain. As the children born during the baby bust become older, their numbers will affect high school enrollments. During the 1980s, enrollments may drop as much as 25%. These statistics represent a basic, nationwide trend, but other demographic factors—those which most concern planners on the regional, state and local levels—make school planning much more complex and uncertain than simple aggregate fertility rates suggest.

Other trends that will affect education:

• Women are increasingly entering the work force and staying longer. This will create more demands to change curriculum and add new school-centered services.

• Continued immigration will place special burdens on school systems in major cities, where immigrants tend to settle.

• Local mobility—the ease with which populations move within this country—will create increasing uncertainty among education planners.

The principal impact of these demographic trends occurs at the state and local levels. Since this is where most education planning is done, improved demographic study must begin at these levels. To see just what problems arise from these trends, it is useful to examine them in detail.

**Left:** Crowds can be fun, but they may not be beneficial to mental development. Children placed together with other children for extended periods of time—as in daycare—may experience slower intellectual growth.
Photo: Joe Di Dio, National Education Association

## The Changing Family

The traditional image of the family—mother, father, and children, around which public policy has been framed—is increasingly at odds with reality. The growth of the single-parent family is one of the major demographic trends affecting schools. Approximately 45% of children born in 1976 will have lived with a single parent for some time before reaching 18 years of age. Between 1970 and 1976, the number of children living with a divorced mother increased by two-thirds, and the number living with a single mother increased by about 40%. The number of female-headed families with children has increased by over 250% since 1950. These families comprise 41% of all poverty-level families; the limited income of these families creates new demands and stresses on all public services, including schools.

Another factor relating to marriage and the family which can influence the school is the tendency of women to defer marriage. In 1970, 12% fewer 20-year-old women had been married than in 1960. The decline in the number of married 24-year-olds was only 7%. This suggests that women are not turning away from marriage in any great number; they are merely delaying it. During that period of deferral, women tend to enter the work force or to continue their education in order to prepare for work.

The entry of women into the work force is perhaps the demographic trend that most profoundly influences curriculum, services, the child's environment and the whole family structure. The shifting roles that women assume as they enter the work force create a demand for curriculum changes to prepare women for their entry. And working mothers need services to take care of their children.

The effects on schools of women in the work force will be great. First, there will be a decline in volunteerism. At a time when the school system is experiencing greater demand for volunteers to meet the pressures for more services, fewer women will be available. An example of this has been experienced by the League of Women Voters. Much of the envelope-licking and stuffing that once was done with free labor now must be done on a fee-for-service basis because so many of the League's members have moved into the work force. Similar effects will soon be felt by schools.

Demographers associate increasing female participation in the work force with a decline in the number of children a family will bear. And education encourages participation in the work force. In the future there will be a cycle in which education promotes work, work promotes a decline in fertility, and declining fertility increases the problems of elementary and secondary schools. The increasing number of dual-income families, especially among middle-class managerial and professional households, provides more discretionary money, money which may lead such families to send their children to private schools or to relocate their residences outside of central cities. The exodus of middle-class families may bring about a big-city public school system whose sole purpose is to educate the underclass.

Female participation in the work force may lead to changes in the purposes and structures of public schools. Schools will face an increased demand to overcome stylized gender roles associated with occupational choices. Career counselling may change to meet new work-sex roles. The new role models for girls will probably increase the number of students desiring vocationally-oriented curricula and counselling. Deferred marriage and earlier entry into the work force may create a demand for curricula that focus upon independent living, and training in financial management and personal affairs. Those who live in the lowest economic strata and are burdened by small children or single parenthood need education that focuses on improving one's economic status through continuation course certification and specially-tailored high-school programs.

The increased demand for day care and nursery care for preschool and young school children of working mothers may be met by the school systems. For children roughly aged 7 to 13, the school day is not quite long enough to accommodate the needs of single-parent working households. There are efforts in some communities to extend the length of afternoon care, not by extending the school day, but by extending the use of school buildings. Some 15% of children in this age group can be usefully served by extending the use of facilities from 3 p.m. to 6 p.m.

The family is becoming less of a dominant factor in the socialization of the child. A child now entering the first grade may have been exposed to nursery school or day care. He may have been involved with Head Start or related programs, or have had extensive exposure to television. The size of his family is different from what it was for children born 10 years ago. Organized religious groups, grandparents and other members of the family, and adult neighbors seem to be playing a declining role in the socialization of children.

## Working Women—and Men

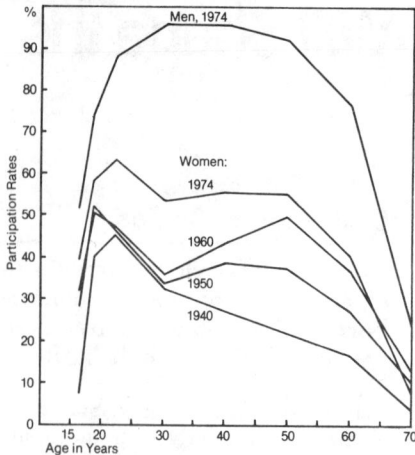

Labor force participation rates for men in 1974—and for women in 1974, 1960, 1950, and 1940. More women are entering the work force, and fewer are dropping out during the childbearing years. This trend is increasing demand for child care.

Chart: Juanita Kreps, ed., *Women and the American Economy*, 1976.

## How Many Will Be Born?

Much of the future will be influenced by present age distributions and birth and death rates that prevail now and in the coming years. The age composition of the population is in a state of continuous flux. As the post-World War II baby boom age group matures, it will create "waves" of expanding and contracting age groups.

Babies produced by the post-World War II "baby boom" generation will create a second-wave effect which is likely to create an upswing in school populations by the mid-1980s. Yet it appears that the long-range trend in the United States is toward fewer children. Recent survey data collected by the Bureau of the Census on the birth expectations of young wives aged 18 to 24 show that nearly 75% expected two or fewer children. If these young wives achieve their expectations—and other fertility surveys have shown a fairly close correlation between the number of children that women say they want and the number that they actually have—then they will experience an average 2.17 births per woman. This works out almost exactly to replacement fertility.

The reduced amount of time available for parenting in families where females work may create a demand for new school services that deal with functions traditionally learned at home. Schools may need to teach the skills of eating, drinking, dressing, social behavior, deportment, manners, self-control, and other functions to compensate for reduced parental care. In view of the underuse of schools and of surplus teacher capacity, the possibility of extending school functions into these areas may seem quite attractive to teachers' unions. However, a word of caution is necessary: Data from social psychological literature indicate that children put together with large numbers of other children for extended periods of time may suffer a reduced mental development.

### Immigration and Non-English Speaking Students

Immigration accounts for one-fourth of net population growth in the United States. Since immigrants tend to settle in metropolitan areas, continuing immigration will create a chronic source of stress for big-city school systems.

There is an interesting relationship between high school dropout rates and the language spoken at home. Where English is the language spoken, or where English is spoken along with some other non-English language, the dropout rate is between 8 and 10%. But where a language other than English is the only language spoken at home, the dropout rate rises to 38%.

Among the specific population of those of Spanish origin, the situation is even worse. The principal non-English language spoken in the United States by people four years old and over is Spanish, spoken by almost 10 million people. Among school-age children, about five million speak Spanish as their primary language. Where English is spoken among families of Spanish descent, the dropout rate of their children is 14 to 15%. Where only Spanish is spoken, the dropout rate is 45%.

Among students who do not measure up to standard performance, non-English speaking students represent the biggest problem. Only 10% of English-speaking students are two or more grades below their peers. In grades one through four, approximately 17% of the non-English speaking students are two grades below mode; at the high school level, some 35% are two or more grades below mode.

The implication of these statistics is significant when they are coupled with the long-term movement of American society toward that of an information society. Approximately 55% of the work force is now in the information business. This situation raises questions about the value of bilingual education, and whether it denies students the chance for an economically useful education. The data suggest that, as now taught, students of foreign origin may be precluded from getting their first foot up on the economic ladder.

If the higher cost of bilingual education of students whose primary language is not English precludes other priorities, the level of education of English-speaking students may be reduced, further accelerating the decline of the urban school systems. Whether or not bilingual education continues, the steady stream of foreign-born students will renew the kinds of cross-cultural stresses associated with students who are hard to acculturate. This often results in delinquency and poor school performance, particularly for urban school systems. And proposed changes in the status of new illegal immigrants might encourage them to make greater use of the school system for their children. This will especially affect big-city schools and the smaller communities in the Southwest and in California.

Preschooler "reads" to himself. The increasing entry of mothers into the workforce will increase the demand for daycare.    Photo: Joe Di Dio, National Education Association

### Local Mobility and Internal Migration

Internal mobility and migration are perhaps the demographic factors that most perturb education planners at the state and local level. Between 16 and 18% of the U.S. population moves annually. The data reveal some evidence that people seem to be attracted to the city for work and other opportunities; but as they enter the childbearing years, people have a tendency to move out of central cities.

The overall effect of internal migration is a trend of movement out of the city and into suburban and rural areas. From 1970 to 1974, cities experienced a net exodus of 1.8 million people. The eight largest cities saw a net out-migration of 1.2%. Population growth in rural areas during this same period was 5.6%, contrasting with a growth of 4% for the nation as a whole. Educational management in these nonmetropolitan and small-community growth centers may run into special problems, because such growth was unexpected. The tax base may be inadequate to meet the demands caused by the influx of people, and the social values of the new migrants may be substantially at odds with those of the local people. The redistribution of population will create an acute problem for education planning in boom towns. In order to come to grips with the energy crisis, we will open up coal resources in Wyoming, the Dakotas, Colorado and other areas in the West, and Kentucky and southern Illinois in the east. One can reasonably anticipate surges in population for which the local communities in these areas will be totally unprepared.

There is a long-term trend toward the equalization of regional incomes. Once the nation's economic backwater, the sun belt areas of the South, the Southwest and southern regions east of the Rockies are all currently undergoing economic growth. In the early 1930s, regional income varied from 50% below average to 50% above the national average. In 1974 this range had narrowed to about 15% to 20%. Equalization may reduce regional differences in cost and quality of education, undercutting regional disparities of funds available per child on a statewide basis.

Migration in and out of metropolitan areas is having the effect of concentrating minority students within the big cities and non-minority students outside of those big cities. This phenomenon, along with concern about the quality of schools, and about the curricula, are increasing white and middle-class dissatisfaction. There are only a small number of options open to middle-class parents who do not wish to have their children experience the effects of the decline in metropolitan school systems. One alternative is to withdraw the pupil to a pri-

### About the Author

Joe Coates is Assistant to the Director of the Office of Technology Assessment for the U.S. Congress. Before joining OTA, he served on the staff of the National Science Foundation and the Institute for Defense Analyses. He has also worked as a research chemist and as a lecturer in philosophy and chemistry, technology assessment, and futurism.

His previous articles in THE FUTURIST include: "Technology Assessment: The Benefits .... the Costs ... the Consequences" (December 1971) and "The Future of the U.S. Government" (June 1972). His address is Office of Technology Assessment, U.S. Congress, Washington, D.C. 20510.

This article is adapted from testimony before the Subcommittee on Elementary, Secondary, and Vocational Education of the Committee on Education and Labor of the U.S. House of Representatives, May 10, 1977, and is based on an analysis he made for the Office of Technology Assessment.

vate or parochial school. The data suggest that families that have the financial option of sending their children to private schools tend to exercise it. Even families with incomes in the $10,000-$15,000 range often send children to private schools.

For families without the income to send their children to private schools, the alternative may be a change of residence. Other options include early graduation and entry into college—a process that may stimulate programs of graduation based on credentials—and tracking, or grouping students by ability. In any case the net effect of all these alternatives open to a white or middle-class population—those dissatisfied with school systems in urban areas—is resegregation.

### Teenage Childbearing

The only group in the United States now undergoing significant expansion in birthrates is that of females under age 15. Of the 3,144,198 live births in the United States in 1975, 12,642 were born to girls under 15 years of age. This situation has several implications for the educational system. Young motherhood interferes with the ability of the mother to continue her education. Children who are born to young mothers are far more likely to suffer a variety of congenital defects. These children born to adolescent mothers are themselves more likely to bear children at an early age, thus further burdening the school system.

Junior high school curricula, services and goals have never come to grips with the onset of puberty. Especially critical is the increasing rate of early sexual activity among boys and girls of junior high school and high school age, creating both immediate and long-term social and educational problems and needs associated with adolescent childbearing.

### Decline in Enrollment

The national decline in enrollments does not imply universal distress—nor is it a universal phenomenon. A decline is occurring predominantly in the Midwest, Mid-Atlantic, and Pacific states,

## Bringing the School to the Worker

Employers around the world are recognizing the need for employees to have more than mere technical training, according to a report by the Organization for Economic Cooperation and Development (OECD).

If an employee is given an opportunity "to develop his whole personality" and engage in "creative self-expression," the report says, he will contribute more to the economy: "Progress towards industrial democracy depends upon the existence of well-informed employees."

Part of the movement to combine education and training is based on the growing belief that changing jobs or social classes is a social right. But the need to absorb greater amounts of information just to keep up with technical matters is barring most employees from taking the time and money initiative to enroll in nontechnical courses. The OECD argues that the employee requires financial support, and the chance to devote some of his working hours—or an extended sabbatical leave—to concentrated study. In the future, the report states, the employer will provide on-the-job study facilities—places where a worker can study during the working day, without loss of income. For those who are unemployed, governments will sponsor training programs that lead directly to available jobs.

A major problem facing most adult education systems is their failure to attract the uneducated. According to the OECD, the majority of adults enrolled in courses have already had more than 16 years of formal education. Present systems often have course prerequisites, or courses that are beyond the capacity of the uneducated. Many courses simply have no practical relevance to workers' careers. The OECD report says that adult education in the future will need to re-design methods of certification and accreditation to meet the needs of those wishing to catch up with the national educational level. Adult school systems will also need to take into account the differences in learning characteristics between adults and children: Too many systems are based on traditional schooling methods that remind former unsuccessful students of their unhappy school careers. Thus many adult dropouts avoid repeating the shame and embarrassment of their youth.

In order to accommodate the undereducated worker, adult schooling will be more accessible and will be complemented with specialized, industry-based, guidance counseling systems. Teachers may be replaced by part-time educators recruited from the ranks of professions and industrial leaders. Courses will be geared toward functional literacy, second-language courses for immigrants, vocational retraining, and civic and cultural literacy. They may be taught in mini-courses conducted at the workplace, with correspondence courses, or through learning machines and texts located in industrial lunch rooms and recreation areas.

Innovative adult education systems, the report claims, may revolutionize world attitudes toward education. Governments and industries may come to see adult education as a means of fostering true democracy by giving all workers the opportunity for personal, career, and cultural advancement.

Lone student works in an empty classroom. Declining enrollment may make scenes like this more common.

Photo: Joe Di Dio, National Education Association

while the South and Southwest are experiencing a boom. To complicate matters further, both enrollment declines and increases often occur in the same state, with different small districts experiencing both shrinking and growing student populations. Especially hard hit by the general trend will be the big cities, already in great fiscal distress.

Thirty-seven states have experienced enrollment declines since 1970. Sixteen of these states have lost at least 4% of their students. Simultaneous with the declining enrollments has been an increase in minority enrollment in big cities. In the period between 1968 and 1974, the average student minority enrollment was 67.1%. School enrollment in the 27 largest cities peaked in 1970, and is now back at the level it was in 1962. The exodus seems to have occurred primarily among middle-class

# Regional Incomes

Change in per-capita personal income as a percentage of the U.S. average, 1929-1974. Regional income levels are becoming more equal as the South and Midwest begin to catch up with the traditionally dominant northeastern and far western states. Broader national distribution of income will tend to equalize regional educational differences.

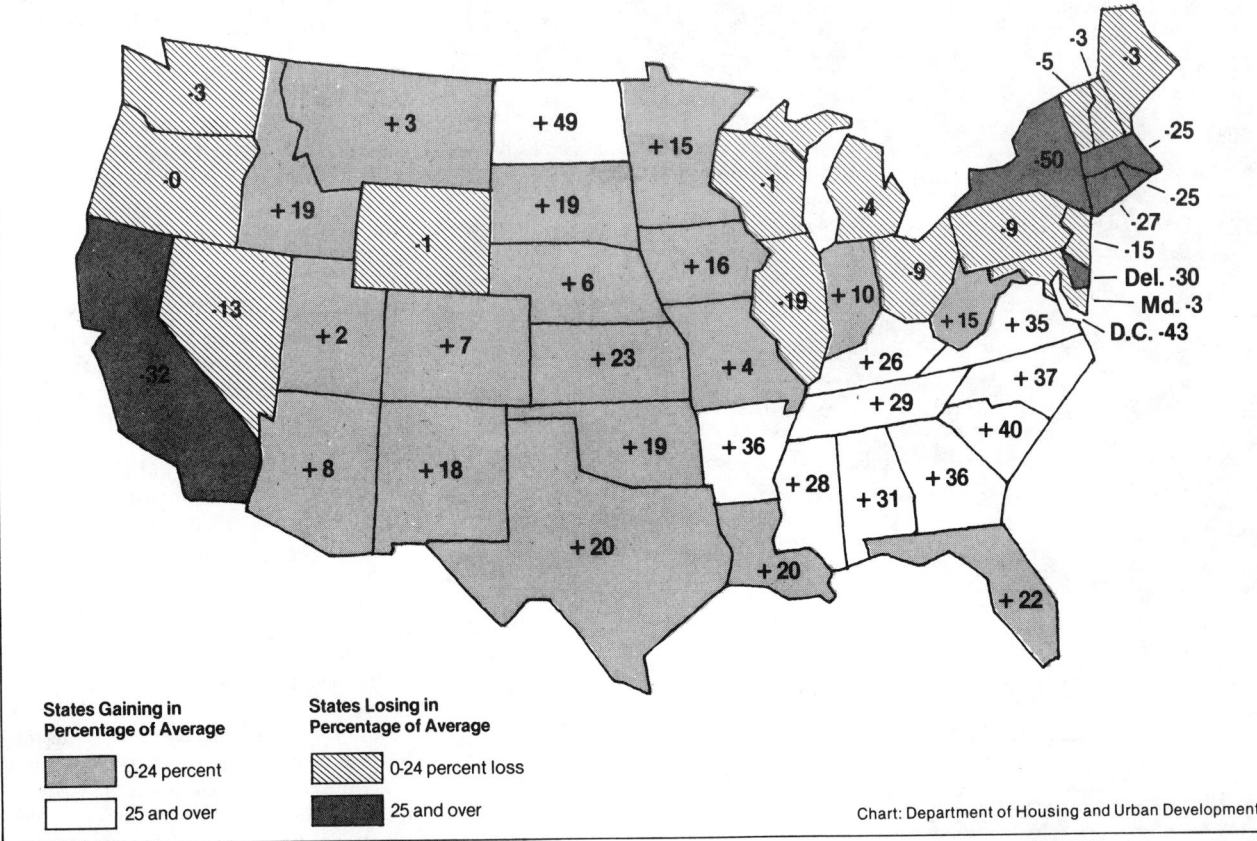

**States Gaining in Percentage of Average**
- 0-24 percent
- 25 and over

**States Losing in Percentage of Average**
- 0-24 percent loss
- 25 and over

Chart: Department of Housing and Urban Development.

# Urban Enrollments

School enrollments in the 27 largest American cities have declined to the level they were in 1962, and they may drop even further. This change may transform urban school systems in the future.

Chart: Council of the Great City Schools.

Students leave school building. Declining population in major cities—along with the exodus of the middle class from urban centers—is causing city schools to deteriorate.

Photo: Joe Di Dio, National Education Association

The traditional image of the family—working father, housekeeping mother, and two children—is becoming increasingly at odds with reality in the United States. Some 45% of children born in 1976 will have lived with a single parent for some time before reaching 18 years of age. Among two-parent families, an increasing number have both parents in the work force.

Photo: USDA

# Other Trends Affecting Education

A variety of non-demographic factors are likely to interact with demographic trends to change the schools of the future.

• **Energy** will have many impacts on education. Direct effects include fuel costs for heating, transportation and busing; long-term effects on the structure and design of school buildings; and a movement toward larger-size school districts to allow for larger buildings. Indirect effects include a reduction in the discretionary income of families, which may affect the amount of expenditures taxpayers will allow schools. Scarce energy may increasingly encourage people to live closer to the areas where they work—and perhaps bring the middle-class back to the city.

• **Civil rights movements** have increased the percentage of children bused to and from school. Increasing busing costs may cause curtailment of other school costs in a time of shrinking budgets and inflation.

• **The rise of the knowledge industries**—trade, finance, real estate, transportation, communication, etc.—has occurred simultaneously with a decline in the percentage of workers in other areas. The major, basic new trend in the labor sector is a movement toward knowledge-based and knowledge-dependent industries. Since the information society puts a great demand on the ability to read and write English, the completion of some level of formal education, either high school or college, is a crucial element in being able to take the first few steps on the economic mobility ladder.

• **Flextime** and other alternative work schedules may enable more women to work and thus may increase the demand for day-care services. On the other hand, flextime may permit more informal familial, neighborhood and other non-institutionalized day-care arrangements, which may *reduce* the demand for childcare services in schools or other formal institutions.

and white students. Looking at a sample of those 27 cities, one finds that the percent of minority school enrollment in almost every case is substantially above the percent minority population in the city. For example, Atlanta has a 52% minority population; minority students there comprised 85% of the school system in 1974. Denver's population is 11% minority; in the schools, 47%. St. Louis is 41% minority; the school system is 70% minority. And the same is true of impoverished families. The percent of students from poor families in the big cities is far in excess of the percent of families in poverty: 33.4% versus 11.6%.

### Response to Decline in Enrollment

In the face of declining enrollment, there are three general strategies available to school administrators: One alternative is to shrink by reducing staff and the so-called "frills" such as sports, music, and art. The second alternative is to expand services to current educational clientele. Places to expand include after-school care, courses in personal development, expansion of curriculum, and smaller classes with more individualized attention.

A third solution for school systems facing declining enrollment is to expand services to include new clientele. Pre-school day-care may be part of this solution. Another is the entry of school functions into health services (such as immunization) and community center functions. But the most important new client for secondary school systems may be the adult. Adults have the need for credentials, courses teaching career skills, hobbies and recreation, and training of economic value, such as car and home repair. And one can anticipate that the coming increase in costs of energy will create a demand for courses teaching home conservation.

### The Need for Improved Demographic Studies

Familiarity with local circumstances can play a major part in determining whether or not a given forecast is useful to policy planners. In general, however, there is not enough expertise at the state and local levels to meet this need. The Census Bureau's state-level population projections are about 10 years old. The upcoming Census of 1980 will give substantial opportunity to improve the means of collecting data on a local level. The need for demographic research relevant to plans concerning adult education, day care, nursery care, and after-school services is increasing along with the increased demand for such services. Such demographic data is essential for the wise policy-making needed to build effective educational systems for the future.

# An Educator Looks Back from 1996

## by Ronald E. Barnes

*An educational consultant imagines a social historian speaking to educators in the year 1996. His description offers an optimistic view of what is likely to happen in education during the next few years.*

Since the mid-1970s, we have moved from a didactic to a heuristic approach to learning—from a knowing to a searching approach. We have put behind us the belief that we can control information and have developed an open system of education that negates the prevalent belief of the seventies that we are successful if we teach our children what our culture already knows. In today's open system of education, teachers and students have become colleagues as they search together for relevant and credible information in this continuing world of change.

There is far less emphasis today on learning facts than on assisting our students to learn how to learn. We have become more anticipatory, since all of us have become learners in an attempt to discover what will happen in the future, or at least what is likely to happen. This transition occurred because of the recognition that so much of what we have taught our students is no longer real or relevant. Of course, there are some facts we want them to know, but primarily our task is to assist students to become self-propelling and self-motivating learners throughout their lives.

### Learning as Discovery

Although there was considerable interest in training people for specific jobs in the late seventies, a renewal of interest in learning as discovery began in the early eighties and is still with us. As you know, training deals primarily with the known; it is the transmittal of knowledge. Learning deals primarily with the unknown; it focuses on the discovery of knowledge. The increasing complexity of the world and the incredible speed with which new occupations and career fields opened up in the early eighties brought pressures on us to better prepare students to deal with nonspecific fields of interest. We began to see that we must equip people to become generalists. While specialists are still necessary, the major task we face today lies in understanding relationships and connections, and in synthesizing information in holistic ways.

In the last two decades we have seen a clear shift from limited schooling to life-long learning. Rather than existing just for persons between the ages of 5 and 18 or so, our schools now assist human beings to learn throughout their lives. The schools have become community learning centers serving the needs of persons of all ages in year-round programs. Perhaps this transition more than any other saved the schools

Computation center at University of Texas.
Photo: University of Texas at Austin

from becoming museums or monuments to irrelevancy.

Another transition of import was the move away from acculturation and socialization of human beings to what we are now calling the person-set goals approach. Those of us who attended any school board meetings in the mid-1970s understood quickly that the primary purposes of schools were to acculturate, socialize, control, and provide custodial care for students. The schools were still required to respond to the industrial age philosophy that initially was intended to homogenize immigrants but became, through mass education, an attempt to produce uniformity for all—a culture factory. The hidden curriculum in the seventies and, of course, throughout the industrial age, was primarily a long course in obedience, in punctuality, and in rote work. These were precisely the skills needed to process youngsters into the work force of the industrial age. This system-centered approach—nurtured, unfortunately, by the myth of the melting pot—was replaced by the individual-centered approach now in its infancy in our schools. This has not been an easy tran-

Commencement 1977 at the University of Texas.
Photo: University of Texas at Austin

sition, as all of you know, because old myths die slowly.

Another transition has been the move from past-oriented curricula to past/present/future-oriented curricula. One clear indication of this change is that in our schools we now find almost as many courses in future histories as we do in past histories. Most of us now understand that the future is where our students will live; no matter how much some of us wish it, they will not live in the past.

One transition I must not leave off my list is the move from an immutable-reality approach to a changing realities approach. More and more educators are finding it difficult to say, "This is the way it is" or "This is what's real." They are becoming more comfortable with the thought that realities differ for each person—that "What is real for me, may not be real for you."

Another important transition we have witnessed is the move from a cognitive to a cognitive/affective approach to learning. We have become more comfortable dealing not only with the mind, but with the hearts and the spirits of people. We now know that a person's feelings primarily determine what he does, how he behaves, how he responds in a given situation. And I find more and more educators unafraid to share with students their personal feelings, matters of the heart, and to let their emotions show.

From a fragmentation-of-knowledge approach we have moved to an integration of knowledge approach. We used to believe, you recall, that all we had to do was give our independent and separate courses and that upon graduation the student would synthesize all of this into some kind of whole. We now realize that fragmentation begets fragmentation and fragmented human beings. This fragmentation approach to knowledge—unfortunately most pronounced at the college and university level—was nurtured by our ignorance, arrogance, and ideology. We have replaced the ideology, and I hope we are not as ignorant or arrogant as we used to be. We are moving toward integrating information in an interdependent world filled with interdependent people.

The next transition that I would like to illuminate may sound strange from a person who wrote several books in the 1980s. We have moved from a book-centered curricular approach to the utilization of unlimited learning resources. Clearly, we rely less on books today than we used to. It is a poverty-stricken classroom that does not use open and closed circuit TV, community resource people, films, tapes, and many other resources. I am happy to report that I know of no school in the country still using textbooks—those now-ancient tools for regulating, controlling, homogenizing, and boring students. Texts went out in the late eighties, I believe, when we finally understood that since all students are unique and different, they need not begin at the same place and end at the same place in a set amount of time.

The next-to-last transition I will mention has been the change from passive to active learning. The move has been away from the belief that students should sit docilely and quietly at desks —a most unnatural position, especially for the young—to a recognition that the more active persons are the more they tend to learn. Experiential learning has come to the forefront of our methodology, and we are not just permitting but rather encouraging students to actively pursue information—wherever it may take them. We encourage and provoke creative divergence among students in our community learning centers. I realize that some of you still long for the "good old days" when classrooms and hallways were quiet, but I also know that you are having more fun in our present environments.

Finally, we have moved from schooling to education. We now understand that these terms are not synonymous: An education is what each of us will have when we draw our last breath; learning is a process by which we acquire that education, and schooling is only one part of that process. Thus, we no longer are school-folks but we have become educators in the truest sense of the word. This realization has been, as much as any other, instrumental in enabling the public to accept us as professionals, not as quasi-professionals, which we indeed were in the prior decades.

## Reasons for Transitions

As the final section of this historical report, let me now turn to the question, "How did these educational transitions come about?" What were the major developments that enabled us to make these—and many more—transitions? The following points are not in any priority order.

• **Diversity:** Because of the actions primarily in the late 1970s of various ethnic groups and other sub-populations within our country, the schools began to actively promote diversity and deemphasize the melting-pot approach. Rather than promoting a homogenization process, which is basic to the melting-pot mythology, the schools began to recognize that students are unique and to treat them accordingly. The schools began to encourage ethnic groups to establish their own identities and live their own life-styles. Only in the last five years have we begun to un-

Learning how things work.

Photo: National Education Association—Joe di Dio

derstand that the basic question involved in this issue is, "Can we love those who are different from us?" The elevation of diversity has been at the root of many of the changes I described earlier—the move to alternative models, to person-set goals, to changing realities, and to the use of unlimited learning resources.

• **Alternatives:** The second major development, closely tied to the first, was the demand for different educational approaches for students. Although initiated by parents, primarily in the late seventies, this move was soon joined by teachers who, in the early 1980s, began to force the National Education Association to examine its rhetoric and use its power to effect change in the educational system. All of us recall the popular slogan the NEA chose as its rallying cry in 1983, "Back to the basics." At first, many people thought that meant the three R's but were surprised to find it meant focusing on the student and on learning.

The increased activism of teachers and parents began to move the United States Office of Education to redirect some of its funds toward alternative models of schooling. Local school districts soon followed suit, although it is unfortunate that only in the past few years have state departments of education provided such support.

• **Questioning of Assumptions:** A third development, what I call "the quiet revolution," is one of the most critical moves we have witnessed in the past decade. It is the questioning and examination of basic assumptions on which the schooling system rests.

During the 1950s and 1960s there were a number of studies focusing on goals and objectives, but rarely any serious questioning of assumptions. This pattern was also evident in the 1970s, although there were fewer studies undertaken. We now know that no real analysis of schooling practices and procedures can take place unless the basic assumptions on which these practices and procedures rest are critically examined.

After the "me-centered" decade of the seventies, during which narcissism was a common malady of so many people, we witnessed in the eighties an awakening to the complexity of the human personality. This move away from simplistic human potential approaches to understanding self toward a more searching approach to understanding self and others had a profound effect on the field of education. We began to understand better how people function, why they behave as they do, what truly motivates them, and how we as educators can best create climates in which students not only wish to learn but enjoy the process. Thus, we began to question some of the classic assumptions such as "Schools prepare students for life," "Knowing makes one better than someone who does not know," "Education equals schooling," "Left on their own, students will not learn," "The young need to be controlled and socialized if they are to adjust to society," etc. We began to develop new assumptions and it was in the process of developing these assumptions that we began to change not only our roles as educators, but the environments of our schools.

• **Reformulation of Policies and Procedures:** The next major development was the questioning and, eventually, the reformulation of policies and procedures within our schools. We began to question, for instance, lesson plans, iron-clad sets of objectives, and assembly line procedures as we moved to diverse learning approaches, alternative objectives, and individualized procedures. We began to emphasize maximum performance standards rather than minimum standards, individual assessment rather than comparative data. There is a litany of these changes you and I could both describe, but suffice to say that the policies and procedures that were established, especially during the past five years, are for the most part consistent with the assumptions I discussed in point number three concerning our understanding of how human personality functions.

• **Future-Orientation:** The fifth development has been the enthusiastic move to have our schools become future-oriented. At the national, state, and local levels we have seen this emphasis take shape. There are few districts in the country now that do not have resource centers for the study of the future. There are few school media centers that do not have sections devoted to journals, books, films, and tapes focusing on this area. The *Futures in Education Newsletter*, initiated three years ago by the NEA, is perhaps as widely read as any other single journal or newsletter in the field of education. I know of 35 states that now have similar newsletters, and I cannot begin to count the number of local school districts which have such publications.

Just as encouraging has been the move of school board members to involve themselves in future-focused thrusts. They, like you, have always been futurists (for what other purpose do they have but to attend to the future needs of the students and public?) but were slow, if not reluctant, to recognize this responsibility.

Most important, of course, has been the response of students as they become aware that they must take responsibility for their own future and prepare themselves as proactive learners. I believe there is a correlation between the decrease in the suicide rate of adolescents, which was so high in the 1970s, and the future-focused approach that now prevails in our schools.

• **Curriculum Renewal Every Three Years:** Another rather quiet development has been the scrutinization of all

An American classroom in the 1970s.   Photo: National Education Association—Joe di Dio

**About the Author**

Ronald E. Barnes is President of Transitions, Inc., a consulting firm. Formerly a university professor and administrator, he now sees himself as a "practicing generalist." His address is Transitions Inc., P.O. Box 4371, Topeka, Kansas 66604.

curricular offerings every three years. You remember that during earlier decades those courses that had been on the books for some time were regarded as sacrosanct and would be passed along year after year without critical assessment. You also remember that every new course that was suggested was subjected to intense analysis. The operational mode was "If it is old, it's good; if it's new, it's suspect, if not bad." Further, any curricular offerings were judged in the past by those whose interests were served by retaining the present curriculum. This resulted in trade-offs and compromises by busy staff members who seldom had the time or inclination to engage in substantive evaluations.

Now, a school's curriculum is wiped off the books every three years and selected representatives of students, teachers, administrators, and parents develop a preliminary curriculum that is presented before the school year begins. Courses selected by students are retained; those that are not are dropped. The involvement of students and parents in this procedure has negated the old myth that "Only the easy courses are popular." Having a stake in the action, families have obviously agreed to pursue those curricular offerings they believe have validity for the future of the young person.

• **Community Learning Centers:** No other single development so aroused the public's interest and enthusiasm as the schools' move to become community learning centers. Opening their doors to persons of all ages 12 months a year and sometimes 24 hours a day brought support to the schools at a time when they could have gone under.

In a world of accelerating change, it became especially clear in the mid-1970s that citizens needed to prepare themselves for new careers by having access to new information and skills. Although school people were slow to respond, by the mid-1980s many had effectively retooled their institutions to provide continuing education programs for the public. One of the problems, of course, was that instructors—many of whom came from the community— needed training, since it was clear that "more of the same" would be insufficient and invalid. In the early eighties, many teachers began to take on new learning experiences in an attempt not only to upgrade their current skills but also to develop new ones that would better serve the citizens. It is clear today that the community learning centers have become a focal point for neighborhoods as well as the primary link in the total educational chain.

• **Accountability:** The final development I will mention here is still in its embryonic stages but appears to be headed toward becoming an actuality: schooling bureaucracies are becoming accountable to the population they claim to serve.

This issue came to a head in 1984 (of all years) when the President of the United States asked how students and teachers would be affected if the federal, state, county, and local schooling bureaucracies closed down tomorrow. While this raised considerable controversy, it was discovered six months later that the only people who were upset with the president's question were those within the bureaucracies. Unfortunately, at that time they numbered several million people, so their protest was substantial.

However, it was becoming clear that the enormous growth of the educational bureaucracies was hindering the transitional processes that had to be made in entering the new age. By 1984 most of these bureaucracies had become unwieldy, unresponsive, self-serving organizations that were placing incredible demands on the time of local school teachers and administrators by giving them endless paper work, reports, and committee assignments. As the bastions of the status quo, the bureaucracies were preventing innovative and experimental approaches by those persons closest to the students.

It was soon after the president's speech that teachers throughout the country pressured the administrative power structure at all levels to recover their sense of dedication to human beings and to the learning process. In response, they did change and restructure their organizations to become more human and learning-centered. While it is too early to determine whether they will be successful, there is good reason for us to have faith in the new process.

Where do we go from here? This historical recitation is intended to encourage you to become proactively involved not only in charting your own personal history but also the history of the educational profession. We are all making history. Those who record history look to you and at you to see not only what you are doing today, but what you are likely to do tomorrow.

Your responsibility is great. You are stewards of a rich educational heritage. But more significantly, you are society's vanguards entrusted with leading and showing the way to the young as they chart their futures. To do so responsibly you must hold a vision of and a commitment to a future that ennobles you, your students, and all children to come. You are the true futurists; may you serve history well.

Library at the University of Texas at Austin.

Photo: University of Texas at Austin

# Education for a Leisure Society

*In the leisure society that some futurists foresee, 15% of the population will be able to provide all necessary goods and services. Consequently, man may need to abandon the idea that dignity and identity are derived primarily from his job. A properly designed educational curriculum would stress interpersonal relations, human development, and man's intrinsic dignity.*

by Robert Strom

Before the Protestant Reformation the concept of vocation and the idea of having a calling applied only to the clergy. This monastic monopoly was unacceptable to Martin Luther, because it placed the responsibility for living the gospel upon too few and because it separated religious life from secular existence. To support his opposition to church structure, Luther urged laymen to fulfill their secular calling for Christian service through their daily labors. Thus, by relating the concept of work to the concept of calling, Luther transformed the popular definition of work from a means of providing for material needs into a strategic arena for the expression of one's religious duty. And this view of life still shapes our values in 1975.

We still retain the Protestant view that each person's mission is to be accomplished through his secular work and that, since work is morally good, unemployment is bad and being unwilling to work is sinful. The decline of religious service as a primary goal of the modern worker has changed the work ethic, which now emphasizes the belief that man must find personal satisfaction and experience meaning on the job. Yet even this modified form of the Protestant work ethic is inappropriate and must be abandoned if we are to deal successfully with some basic conflicts created by automation:

The productive capacity of automation makes full employment unnecessary; but to be unemployed is shameful.

Paid employment is the only way for a person to obtain dignity; but automation promises to displace many job holders.

Workers are expected to find their sense of self-worth from a job; but automation makes jobs routine and boring.

> *"In a relatively jobless society, the question of life purpose becomes crucial and a new educational structure is needed to help people find the answers."*

Automation leads to an abundance of leisure; but since people regard nonwork activity as lacking in value, they naturally experience guilt and self-recrimination when leisure is extended.

Simply stated, our problem is how to ensure that each individual participating in an automated society experiences dignity and purpose, while at the same time his culture has a rationale for distributing the results of its high productivity. To accomplish these enormous but necessary tasks, we must revise our concept of work.

### Automation and the Replacement of Man

In his 1971 testimony before the U.S. Senate Subcommittee on Employment and Manpower, John Snyder, president of U.S. Industries, suggested that it is time for popular myths about automation to give way to some unpleasant facts. The most seductive myth alleges that automation will not displace workers. But Snyder contended that automation is a major factor in the elimination of 40,000 jobs per week. The Department of Labor's more conservative estimate is 4,000 jobs per week. In either case, the figure is large enough to warrant concern.

A second myth contends that the need to maintain and operate automated equipment will actually create more jobs than presently exist. But, in fact, computers require little maintenance and if workers were not displaced, automation would lack economic feasibility. Nevertheless, some groups still point to what they regard as equally drastic labor changes in the past—like the introduction of knitting machines to textile manufacturing—and remind us that in time these machines increased employment. However, labor-saving devices introduced during the industrial revolution also led to riots, turmoil, and war. Moreover, since these changes occurred in basically rural societies, the land guaranteed food and a place to live for the unemployed. In an urban society like ours, the alternative of becoming a

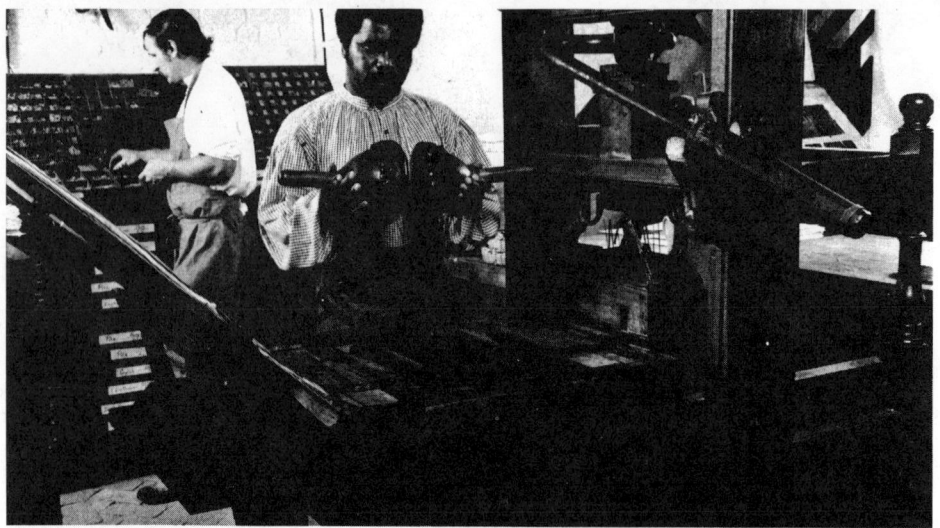

In the 18th century, printers produced newspapers by hand, using presses like this one. Today, automation has largely replaced printing craftsmen. In the future, many experts think, no more than 15% of the population will need to hold jobs in order to provide for society's needs. In the face of widespread unemployment, author Strom believes the Protestant work ethic will have to be abandoned. In the photo: Costumed craftsmen use old-style presses on the site where William Parks first published the Virginia Gazette in Williamsburg, Va. in 1736.

PHOTOS: COLONIAL WILLIAMSBURG

A bootmaker in Colonial Williamsburg, Va., using hand tools and age-old methods, shows how boots were made in the 18th century. In the past, when a craftsman was driven out of his trade by technological advancements, he alone left his job in an otherwise healthy town. Today, in the era of big business and assembly lines, thousands of people lose their jobs at one time.

farmer does not exist.

A half-century ago when the blacksmith was driven from his trade by the automobile, he alone left his job in an otherwise healthy town. But technological advancements and business failures now affect thousands of people 350,000 jobs lost in Detroit in the past year 60,000 jobless aircraft personnel in Seattle). When layoffs of this magnitude occur, as they increasingly do, masses of people are left in a state of volatile misery which cripples both family and community. Despite emergency help projects, the closing of the Hudson Motor Company in South Bend, Indiana resulted in 15 suicides and the breakup of 300 marriages.

Many experts think that automation has only begun its replacement of people, that

> *"To the question 'What are you going to be?' youngsters now say, 'I already am—and you should recognize me as a person whether I'm employed or not, whether I'm through with school or not.'"*

within the next two decades we shall see an unprecedented rise in unemployment among the skilled and middle-management groups as well as the uneducated. They predict a society in which no more than 15% of the population will be needed to provide the basic necessities and services for all. In such a society, it would be cruel and unreasonable to retain the notion that only through a job may an individual discover contentment and define who he is. One's identity, status, and sense of potency would all be expected to derive from the job, but, because the majority of people would be unneeded for employment, they would have to accept the social and psychological consequences of being regarded as worthless.

**Distinction Must Be Made Between Job and Work**

To reconcile the leisure society with an individual's need for dignity we must stop perceiving a person's work and his job as inseparable activities. In a relatively jobless setting it is no longer appropriate for paid employment to be a prerequisite for dignity. If a distinction between job and work were generally accepted, the result would be in everyone's best interest. We could enlarge our inquiry of self and others from "What is your job?" to "What is your work?" (that is, your mission as a person, the activity you pursue with a sense of duty and from which you derive self-meaning and a sense of personal worth). It would be understood that given the meaninglessness of some jobs, numerous people would necessarily identify their work as something apart from their employment. This would release them from the self-delusion and guilt which comes from working at a job which they abhor, but from which they are expected to gain satisfaction.

Industrial sociology studies have shown that the monotonous tasks being created by automation have caused an increasing number of job holders to begin to find their major life interests outside their jobs. The idea that everyone needs a job to feel good about himself and that job holding brings satisfaction is erroneous. When someone says, "Thank goodness it's Friday," what does he mean? Does he mean that he achieves so much pleasure and extracts so much significance and self-fulfillment from his job that the ecstasy of it cannot be sustained for more than five days at a time? Or does he mean that the job lacks importance to him, fails to satisfy his need for potency and forces him to look to the weekend for fulfillment? Does he mean it would be nice not to have to hold this job but the need for income and social status demands it? The inner turmoil of this person and millions of others does not suggest that they are lazy or that constructive achievement doesn't interest them. It means that work and job are being distinguished and alienation from the job is becoming common. In a leisure society the incidence of such behavior is destined to rise as industry shifts to the four-day week and people can give more attention to other interests.

### "Thank God It's Thursday"

More than 700 U.S. companies currently have all or most of their workers on a four-day week and at least 1000 other companies are contemplating such a shift. In 1973 the nation's largest employer, the federal government, began to experiment with a four-day work week, starting in the Baltimore headquarters of the Social Security Administration. During 1974 municipal employees in Atlanta, Long Beach, and Phoenix made the transition. A dozen companies, including Metropolitan Life Insurance, have gone even further, assigning some of their workers a three-day week.

In a leisure society, for the first time in history, most of a person's time would belong to himself and he could live far away from the city where he is employed; however, confidence in the leisure society seems to be declining as its arrival draws near. Previous generations believed that a relatively jobless economy would introduce greater contentment than ever before, but only 23 percent of the Americans recently polled in a national survey assume that labor union proposals for a four-day week and three-month annual vacation will result in happier homes. Evidence from industrial sociology supports this popular doubt by indicating that the shorter work day does not necessarily increase family interaction or insure other forms of constructive activity. Many physicians have stopped prescribing holidays and vacations for tense and anxious patients because leisure could bring disaster rather than relief. Suicides, depressions, and other self-disabling behavior increase over weekends and holidays when inner conflicts can no longer be repressed by the rigors of routine. In many cases leisure appears to generate domestic conflict or withdrawal. Reinforcing the danger are gerontological studies which intimate that many marriages are sustained during the career years because the people seldom see each other. Extended interpersonal contact is unpleasant unless people know how to relate well.

### A Man's Work Should Last a Lifetime

Slowly our society is realizing that what is important is not that each of us holds a job but that all of us have work. Many people who have jobs lack work and therefore a sense of satisfaction and self-pride. The problem cannot be solved just by making jobs more meaningful because there is a significant difference between having a work and holding a job. Nothing framed in a period shorter than a lifetime can be termed a man's work, but he may never have a job or may retire at age 60. If he has not discovered a work, a retiree may move to Florida and die sooner because he has lost a respected role and is unable to view his life as important apart from the job hierarchy. The number of people facing this prospect is growing; already in 1975 over 20 million Americans are at least 65 years old. If the increased lifespan is to be satisfying rather than cruel, we must abandon the tradition which limits self-validation to one's job.

Recognizing that people are disenchanted

**Educator Robert Strom has done research on children's play and parent education and has written ten books on child development and mental health. He has edited two books:** *Values and Human Development* **(1973, Charles E. Merrill Publishing Co.) and, with E. Paul Torrance,** *Education for Affective Achievement* **(1973, Rand McNally and Co.).**

with certain jobs, management has responded mainly by inventing rationalizations for investing jobs with inherent worth or greater social meaning. We all expect "What do you do?" as the first question to be asked after introduction to a stranger. However, the answer becomes more difficult as a technologically advancing industry creates jobs that are new, nameless, and hard to describe. What status is there in saying, "I am a relay transmitter maintenance technician on the 609 power mag." The substitute answer is then offered not in terms of what one does but where he does it: "I am employed at Sears Roebuck." Despite these obstacles, the game of appealing job titles continues to expand. A person who joins a chain of department stores may immediately be given the title of assistant manager, thus temporarily meeting the beginner's need for status. In some occupations it is an accepted practice to uproot a man and his family and transfer them 1000 miles from friends, relatives, and preferred location and actually lead them to feel honored because the reassignment is termed a promotion. Each of us has a need to feel significant, potent, and useful. This need will persist in an automated society; and since the need will not be met by jobs, work is urgently required.

If more work and less jobs are the design for mental health in an automated society, we must soon deal with the related problems of income distribution and education. In terms of sharing our national abundance, we

---

*"Today there are many people whose training and income qualify them as successful but whose lack of maturity and concern for others label them as failures."*

*"Under competitive conditions people are taught to resent or fear the talents of peers instead of recognizing the talent as an asset for the group."*

> *"We could enlarge our inquiry of self and others from 'What is your job?' to 'What is your work?' (that is, your mission as a person, the activity you pursue with a sense of duty and from which you derive self-meaning and a sense of personal worth)."*

can choose between two inconsonant values. One value states that people gain virtue and dignity from job-holding and therefore no one without a job should be judged acceptable or given assistance lest his chance for dignity be jeopardized. A second and more recent principle asserts that if a man is unable to hold a job or if his vocational skill is unneeded, he still should receive a guaranteed income so that his family is comfortably cared for. A Gallup Poll taken several years ago revealed that about 70% of Americans agreed with the latter principle. But it is apparent that as automation eliminates jobs, these values will clash. The public will resist paying the unemployed and the jobless will feel guilt and self-derogation from accepting money they have not worked to earn. To escape from this dilemma we must prepare tomorrow's adults for life in a leisure society.

### Enlarging Educational Goals

Affluent people will not willingly share their wealth unless they are convinced that greater importance should be attached to off-the-job work. Perhaps the schools can begin this process by presenting students with two basic questions throughout the learning process. Unlike the present arrangement which urges young people to decide "What is to be my job?", the goal could be enlarged to "What is to be my work?" and "What am I going to do with my life?" By raising both inquiries we may free the student from identifying who he is with the occupation he chooses. We painfully recognize the mental health outcomes when success has too narrow a definition, when the vocational side of man is considered the whole of his obligation. Today there are many people whose training and income qualify them as successful but whose lack of maturity and concern for others label them as failures. The fact that more people in business and industry are fired for interpersonal relation problems than for job incompetence underscores the need for schools to help facilitate the growing up process, the affective or emotional aspects of development.

With these goals in mind, the Danforth Foundation in 1974 gave St. Louis University a multi-million dollar grant to redesign university curricula to prepare students for life in the twenty-first century. Efforts are also underway to help younger students redefine achievement, an example being my own research on using play as a medium for peer teaching. In these studies (supported by the Rockefeller Foundation and the Toy Manufacturers of America) parents, grandparents, and middle-grade children have been trained to teach preschoolers and kindergarteners.

The system, Toy Talk, uses toys as a medium for adult-child conversation. Play, the child's favorite activity, becomes his focus for learning. The child chooses a play theme which the teacher then employs to increase desired affective behaviors, assess vocabulary comprehension, introduce new words in context, and immediately correct speech and misconceptions. Teachers participating in Toy Talk also made important self-concept gains and achieved a better understanding of the teaching-learning process.

If students are expected to teach as well as learn, their definition of accomplishment can grow to include helping other people to achieve. If children learn early to share themselves, it also seems likely that they will be more willing as adults to share their affluence. It is unwise to complain that the modern market place does not offer children an opportunity to learn responsibility as some of us learned it through youthful employment. In fact, having to work may have trained us to view responsibility in its most narrow sense; surely it did not teach most of us to share with people outside our family. Instead it taught us to feel proud that no one needed to share with us. Children today must learn responsibility in school or they may not learn it at all. The consequences of allowing students to be only learners shows up in higher education. Many university students prefer not to participate in groups and share what they know with fellow students. Typically they reason that since peers know less than the instructor, he alone should be responsible for teaching. When only one person in the class is expected to share his knowledge and be responsive rather than selfish, accomplishment reverts to its narrow definition—competition. Under competitive conditions people are obliged to resent or fear the talents of peers instead of recognizing the talent as an asset for the group. I believe peer teaching and play education can help young people improve the ways they see themselves and each other.

### Curriculum Will Emphasize Human Relations

Some futurists believe that a relatively jobless society would not need public schools, that without an occupational focus any curriculum would be meaningless. I regard this perception as inaccurate, for we are clearly undereducated in child-rearing, community service, personal development, and understanding one another. Our lack of skill in the art of relating is demonstrated by our divorce rate, our treatment of the poor, and our neglect of the elderly. Ostensibly these matters of relating have not been given attention because there was insufficient time

**The boring, monotonous tasks created by automation have forced many workers to look outside their jobs for fulfillment. Strom predicts that alienation from the job will become common as we move into a leisure society. However, a few companies (such as Tandbergs Radiofabrikk (radio factory) in Norway, shown here) have made concerted efforts to make assembly line work more pleasant.**

PHOTO: NORWEGIAN INFORMATION SERVICE

Classrooms might stand empty when automation makes work unnecessary, some futurists believe. They argue that many people would find education meaningless without an occupational focus. Strom disagrees, noting the need for learning how to raise children, serve the community, attain personal development, and understand other people. In the photo: A new lecture hall at Denmark's Roskilde University.

PHOTOS: ROYAL DANISH MINISTRY FOR FOREIGN AFFAIRS

A retired person who has depended entirely on his job for status, identity, and fulfillment often feels that his life is empty and meaningless. Unless society abandons the belief that dignity and self-esteem can only be earned through economic production, the leisure years will seem burdensome to millions of retired people. This photograph shows a retired worker relaxing at his summer cottage in Denmark, a pioneer in programs for the aged.

in a schedule already filled with job-oriented studies. Now that more time will be available, the relevance of such curricula cannot be so easily dismissed. Of one thing we may be sure: Our schools currently devote much more effort to helping young people learn how to make a living than to finding out what their work is to be. In a relatively jobless society, the question of life purposes becomes crucial and a new educational structure is needed to help people find the answers.

I believe that the family will survive in the coming leisure society, even though current divorce statistics reflect a high ratio of discontent among the married. The high divorce rate comes from the very high expectations that people now have for marriage. The recently divorced seldom complain of desertion or physical abuse; instead the unacceptable behavior is usually a lack of understanding or communication, insufficient companionship or romance, or a failure to share goals. Many husbands and wives expect their partner to behave more maturely than is taught in the schools. As curricula are revised to emphasize the previously ignored arenas of human relations and continued personal development, the proportion of successful marriages will probably increase. It also seems likely that in the future fathers will be expected to play a more active role in the family. Until now, fathers of young children have justified their absence because of the job; in the leisure society they will not have that excuse.

Many adults cannot envision a future of peace and equity because they daily observe man's obsession with status, unwillingness to share, and readiness to ignore the needs of others. Yet, why should we find it strange that people unschooled in personal development seldom manifest signs of maturity? Under conditions which define success more in terms of personal growth, student motivation is necessarily modified so that status becomes less a need than does service to others. Accomplishment will be defined in terms other than acquisition. Status is presently an accomplishment, but if status were assumed rather than earned, accomplishment would relate to beneficial influence. Many older people, after a lifetime of pursuing materialistic goals, begin to ask themselves a different kind of question: "What has my life meant? How can I live the remainder in a humanistic way?" Because these questions are being asked at a younger age than ever before and since one's self-concept rests upon the answer, there is reason to believe that maturity will arrive much earlier in the individual lifespan in the future. Even a casual observer is aware that the financial motive has less appeal to youth than in the past. The mature person sees sharing, respect, and service as his chosen behavior.

**Human Dignity Is Intrinsic, Not Earned**

Young people are already abandoning the Protestant work ethic, the belief that a man's dignity is dependent upon his economic production. To the question "What are you going to be?" youngsters now say, "I already am—and you should recognize me as a person whether I'm employed or not, whether I'm through with school or not." To suggest that a person without a job has no dignity is like saying a slow learner is undeserving of respect. Neither teacher nor society can dispense dignity; it is not extrinsic; it need not be earned but rather should be assumed in every act of relating. Today increasing numbers of people see themselves as less than somebody, an underevaluation which has been thrust upon them by an archaic dictate urging each individual to derive his self-worth from being defined as employed, unemployed or unemployable.

To satisfy the human desire for happiness, a society must consider the mental health, aspiration, self-concept, and dignity of individuals. Once we thought dignity came through biology, being well born; later we decided it occurred as a product of labor, having a job. A proper redefinition of the status of the individual must include the assumption that dignity begins with conception. Only then will man feel comfortable in a leisure society.

ROBERT STROM IS DIRECTOR OF THE PARENT CHILD LAB AND PROFESSOR OF EDUCATION AT ARIZONA STATE UNIVERSITY, TEMPE, ARIZONA 85281.

# Beating Unemployment Through Education

### by William L. Abbott

**Workers need almost constant retraining to survive in the modern labor market. To provide this training, both labor and management in the United States have turned to community colleges for help, and the results have been encouraging. Meanwhile, a Swedish innovation known as the "study circle" is also getting attention as a partial answer to worker obsolescence.**

Perpetual retraining is becoming a fact of life for modern workers as old jobs disappear and new jobs develop. About 8,000 types of jobs vanished from the U.S. labor market during the period from 1949 to 1965, due largely to the spread of automation. At the same time, more than 6,000 new jobs developed. And the same trends are continuing today: An electronic tomato-harvesting machine is expected to displace 11,000 farm workers in the near future, and all told, the automation of farm equipment will eliminate between 100,000 and 250,000 farm labor jobs in the U.S. during the next 10 years, according to union leader Cesar Chavez. The same pattern may be seen in industry: Rubber plants in Akron, Ohio, now employ fewer than half as many workers as they did 20 years ago.

Many workers now must retrain three or four times during their careers. Take electrical workers as an example: The integrated circuit was introduced in the 1960s. By 1970, microelectronics had become a billion-dollar-a-year industry; by 1976, it was a three-billion-dollar industry. By 1986, its incorporation into other industries and products is expected to make the industry 100 times larger than it is today. Circuits have rapidly become complex. In 1970, there were 256 bits per circuit. Today there are 16,384 bits in every circuit. The entire electrical industry has become so complex that the International Brotherhood of Electrical Workers, AFL-CIO, has 57 members constantly updating textbooks.

The person most affected by rapid changes in the workplace is the older worker. A number of union business agents have remarked that a young apprentice often knows more about new developments in his trade than an experienced journeyman. The apprentice has the advantage today of going to school and being taught the latest techniques.

Because of this increasing problem of worker obsolescence, retraining may one day account for more enrollment in vocational courses than original training does throughout the United States. Already, 130 commun-

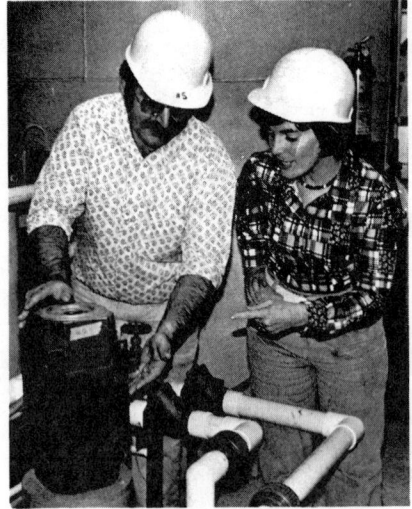

Instructor in water and wastewater technology program discusses a mechanism with one of his students.
Photo: Kirkwood Community College, Cedar Rapids, Iowa

For practical training, construction engineering students at the Community College of Baltimore build a storehouse adjacent to the college.
Photo: Community College of Baltimore

Elderly woman studies mathematics at Kirkwood Community College in Cedar Rapids, Iowa. Community college courses are becoming increasingly popular with older Americans.
Photo: Kirkwood Community College

ity colleges are heavily involved in retraining displaced workers.

## Community Colleges Enjoy Rapid Growth

Community colleges have prospered in recent years by responding to the demand for worker retraining courses and by preparing students for jobs that actually are available. Enrollment in community colleges has soared from 660,000 students in 1960 to over 4.3 million today. There now are one million more students enrolled in community colleges than in universities. In addition, another three million students are enrolled in non-credit adult education activities in public community colleges —a 463.5% increase over the past decade.

Employers, unions, and workers have converged on community colleges for help in coping with rapidly changing occupational demands. The community colleges now offer two-year degrees in a multiplying number of technologies, trades, professions, and paraprofessions. In 1965, only 13% of community college students were enrolled in occupational training programs; this year, half of all two-year college students are in vocational education programs. An appealing feature of community colleges is their reasonable price. The national average for tuition at community colleges is only $332 per year—about half the cost of a state university and far below Harvard's $4,400.

According to the state of Washington's *Job Opportunities Forecast*, community colleges will continue to be the best place to go to get training for the types of good jobs that will be plentiful in the near future. The *Forecast* concluded:

> It is significant that only four of the high-demand occupations require a (four-year) college degree for entrance. Though the professional, technical, and kindred group is growing the fastest, the overwhelming majority of opportunities will be in occupations needing less education. That fact, however, does not eliminate the need for some post-high school training. Post-high school experience will continue to be a requirement for entrance into most of the high-demand occupations.

Striving to reach more adults, community colleges in the United States and Canada have pioneered in educational innovations. For example, classes at Coastline Community College in Orange County, California, are conducted via nine television courses and 115 education centers in banks, hospitals, and even at a dance studio. The college has no campus of its own. Students enrolled in the TV courses take tests by filling out cards which are mailed in for processing by a computer and mailed back the same day. When Coastline began operations in 1976, 20,000 students immediately enrolled, apparently unconcerned about the college's lack of a campus. Vermont Community College, which serves the entire state of Vermont, also has no campus.

Throughout the United States, community colleges offer classes in factories, union halls, and even aboard ship. Besides day and night classes, many community colleges also provide special weekend courses for people who have no time during the week.

In Wisconsin, teachers go from village to village—like the circuit riders of old—training people in useful occupations.

## New Coalition Emerges

The community colleges are part of a new coalition of employers, unions, and educational institutions that is emerging to meet the pressing employment needs of the evolving post-industrial economy.

Labor-management joint apprenticeship committees have been advising community colleges for years on programs in various trades, technologies, and professions. Only in recent years, however, has the new coalition truly taken shape, and the catalyst was the heavy unemployment suffered by some communities in the 1970s. Both labor and management agreed that training and retraining of workers was a key to attracting new industries and saving established ones; consequently, in their contacts with community colleges, the labor-management advisory committees began to concentrate more on seeing that people received up-to-date training for existing jobs.

In Milwaukee, for example, a survey showed that many good jobs were going begging while thousands of people were looking for work. To match up unemployed people with salable skills, Milwaukee's huge technical college now is using a wide variety of labor-management advisory committees. A labor-management committee in Jamestown, New York, worked with Jamestown Community College in retraining

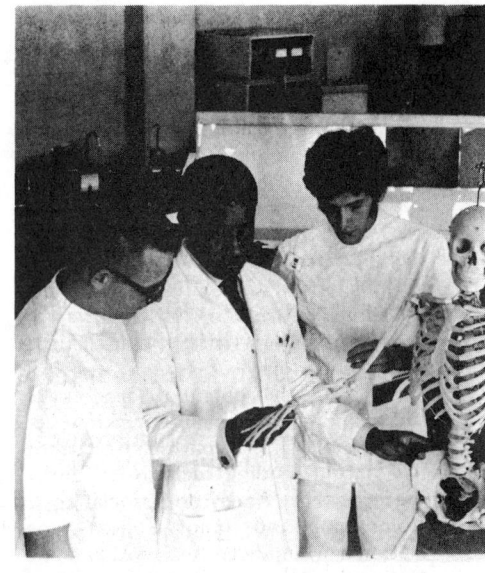

Radiologic (X-ray) technology students at Montgomery College study bones of a skeleton.
Photo: Public Information Office, Montgomery College

Printing technology students at Montgomery College in Rockville, Maryland, examine copy they have just run through a printing press.
Photo: Public Information Office, Montgomery College

workers for new jobs and thus helped restore that community's fast-fading economy.

The state of Washington now produces a job opportunities forecast which predicts the number of jobs in leading occupational categories up to 1985. The 10 state agencies which jointly prepare the forecast later survey the schools to see how many students are training for various jobs. If an institution is training too many students for jobs in a certain category, students are encouraged to shift occupations.

Realizing the potential benefits of such labor-management-education coalitions, the U.S. Department of Labor has started funding such efforts under the aegis of the American Association of Community and Junior Colleges, the National Manpower Institute, and the National Alliance of Businessmen. These joint ventures, often taking the form of "community education/work councils," will attempt to coordinate work-education activities in a community so that duplication of efforts will be eliminated and all of the available training and counseling and placement resources are identified and made accessible to those who need them.

The emerging work-education alliance has expanded to include representatives of minority groups in Oakland, California, whose decaying inner core gave birth to the Black Panthers. The city's labor unions are so militant that they once shut down the city with a general strike. But recently, minority groups, labor, and management jointly formed the New Oakland Committee to help rejuvenate the city. Each group—labor, management, and minority representatives—holds a caucus to decide what its policy should be on issues before the committee; then all of the groups meet together. Having identified education as one of the keys to overcoming youth unemployment, the committee worked with Peralta Community College to create a New Careers Council to train young people for jobs available in the area.

### Colleges Work with Employers

Students at Orange Coast College in Costa Mesa, California, now get college credit for planning their careers, and that task is helped considerably by a computer shaped like a television set, which carries on a "conversation" with a student regarding his future career options, talents, and interests.

When students decide on a career, their chances of getting a job through the college's career center are excellent. Employers know that the quality of instruction at Orange Coast College is first-rate, so the walls of the center are plastered with notices of employment opportunities.

LaGuardia Community College in Queens, New York City, is accomplishing the seemingly impossible task of taking incoming freshmen, 40% of whom cannot read above an eighth-grade level, and turning them into competent, literate people. LaGuardia attributes its success to several factors, including (1) intensive tutoring for those who need it; (2) a job internship program; and (3) the dedication of the faculty and administrators to serving the needs of the students. Students get additional emotional support from a peer counseling program under which certain students are trained to advise and assist classmates with personal problems.

**About the Author**

William Abbott, editor of the World Future Society's CAREERS TOMORROW newsletter, is the author of "Work in the Year 2001" (THE FUTURIST, February 1977). He is Director of the Service Center for Community College-Labor Union Cooperation of the American Association of Community and Junior Colleges, 1 Dupont Circle, N.W., Washington, D.C. 20036, U.S.A.

# Cooperative Education:
## A New Approach to Job Training

New York's Board of Higher Education wanted a completely new kind of college—one that would really prepare students for the world of work. So, in 1970, it created Fiorello H. LaGuardia Community College as the state's first postsecondary institution to offer a comprehensive program of cooperative education, an educational approach that interrelates classroom instruction with practical career-related work situations.

LaGuardia's President, Joseph Shenker, reports that 98% of all graduates seeking work find jobs. In one sample analysis of 430 graduates, none said they were unemployed.

What makes this record of placement remarkable is that LaGuardia, located in Queens, New York City, has a high proportion of low-income students. Forty percent of all freshmen cannot read above an eighth-grade level or handle basic math.

When freshmen arrive at LaGuardia they go through an advisory orientation program conducted by a team consisting of a counselor, a co-op education instructor, and a faculty member. They learn in these sessions how to explore the career field and how to use the college's resources to identify a vocation that suits their goals and personalities.

Some students are specially trained to conduct counseling sessions to help their fellow students overcome personal problems. Students are made to feel wanted.

After an initial stint in classrooms, the college finds the student an internship. During the course of the co-op program, each student must intern at three different jobs.

In their second or third quarter, students are taught job-coping skills, resume writing, and other practical ways of getting and holding a job.

"We are always under pressure to do our best," says Harry Heinemann, Dean of Cooperative Education. "We get immediate feedback from employers if our students are not making the grade." At one time, he adds, a big expansion in enrollment overtaxed the staff, causing some students who were inadequately prepared for secretarial work to slip into jobs. The college was jarred with quick complaints from employers. Faculty and administrators met and worked out a simulated testing system which corrected the situation.

When one talks to LaGuardia's staff, there is an aura of winning-team confidence when they speak of "our mission" as pioneers in an educational experiment which involves "substantial commitment." The faculty had no models to emulate when they completely rewrote texts and courses to relate subjects like philosophy and sociology to the experiences and interest levels of the students. Faculty and other employees of the college often teach as a team; they are encouraged to work for the common cause, keeping student needs foremost in their minds.

In LaGuardia's busy career counseling center, a computer gives students useful information about career options and job prospects. Like most community colleges, LaGuardia emphasizes service to the entire community: Anyone—not just students—can walk into the career center and receive vocational counseling.

LaGuardia finds good, satisfying jobs for 98% of its graduates seeking work. The college owes much of its success to a pre-graduation job placement program which involves career exploration, counseling, and the cooperation of the business community. More than 300 employers have provided jobs for LaGuardia students, thus giving them an opportunity to prove themselves on the job while still in school. Students alternate periods of full-time work with periods of classroom instruction. Such work greatly improves a student's chances of being offered a permanent position upon graduation. While working full time, students are required to participate in weekly evening seminars in which they try to mesh what they are learning in the world of work with humanities and social sciences concepts.

Classroom instruction at LaGuardia emphasizes practicality—even in liberal-arts courses. A philosophy course, for example, includes a section on work ethics. Many teachers at the college hold full-time jobs in industry and therefore can provide practical, up-to-the-minute insights into the world of work. Whether they work in industry or not, the faculty and administrators have convinced the students that they really care about them, and their genuine interest is another reason for the college's outstanding success.

Progress is clearly being made, as indicated by the previous examples, but there are still some unanswered questions regarding the educational system being shaped by the emerging education-work coalition. One unanswered question concerning the education-work alliance is whether the right balance is being struck in the training received by apprentices. Many vocational educators argue that occupational education should be directly related to the trade, because the amount of technical knowledge that must be mastered leaves no time for liberal-arts "frills."

But other educators argue that precisely because of the modern knowledge explosion, on-the-job training must be supplemented with language skills and liberal-arts type information so that students can cope with rapid changes in society in general, as well as the world of work.

The danger also exists that the coalition will concentrate too much on training people to meet employer labor market needs and not enough on the needs of individual workers. And such councils have one additional drawback: The amount of time that very busy community leaders can spend away from their work and other activities is limited. One solution to this dilemma would be to open the decision-making process to mass participation; the workers themselves could be encouraged to actively participate in solving societal (as well as personal) problems such as unemployment and job dissatisfaction.

### Study Circles in Sweden

Recent innovations by American community colleges could be combined with the "study circle" concept popular in Sweden to create a really superior educational system.

## Valencia Community College: Serving the Community

Community colleges in the United States have grown rapidly in recent years, and a brief description of the services offered by Valencia Community College in Orlando, Florida, reveals some of the reasons for their success.

Valencia Community College has an East Campus and a West Campus on opposite sides of Orlando, plus an Open Campus, headquartered in downtown Orlando. As its name implies, the Open Campus offers courses throughout the district—at various educational complexes, at police and fire departments, at high schools, churches and nursing homes, at art centers and recreational facilities, at Walt Disney World, and at major industrial and business sites. The college offers courses daily from 7:00 a.m. until 10:00 p.m., on weekends, over television, and through newspapers, thus giving citizens a wide variety of ways to get postsecondary education, regardless of work or family responsibilities.

In addition to its courses, the college offers a full range of supporting services—professional counseling staff, career development center, office of veterans affairs, financial aids program, tutoring assistance, credit by examination, assistance in finding part-time employment, student-centered learning laboratories, student organizations and publications, intramural and competitive athletics, cultural and social activities, and many other services to meet student needs.

Students range in age from 16 to 100, and the average age of students enrolled in credit courses is 27.

Approximately 80% of Valencia students hold jobs.

Valencia offers a variety of locally-needed occupational programs and also has a continuing education program that focuses on updating the skills of people working in various fields.

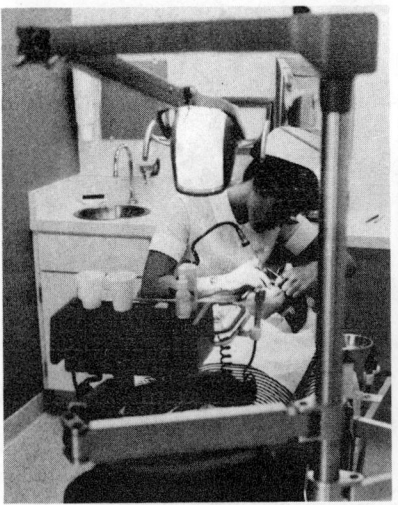

Dental hygiene student at Valencia Community College in Orlando, Florida, cleans patient's teeth.

Horticulture technology students work in greenhouse at Valencia Community College. Photos: Valencia Community College

Swedish study circles grew out of a popular-education movement pioneered by Social Democratic youth clubs in 1908 and the Workers Education Association, a group associated with unions, the cooperative movement, and the Social Democratic Party. Later, groups such as the Center and Liberal Parties, the Lutheran State Church of Sweden, and a union of white-collar workers organized their own educational circles.

Each circle consists of about 10 people who meet periodically for joint learning. Each study circle decides the direction of its own studies and determines its working method and pace. However, a trained moderator is on hand to keep things moving.

Government grants cover the study circle moderator's salary and 75% of the cost of materials; fees and members' dues take care of the remaining expenses. There are also "high priority study circles" for which the government pays 100% of the cost; their purpose is to narrow existing educational gaps among the population, and the subjects offered are Swedish, English, and social studies.

Among the regular circles, languages (particularly Swedish and English) are most popular. The other subjects studied tend to reflect the specialized interests of the parent organizations; for example, the church-affiliated groups concentrate on religion, philosophy, and psychology.

In Sweden, there are now some 200,000 study circles involving over two million participants—an impressive participation level for a country of eight million people. Study circles are therefore the most pervasive method of bringing education to Swedes of all ages and walks of life.

William Strawn, an American who writes for Swedish publications, believes that one reason for the popularity of the study circle is that in small towns it becomes a social center. Also, the circles constitute an "easy-going, friendly way of disseminating knowledge," Strawn says. People make friends in the circles—and sometimes even have an impact on government policy. Reports on discussions by study circles on whether or not Sweden should use nuclear energy as a future power source were transmitted to the government. In this way, reports Strawn, "Swedish leaders received highly accurate readings of current popular thinking on this volatile issue."

A combination of the study circle idea and the community colleges could lead to a golden age of adult education in North America. All that is needed is for some interest group to take the initiative and, as in Sweden, the unions may make the first move. Already some U.S. unions negotiate contracts with colleges to provide desired courses. For instance, District Council 37 of the American Federation of State, County, and Municipal Employees (AFSCME), which represents the New York City government workers, shops around at the local colleges and universities and chooses the schools offering the best deal in terms of quality and price. With a $1.5 million education fund, the union can afford to offer its members a wide variety of top-notch courses. Throughout the United States, labor and management invest enormous amounts of money in negotiated tuition-aid programs which could be funneled into mass education of workers.

### Will U.S. Workers Join Study Circles?

The money and the technology for this American adaptation of study cir-

Culinary arts student decorates cake at Los Angeles Trade-Technical College.

Community college student in Los Angeles practices welding under the watchful eye of an instructor.

Photos: Los Angeles Community Colleges

cles seem to be potentially available, but are American workers really interested in furthering their education? Will they respond favorably to the study circle concept?

A few years ago, the United Auto Workers negotiated a tuition aid program which provides a worker with up to $900 a year for college expenses, but only about 1% of the workers have taken advantage of the benefit. On the other hand, a study of workers in Michigan and Pennsylvania revealed that 70% of union members felt that their unions should be doing more to help them improve their skills.

One reason for the mixed response of workers to educational opportunities is

Carpentry student practices his trade at Los Angeles Trade-Technical College.

# Miami-Dade Community College

With more than 54,000 students, Miami-Dade Community College in Florida is the largest two-year college in the United States. The college offers 124 different programs and 1,273 courses. It has four campuses, including the New World Center Campus shown at left. Woman at right is taking a secretarial course at the college's South Campus, which has a simulated office course in which all kinds of business papers are processed in an organized paper flow through five departments, from sales to accounting. In other pictures: Fire-science students (below) battle blaze under controlled conditions. Engineering students learn in ultra-modern laboratory (bottom).

Photos: Miami-Dade Community College

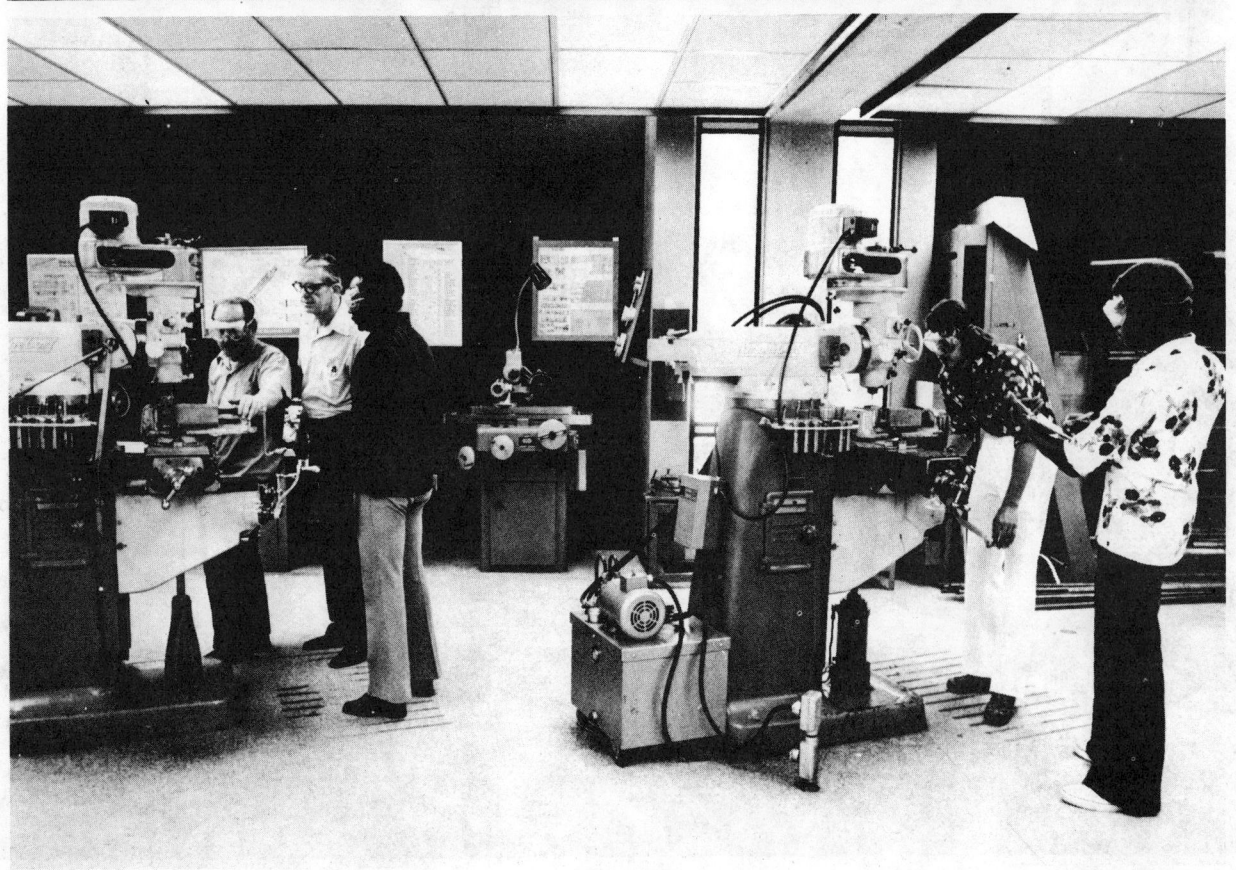

the delivery system. Workers are tired after a hard day of work, so it takes above-average motivation to battle traffic in the evenings, search frantically for a parking place, and then sit in a classroom filled with strangers. Also, the word "college" is intimidating; it has elitist connotations, and many adults don't relish the prospect of competing with youngsters. A survey conducted by Cornell University in New York found that the great majority of workers preferred to learn at the workplace; their second choice was community colleges.

If workers could have study-discussion groups made up of like-minded peers in their own neighborhoods or factories—perhaps even in their own homes—and know they would get college credit, worker participation in adult education almost assuredly would leap upward.

### The Value of Study Circles

Study circles offer a way for millions of people to study public issues like unemployment, energy, and transportation and discuss solutions, which could then be passed on to their government officials. What politician would overlook the recommendations of constituents who spent an entire semester studying and discussing an issue? Workers could play a role in planning their nation's future, thus ushering in an era of direct democracy.

Courses could also be designed to stimulate employees to think of ways to improve the quality of worklife and productivity. Jamestown Community College currently offers a three-credit course, jointly sponsored by labor and management, called "Improving the Quality of Working Life." West Virginia Northern Community College offers a seminar on "The Problems of Worker Discontent." During World War II, tens of thousands of workers on production committees helped identify ways to increase production. In New York City, city workers sit on 40 productivity committees along with management representatives; in 1976, their union (District Council 37, AFSCME) credited them with saving the city $7.8 million.

Most importantly, study circles could encourage adults to develop learning habits; every study of adult learners shows that the more education a person has, the more he wants. In the knowledge society now emerging, people must get accustomed to learning if they are to avoid obsolescence—and that constitutes the strongest argument for study circles or for any other type of "fun" adult learning.

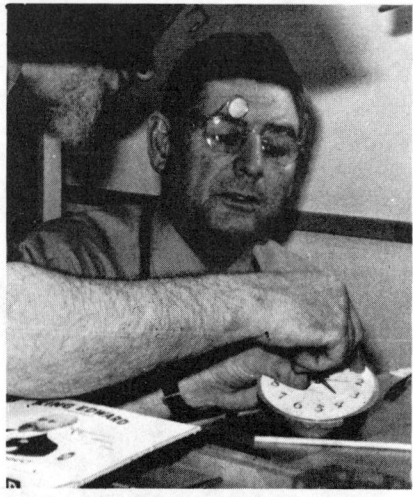

Student receives instruction in horology (the science of time and timekeeping instruments). In the one-year certificate programs offered at Mountain View College in Dallas, Texas, students study the design, construction, and mathematics of individual parts in antique and modern timepieces.
Photo: Mountain View College

The study circle concept has proved successful in Sweden. Uniting it with the awesome potential of the educational technologies now available could add a powerful new weapon against unemployment to the arsenal of human progress.

Study circle meets in Dalarna, Sweden. The average age of the students in this study circle is 82.
Photo: Swedish Information Office

# Is going to college worth the investment?

*by Andrew Spekke*

Since World War II, a college education has been thought of, and depicted in advertising campaigns, as an intrinsic investment in a child's future. And until recently there was solid evidence to support the claim that a college education would pay off handsomely. Recently the claim has been challenged, and the value of the college education for today's high school graduate is now an open question.

Throughout the 1950s and 1960s, an ample demand for college graduates existed in private industry, as well as government. During this period, a shortage of teachers at all levels provided job openings to graduates of all kinds. But the supply of graduates caught up with the demand as the children of the post-World War II baby boom left the universities to enter the world of work. This influx alone would have created an oversupply, but the recession simultaneously reduced the demand for college graduates in government and industry.

The effects began to be seen clearly in 1970, when the College Placement Council reported that offers of employment to June graduates were down 20% from the previous year. The decline continued in 1971 and, with the exception of a brief recovery in 1972, the prospects for employment of U.S. college graduates have remained bleak throughout the 1970s. By the end of the 1976 academic year, about 1.3 million people had bachelor's, master's, and Ph.D. degrees, nearly double the figure of ten years ago. During the same period, the number of professional, managerial, technical, and administrative jobs in the United States grew only by about one-third.

The financial returns on the college investment now have gotten smaller. As recently as 1972, according to a Census Bureau study, the average white male college graduate could expect nearly $200,000 more in lifetime earnings than the average male high school graduate. Today, when many blue-collar technicians earn $15 an hour, sanitation workers in some major U.S. cities annually gross $14,000-$18,000, and many Ph.D.'s drive taxicabs, the straight economic argument supporting the college degree no longer points in a clear direction toward higher social status and greater lifetime earnings. In a recent study for MIT's Center for Policy Alternatives, Harvard economist Richard Freeman and MIT Professor Herbert Hollomon noted the following:

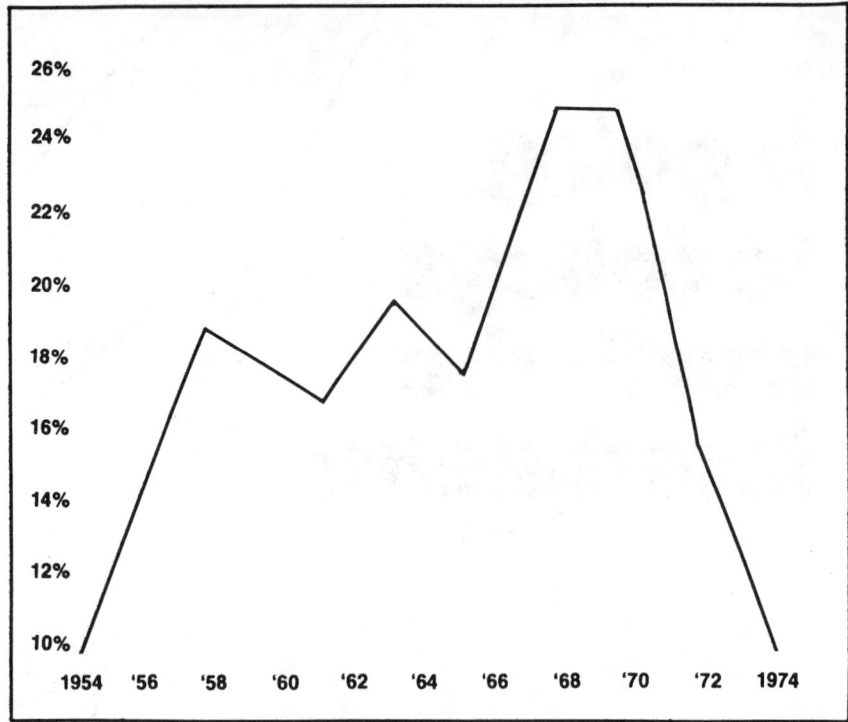

**Starting salary advantages of college graduates over average wage and salary earnings. Reprinted with permission from Vol. 7, No. 7, Change Magazine.**

- The rate of return on a college investment fell from 11-12% in 1969 to 7-8% in 1974, an unprecedented decrease. The rate is computed from the projected lifetime earnings of the college grad, minus tuition and other costs and lost income while in college.
- Incomes of college graduates still exceed those of high school graduates, but the ratio, stable since World War II, dropped from 53% to 40% between 1969 and 1974. Among 25- to 30-year-olds, the ratio fell from 39% to 23%.
- In comparison with 1969, the starting salary advantage for college graduates last year had dropped by 23% for social-science and humanities majors and by 21% for mathematics majors.
- Between 1969 and 1974, the proportion of 18- to 19-year-old males enrolled in higher education declined from 44% to 33.4%.
- The ratio of professional and management jobs to the number of graduates fell 2.8% per year from 1969-74.
- In the early 1970s, one-third of the men and two-thirds of the women took jobs unrelated to their college majors, compared with 10% and 13% in the early 1960s.

Under these circumstances, it is not surprising that the basic tenets regarding college attendance are being challenged and reevaluated.

Caroline Bird, a former instructor at the New School for Social Research, in *The Case Against College* (McKay, 1975), argues that going to college is "the dumbest investment you can make." One of her central arguments—somewhat tongue-in-cheek—goes as follows: The cost of four years at an Ivy League institution for a member of the Class of '76 is $34,181. (This total includes earnings accrued while working four years and not attending the University.) If, instead of investing this amount for a B.A. diploma, an 18-year-old youth were to invest the lump sum in a savings account or savings certificates at 7.5% interest compounded daily, he would have a sum of $1,129,200 at retirement—a sum nearly twice the expected life-time earnings of a college graduate. This, of course, would be in addition to his own lifetime earnings at this point.

There is, however, an unrealistic aura to this kind of reasoning in that most high school seniors do not have the $34,000 in a lump sum to invest, but Bird gets around this by having a rich uncle donate the total required amount. Many educators see *The Case Against College* as thinly disguised anti-intellectualism, but others believe that at least some of her arguments are valid.

## The Middle Class Pinch

The sharp public reassessment and critique of college has not seriously altered the fact that an overwhelming majority of Americans still want all possible educational opportunities and advantages for themselves and, especially, for their children. Public opinion polls show that the number one regret of adult Americans is that they did not attend college or did not get enough education; the number one hope continues to be that their children do so.

A recent survey conducted by Citicorp in New York pointed out, however, that "more than a third of those who plan to send junior away to college say they face an extreme financial hardship when the time comes." The total cost of enrollment is nearly double that of a decade ago. A year's tuition, room, board, and fees at an average private college costs nearly $5,000; even at many tax-supported institutions, the costs have doubled in the last 10 years as well, and parents are now paying an average $2,790 at a four-year college.

The Bureau of Labor Statistics (BLS) confirms that very few families have adequate funds to meet college costs. BLS estimated in the autumn of 1974 that families living on "low budgets," estimated at about $9,000 annually, and "intermediate budgets," estimated at about $14,000 annually, had very little "miscellaneous consumption" income left over after meeting their living expenses and other basic needs. Families earning less than $15,000 a year can usually qualify for help from the federal government. But middle-class families with incomes above that range have difficulties obtaining financial aid and meeting the costs of a college education, particularly when more than one student is concurrently attending college.

At the federal level, legislation has been proposed which would somewhat relieve the burdens of middle-class, college-attending households. A bill was introduced this year by Senator James Buckley of New York that would have allowed every taxpayer to deduct up to $1,000 for each dependent student. The bill, which did not pass this year, is in keeping with the sentiments of 63% of parents of college-age children, who strongly believe that government should help with their educational expenses.

## Temporary, Cyclical, or Long-Run?

Something, then, seems to be wrong at the education and employment crossroads. Are the developments of the 1970s a major break with the past or simply a temporary or cyclical phenomenon? It is very difficult to determine whether one is looking at a temporary deviation from a long-term trend or the beginning of an entirely new one when the figures available are but a few years old. However, analysis strongly suggests that the apparent collapse of the college job market is part of a long-term change in the existing supply and demand balance.

During the 1950s and 1960s, the world experienced exponential economic growth that is not likely to be equalled in the future. The growth rate of most sectors of the economy has now slackened. Two activities, for example, that employ large numbers of college-trained people—education and research and development—declined at the turn of the decade; the government reduced its outlays for research, and the number of school-age children declined, along with the birth rate.

While the demand for college graduates was leveling off, the supply of new graduates seeking work was increasing. Freeman and Holloman calculated that "estimates of the number of new B.A.'s seeking work, obtained by subtracting those going to graduate school, suggest that the number of new male B.A.'s 'on the job market' increased by 8% per year (relative to the male work force) from 1968 to 1973, compared to a modest 1.75% per year in the 1960s. In addition, the flow of new graduates was so much greater throughout the period than the number of retiring B.A.'s that the total supply of college-trained workers increased rapidly as a fraction of the work force—a development almost certain to continue into the 1980s due to the continued small number of college graduates nearing retirement age."

## The Economy in 1985

What of the future? Turning to the 1976-77 edition of the *Occupational Outlook Handbook* compiled by the U.S. Department of Labor's Bureau of Labor Statistics, we see that total employment is expected to increase by approximately 20% between 1974 and 1985, from 85.9 million to 103.4 million. Throughout the mid-1980s, BLS predicts the continued growth of white-collar and service occupations, a slower than average growth of blue-collar occupations, and a marked decline of farm workers.

Discussions and graphs of future employment opportunities by the BLS are primarily based on estimates of projected growth in employment and replacement needs because of deaths and retirements. Compared with replacement needs, employment growth is expected to account for only 30% of all job openings between 1974 and 1985. (See table.)

The projections published by BLS regarding overall 1985 employment and specific occupational projections are based on the following fundamental assumptions:

- The institutional framework of the U.S. economy will not change radically.
- Current social, technological, and scientific trends will continue, including values placed on work, education, income, and leisure.
- The economy will gradually recover from the high unemployment levels of the mid-1970s and reach full employment (defined as 4% unemployment) in the mid-1980s.
- No major events such as widespread or long-lasting energy shortages or war will significantly alter the industrial structure of the economy or alter the rate of economic growth.
- Trends in the occupational structure of industries will not be altered radically by changes in relative wages, technological changes, or other factors.

What about the demand for college graduates in the labor force of the 1980s? The Bureau of Labor Statistics expects the supply of graduates to exceed the demand throughout the mid-1980s. Even though the professional/technical category of workers will probably expand to 20% of the work force by 1985, there may be as many as 2 to 2.5 college graduates competing for every available job.

The Bureau believes that this situation may lead to rising entry requirements—i.e., desperate Ph.D.'s take jobs that M.A.'s could readily command; the M.A.'s accept positions usually held by B.A.'s, and so on to the bottom of the ladder, where people with little or no education are left competing for the most undesirable jobs.

It is no understatement to suggest that an unfortunate effect of underemploying the well-educated is an increase in morale problems and job dissatisfaction throughout industry and government.

### The Future of Work

Myron Clark, former President of the Society for the Advancement of Management, estimates that nearly 80% of all American workers are underemployed. The figure must include workers who are working at less than their full productive capacity, although that is not clearly stated. Many jobs have been "upgraded" (that is, Ph.D.'s and M.A.'s are employed in positions not previously held by Ph.D.'s and M.A.'s).

All workers in the category of the underemployed share a common problem—boredom. Most minds have great difficulty tolerating a steady diet of boredom, and unfortunately, boredom seems likely to increase in the future. Automation is a factor, but the problem more specifically is that the tolerance for routine decreases as the labor force becomes more highly educated. The increased expectations produced by exposure to TV and other media are also partially responsible for this trend. Furthermore, the types of jobs likely to be available in a post-industrial society will, if anything, exacerbate the underemployment problem.

Contemporary social observers Daniel Bell and Peter Drucker note that our society may be in the throes of creating a new meritocracy. The "elite" are the 20% or so holding the better jobs in the economy. The new, and possibly dangerous, feature of this meritocracy is that their superiority, skill, and education are not much greater than that of the "masses."

In a recent article, Fred M. Hechinger of the New York *Times* asks the penetrating question—"Will we turn out useless, and therefore disgruntled, graduates? Will the United States repeat the dangerous error of Germany and Italy in the 1920s—create an unemployed, alienated, and politically menacing proletariat?" (One-third of the SS officers in Nazi Germany had Ph.D.'s.) Although there is little hard data to support this development, one can see signs of disenchantment among educated men and women who have been relegated to menial jobs or unemployment, accompanied by loss of social status and their claim to the good life.

### Vocationalism Gains in Colleges

Institutions of higher learning are re-examining their curricula with a view toward providing more realistic "occupational preparation" or career-oriented studies. The response to newly perceived needs is not occurring easily or quickly. Debates rage. Critics see the trend towards "rampant vocationalism" threatening traditional academic pursuits, especially the liberal arts. Students everywhere reiterate the familiar—"I've learned a lot of useful things in college, but none of it had anything to do with getting a job."

Within colleges and universities throughout the U.S., shifts of student interest, from the "pure humanities" to career-related programs such as

## Projected Employment Growth by Major Occupational Group, 1974–85

(In thousands)

| Occupational Group | 1974 Employment | Projected 1985 Employment | Percent Change | Openings Total | Openings Growth | Openings Replacements |
|---|---|---|---|---|---|---|
| Total | 85,936 | 103,400 | 20.3 | 57,600 | 17,400 | 40,200 |
| White-collar workers | 41,739 | 53,200 | 27.5 | 34,300 | 11,500 | 22,800 |
|   Professional and technical workers | 12,338 | 16,000 | 29.4 | 9,400 | 3,600 | 5,700 |
|   Managers and administrators | 8,941 | 10,900 | 21.6 | 5,200 | 1,900 | 3,200 |
|   Salesworkers | 5,417 | 6,300 | 15.7 | 3,400 | 900 | 2,600 |
|   Clerical workers | 15,043 | 20,100 | 33.8 | 16,300 | 5,100 | 11,300 |
| Blue-collar workers | 29,776 | 33,700 | 13.2 | 12,500 | 3,900 | 8,600 |
|   Craft and kindred workers | 11,477 | 13,800 | 19.9 | 5,100 | 2,300 | 2,800 |
|   Operatives[1] | 13,919 | 15,200 | 9.0 | 6,000 | 1,300 | 4,800 |
|   Nonfarm laborers | 4,380 | 4,800 | 8.8 | 1,400 | 400 | 1,100 |
| Service workers | 11,373 | 14,600 | 28.0 | 11,000 | 3,200 | 7,800 |
| Farm workers | 3,048 | 1,900 | −39.0 | −200 | −1,200 | 1,000 |

[1] Includes the 1970 Census classification: operatives, except transport and transport equipment operatives.
Note: Details may not add to totals because of rounding.

business administration and computer sciences, are being widely reported. The U.S. Commissioner of Education, Terrel H. Bell, recently stated: "The college that devotes itself totally and unequivocally to the liberal arts today is just kidding itself. Today, we in education must recognize that it is also our duty to provide students with salable skills."

Critics assert that the use of the universities for more and more career education is nothing more than "aggrandizement of the managerial class." This refers to the widely held belief that American industry has created an artificial demand for diplomas by using the degree to screen potential employees—regardless of the relevance of the diploma to their employment. But if the diploma serves only to identify and screen potential corporate employees, it becomes, in the words of Harvard's Christopher Jencks, "a hell of an expensive aptitude test." And if everyone has one, so to speak, it becomes more and more an empty credential, and further devalues a college education.

A manpower report prepared by the Department of Labor in 1971 reached some revealing conclusions regarding the relationship between education and employment:

1. In eight of ten occupations, there was *no* relationship between the workers' educational attainment and their degree of job success.

2. Widely different educational requirements are used for the same jobs.

3. Turnover tended to be high where there were significant differences between industry hiring standards and the actual requirements of the job.

4. Reliance on educational attainment as a main screening device can have serious consequences and high turnover rates, as well as poor morale and job performance among the better educated employees.

5. Elimination of artificial hiring requirements can have positive effects for employers and employees.

There are obvious pitfalls to vocational or career training in higher education. "This whole business of trying to pick a major to match a job is just Russian roulette," says Harvard economist Freeman. Today's "hot" fields in the computer sciences, accounting, and nursing, for example, could be glutted in a few years, just as the aerospace industry, very glamorous in the early 1970s, dried up by the end of the decade.

Students are flocking to community and junior colleges; many find the vocational nature of the curriculum the surest route to a good job. Between 1960 and 1974, enrollment at two-year colleges went from 660,000 to a staggering 3,257,000. Many of the programs frequently give the students on-the-job training away from the campus.

President Ford, among others, has heartily endorsed the concept of "career education." A year ago, he told a graduating class at Ohio State University: "You spend four years in school, graduate, go into the job market, and are told that the rules have changed. To succeed you must acquire further credentials, so you go back to the university and ultimately emerge with a master's or even a Ph.D.... And you know what happens next? You go out and look for a job and now they say you are overqualified... The fact of the matter is that education is being strangled—by degrees."

**Jobs Present/Jobs Future**

Where are the jobs today? Most employers look for individuals who can provide specific talents, such as accounting, secretarial, and nursing skills. Demand is high in certain engineering fields (petroleum, energy), as well as for computer scientists and technicians. Other so-called "hot" occupations include hotel and restaurant management, fast food services in general, pharmaceutical technology, and sales.

Private industry is quite eager to employ women and blacks. The 1976 Endicott Report shows that 45% more graduates would be hired from both of these groups this year than last. To the question of what liberal arts graduates can do to make themselves more employable, the majority of the *Fortune* 500 companies say: "Take business-related courses. Minor in a business subject. Take economics, accounting, business administration, computer science, statistics, and finance."

The BLS *Occupational Outlook Handbook, 1976-77 Edition*, identifies the following occupations for college graduates where the employment prospects, in terms of average annual openings, will be the greatest in the next ten years: engineering, social work, personnel and labor relations, accounting, computer operators, programmers, and systems analysts. The field of nursing will provide unprecedented opportunities in terms of average annual openings during the forthcoming decade. In fact, if therapy and rehabilitation occupations are included in the projections, the annual growth and replacement rate for the nursing field exceeds 300,000.

Not surprisingly, the largest group, with the greatest prospects for future employment, continues to be clerical. Vast armies of college graduates, especially female, will be found in the secretarial and typing pools; the combined annual openings for secretaries, stenographers, and typists will exceed the 560,000 mark. (See table.)

**Options for High School Graduates**

With respect to the question, "Is college necessary—and for whom?", the consensus among career counselors and educators is that the most positive way out of our present troubles is to stop selling college education as an economic investment and to emphasize that general education and career education are not mutually exclusive.

Many educators believe that the public should gradually be persuaded that higher education should not be limited to—much less dominated by—high school graduates. Colleges and universities should become centers for life-long learning. The president of Yale University, Kingman Brewster, for example, warns against "the assumption that formal education is best received in continuous doses."

Today's high school graduate has at least five distinct options:

- Continue and pursue formal education.
- Find employment—full time or part time (work study).
- Get involved in volunteer work (any field of interest).
- Enlist in any of the armed services.
- Take the "grand tour" (travel in U.S., Europe, etc.).

The second and third alternatives have found increasing favor among counselors advising prospective college students. The counselors' message to many high school graduates is: "Get work in your field of interest first, pick up practical knowledge and income, then see if your career requires further degree study." Frequently part-time or summer jobs or volunteer work may turn into full-time employment.

Fewer students should commit themselves to immediate college enrollment upon graduation from high school, many counselors believe, but many high school graduates who do not immediately go to college

## Where the Jobs Will Be

The following table, excerpted from the U.S. Department of Labor's *Occupational Outlook Handbook in Brief,* 1976-77 edition, lists some of the areas that will provide the most jobs for college graduates in the next 10 years.

| Occupation | Estimated employment 1974 | Average annual openings[1] 1974-85 | Employment trends and prospects |
|---|---|---|---|
| **Engineering occupations** | 1,100,000 | 52,500 | Employment expected to grow faster than average for all occupations. Very good opportunities for engineering school graduates as supply is likely to fall short of demand. Many openings also will be filled by upgraded technicians and graduates in related fields. |
| **Social workers** | 300,000 | 30,500 | Employment expected to increase faster than average for all occupations. Best opportunities for those with professional social work training at all degree levels. |
| **Personnel and labor relations workers** | 320,000 | 23,000 | Employment expected to increase faster than average for all occupations as employers implement new employee relations programs in areas of occupational safety and health, equal employment opportunity, and pensions. Although growing public employee unionism will spur demand for labor relations workers, keen competition is anticipated. Best opportunities for applicants with advanced degrees. |
| **Accountants** | 805,000 | 45,000 | Very good opportunities. Because of growing complexity of business accounting requirements, college graduates, particularly those who worked part time for an accounting firm while in school, will be in greater demand that nongraduates. Employers also prefer applicants trained in computer techniques. |
| **Computer and related occupations** | | | |
| **Computer operating personnel** | 500,000 | 27,500 | Employment of keypunch operators expected to decline because of advances in other data entry techniques and equipment. Employment of console and auxiliary equipment operators should grow faster than average for all occupations in response to the expanding use of computer hardware, especially terminals. |
| **Programmers** | 200,000 | 13,000 | Employment expected to grow faster than average for all occupations as computer use expands, particularly in medical, educational, and data processing services. Best opportunities for programmers with some training in systems analysis. |
| **Systems analysts** | 115,000 | 9,100 | Employment expected to grow faster than average for all occupations in response to advances in hardware and computer programs resulting in expanded computer applications. Also, as users become more familiar with computer capabilities, they will expect greater efficiency and performance from their systems. |
| **Nursing occupations** | | | |
| **Licensed practical nurses** | 495,000 | 93,000 | Very good opportunities as public and private health insurance plans expand and as LPN's assume duties previously performed by registered nurses. |
| **Nursing aides, orderlies, and attendants** | 970,000 | 123,000 | Employment expected to increase much faster than average for all occupations. Although most openings will arise from replacement needs, many new openings will be in nursing homes, convalescent homes, and other long term care facilities. |
| **Registered nurses** | 860,000 | 71,000 | Favorable opportunities, especially for nurses with graduate education seeking positions as teachers and administrators. Strong demand in some southern states and many inner-city locations. |
| **Secretaries and stenographers** | 3,300,000 | 439,000 | The increasing use of dictating machines will limit opportunities for office stenographers. Very good prospects for skilled shorthand reporters and secretaries. |
| **Typists** | 1,000,000 | 125,000 | Employment expected to grow faster than average for all occupations as business expansion results in increased paperwork. Very good opportunities for typists, particularly those familiar with automatic typewriters and new kinds of word processing equipment. |

*Footnote*
[1] Due to growth, deaths and retirements, and other causes of separation from labor force. Does not include transfers out of occupations.

Source: Bureau of Labor Statistics, U.S. Department of Labor

should do so when their personal interests and aspirations have matured and crystallized. In other words, the counselors are saying: "Don't get a diploma and then start looking for a job. Try to get work experience *before* you have your diploma."

Other practical advice from the experts:

• Be wary of fields which are touted to be wide open, either now or in the future. Overcrowding in any field tends to be cyclical, warns Freeman. "What you want to do is to see what everyone else is doing and then do something different."

• Be aware of geography. Generally, one should avoid cities like San Francisco, where "everyone wants to live." Large urban centers experiencing fiscal problems—New York, Boston, and Detroit, for example—are also likely to have relatively few openings.

**Where To From Here?**

The increasing disparity between the number of new college graduates entering the job market and the number of new openings in professional/technical occupations requiring a college degree has led to calls for the reform of entire systems of education. In the United States, as well as other industrial nations, there is increased pressure for some sort of "manpower planning." Though hotly debated, the issue remains unresolved.

In Sweden, for example, reforms which will take effect in 1977-78 will channel students into one of five vocational sectors, based on predictions of the number of jobs required in each. In the 1977-78 school years, the 38,000 new college students will be distributed in the following way among the five sectors, according to a recent article in the *Chronicle of Higher Education:* teacher training, 10,000; administration and economics, 8,900; welfare sector (including medicine, nursing), 8,100; technological fields, 5,400; culture and information, 2,800. The distribution of the remaining 2,800 students will be determined by local needs as required. In recent years, Sweden has experienced a declining enrollment in universities, easing its manpower distribution crisis somewhat. The new program, hopefully, will make the problem largely a thing of the past.

Even in the Soviet Union, where manpower planning has long existed, authorities are finding "vexing imbalances" in the supply and demand ratio of needed professionals.

In the U.S., many are calling for the federal government to step in, as in the 1930s, to correct the imbalances. New versions of the Work Projects Administration (WPA), Civilian Conservation Corps (CCC), and National Service are being proposed to make constructive use of the various skills of America's unemployed. Manpower experts are also suggesting a variety of schemes whereby the private sector might provide more effective career counseling to schools and communities.

*"Even though the professional/technical category of workers will probably expand to 20% of the work force by 1985, there may be as many as 2 to 2.5 college graduates competing for every available job."*

The Carnegie Commission, headed by former University of California President Clark Kerr, has supported this view by proposing that every high school graduate be given "two years in the bank" to spend on higher education at any time—suggesting an alternating pattern between education and work.

Sociologist James Coleman, in a report to the President's Science Advisory Committee, recommended more work and less school for America's youth, aged 14 to 24. His team of nine social scientists and educators proposed programs to alternate study with work, a move toward an old pattern—apprenticeship.

Willard Wirtz, former U.S. Secretary of Labor, in a recent study, *The Boundless Resource* (New Republic, 1975), proposes that "a break of one or two years in the formal education sequence—taken between ages 16 and 20—be recognized and established as a standard optional phase of the youth experience." Wirtz calls for a careful review of all laws and regulations that now impede the movement from study to work and vice versa.

Discrimination on the basis of a college education may be illegal in the U.S., many manpower experts believe, as it already is for secondary level education. In a 1971 Supreme Court ruling (*Griggs v. Duke Power Co.*), the requiring of a high school diploma was outlawed on the grounds that an employer cannot demand a qualification which systematically excludes an entire class of applicants, unless that requirement can be specifically and unequivocally shown to be a prerequisite for the successful performance of a particular job. To date, this has not been tested on a college level, but eventually the Supreme Court may extend the principle, enunciated in *Griggs v. Duke Power Co.*, to cover college education.

"We need a new rationale for why students should go to college and for why society should support higher education," says Frank Newman, President of the University of Rhode Island. The rationale of the '50s and '60s, Newman says, was the "theory of trained specialists. It fit the needs of the society, of the students, and of the universities in an era of growth, but it will not work when the need for 'trained specialists' stops growing."

What really is most urgently needed, the experts generally agree, are broader alternatives and options for high school graduates. One benefit of the current debate is that Americans are challenging old assumptions and cliches, connected with middle-class prejudices and pride. College has never been for everyone, and this may be all the more true in the years to come. High school students need to look more closely and critically at college, and decide if the heavy investment is likely to yield adequate dividends, financial or otherwise, in the future.

---

## Help in Choosing a Career

A student seeking help in choosing a career should consider a career counseling service. A career counselor uses a series of tests and interviews to identify a person's aptitudes and interests, assets and limitations. The counselor also provides information on the number of openings in a particular field; the amount of education and experience that are required; pay scales; and opportunity for advancement. He can also provide information about the values, life-styles, and cultural aspects of various occupations. The cost of career counseling ranges from $75 to $500; a typical short-term counseling package might involve three or four interviews and six hours of testing. (Free counseling is available for students at most university counseling centers.)

For a list of accredited counseling services in the United States (plus a few in Canada), see the *Directory of Counseling Services,* available at many libraries or from the publisher, the International Association of Counseling Services, Inc., 1607 New Hampshire Avenue, N.W., Washington, D.C. 20009, at a cost of four dollars. Each listing includes clientele served, fees involved, business hours, method of applying, staff, and the credentials of the director.

For information on job duties, educational requirements, employment outlook, and earnings for more than 850 occupations, see the *Occupational Outlook Handbook, 1976-77 Edition,* compiled by the U.S. Department of Labor's Bureau of Labor Statistics. The handbook is available for $7 from the Superintendent of Documents, U.S. Government Printing Office, Washington, D.C. 20402. The Bureau has also compiled the *Occupational Outlook Handbook in Brief, 1976-77 Edition,* which summarizes the employment outlook to 1985 for about 275 occupations selected from the larger handbook.

---

Andrew Spekke, a consultant-editor in the Washington, D.C., metropolitan area, writes a monthly "Future Focus" column for *Intellect* magazine and was the editor of *The Next 25 Years: Crisis and Opportunity* (World Future Society, 1975). He lives at 4403 Bradley Lane, Chevy Chase, Maryland 20015.

---

EDUCATION TOMORROW is a bimonthly newsletter of the World Future Society that features trends, forecasts, and innovations in traditional and non-traditional learning at every level from pre-school to post-retirement.

EDUCATION TOMORROW is for teachers, students, parents, government officials, businessmen, community leaders; everyone in fact who cares about expanding and improving opportunities to learn.

Topics in past issues of EDUCATION TOMORROW have included:

- Special education for gifted children
- Why some colleges are dropping traditional honor codes, but bringing back "old-fashioned" D's and F's
- High school experiments with a 4-day week
- Liberal arts may still be "the most practical" education for the future
- Indonesia's satellite for educational TV

Enroll yourself today in EDUCATION TOMORROW.
EDUCATION TOMORROW (Price: $12; $9 for members of the World Future Society)

# Illiterates with Doctorates:
# The Future of Education in an Electronic Age

### by Peter H. Wagschal

Many educators and parents are demanding that schools return to "the basics." But reading, writing, and arithmetic may be skills without a future, an educator suggests. Increasingly sophisticated audio, video, and computer technologies will soon replace the three R's as the basic tools of communication. Hence, the citizen of the future may be knowledgeable and effective—but largely illiterate.

Apparently, everyone who has anything to do with American education agrees that it's time to go back to the basics. Standardized test scores are down, reading test scores are down, and students don't write as well as they used to. So, obviously, we have to go back to the basics.

This may sound like compelling logic, but in a society that stands on the brink of a communications revolution, I would suggest that equating "the basics" with "the three R's" is a grievous and short-sighted error. Few educators insist on reading, writing, and arithmetic for their own sake. Rather, most argue that these skills are necessary because they give people access to the stored knowledge of humanity, or that they are abilities required to survive and succeed in modern societies, or perhaps, that they "train the mind" for the kind of critical thinking that teachers encourage in their students. The "basics," in short, have always had something to do with knowledge, communication, and maybe even wisdom, and we have always assumed that the ability to read, write, and compute were necessary prerequisites for achieving those ends.

In the past, this facile assumption made some sense—even if it was wrong in many instances. After all, printed words and numbers were the only way for people to pass their wisdom on to posterity, or to communicate over distance, or to store reliably their thoughts for inspection at a later time. Until recently, the printed word was the only trustworthy way to send our thoughts through time and space.

But computers and video-cassettes have clearly put an end to all that. Not only is the written word no longer the only means of storing and sending information, it is no longer even the best way. The present generation of computers can store more information in less space and communicate more quickly and reliably than any form of printed matter. And the next generations of computers will be still faster, lighter, cheaper, and more reliable. What I am suggesting is that we are witnessing the demise of the written word as our primary means of storing and communicating information. By the time my four-year-old son reaches adulthood, there will be hardly any compelling reason for him to be able to read, write, and do arithmetic. He will have more—not less—access to the accumulated wisdom of the peoples of the globe, but the three R's will have succumbed to the influence of inexpensive, fast, reliable computers that call up information instantly in response to the spoken word.

We are so accustomed to equating knowledge, intelligence, and wisdom with the written word that the modern transition from printed to electronic media is catching us by surprise and challenging our preconceptions. For example, despite its obvious advantages, the printed word has always had serious flaws. One is that a book is inherently passive: You can ask it all the questions you want, but it simply cannot respond. Furthermore, reading and writing are inherently solitary activities. You can't read or write a book and talk about it at the same time. And, of course, books can offer only words and still photographs, which together convey only a paltry fraction of what human beings have to communicate to one another. How much more would we know of Freud's thought and work if we had videotapes of his therapy sessions instead of only his books?

The printed word has always had another serious disadvantage—one which is reflected in our present worries over declining reading and writing abilities and in the continued failure of global literacy programs—the three R's are, by their very nature, tools of the affluent and elite. They are time-consuming modes of communication and inherently difficult to learn. The illiteracy of the majority of the globe's population has never been a reflection of species-wide stupidity, but rather of the limited and limiting nature of print as a medium. Only a minority of the globe's population can afford the time and resources required to learn and use the three R's.

The electronic media, on the other hand, possess no such built-in limitations. As soon as they become economically competitive with the printed word (audio technologies already are; video technologies are sure to be within a decade; and computer technologies will be within two decades), electronic media will make everything there is to know **universally** accessible to all peo-

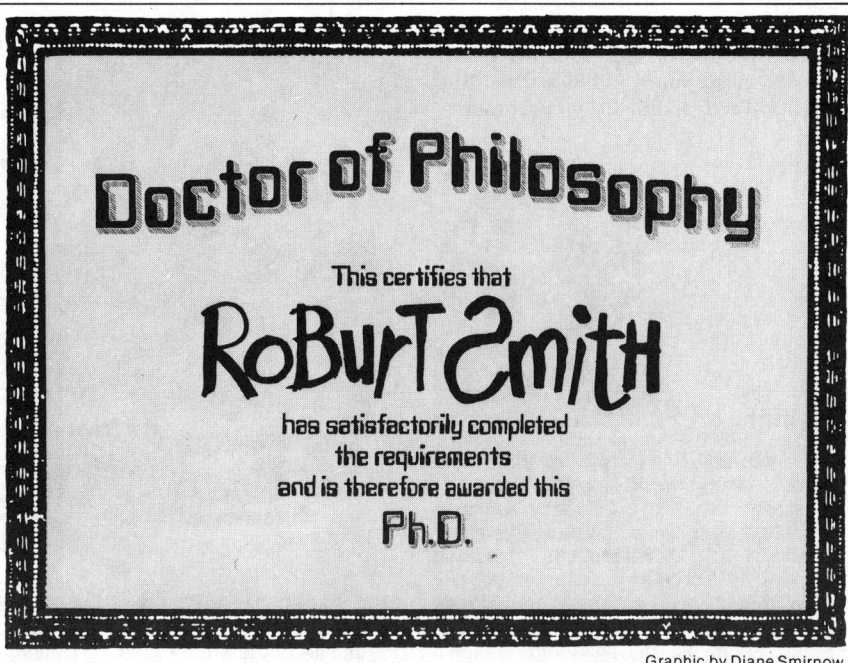

*Graphic by Diane Smirnow*

ple of the globe. Knowledge will then be everyone's property, rather than being restricted—as it currently is—to the minority who can afford the luxury of reading and writing.

Our fears about the computer revolution, of course, are phrased in quite the opposite manner—we see The Computer as an inherently centralized technology which enables a few to dictate to the many. But computers now are becoming more individualized and decentralized, thanks to minicomputers and microcomputers, whereas print remains *inherently* centralized and elitist. Computer technology is increasingly accessible to the average person; if you own an electronic calculator, you already own a computer.

So, yes, let's go back to the basics. But let's recognize that this does not mean placing *more* emphasis on the three R's. Rather, it means placing *less* emphasis on those skills and more on the goals they were originally intended to serve. For every indication suggests that 21st-century America can be a society in which knowledge, ability, and wisdom are exceedingly widespread in a population that is substantially illiterate.

### About the Author

Peter Wagschal is Director of the Future Studies Program at the University of Massachusetts. He is currently editing a collection of speeches given at the recent University of Massachusetts "Learning Tomorrows" conference, for publication by Praeger Publishers next spring. His address is Future Studies Program, Hills House South, Room 162, University of Massachusetts, Amherst, Massachusetts 01003.

Electronic educational systems may provide tomorrow's students with a first-class education without requiring them to read or write. The advent of electronic learning may lead to the demise of the written word, says educator Peter Wagschal.

Photo: National Education Association

# Tomorrow in Brief

Forecasts
Trends
Innovations
Ideas

### The Abacus vs. the Calculator

Despite the advent of cheap electronic calculators, the abacus still has a bright future in Japan. Until a few years ago, almost no one in Ono, the acknowledged abacus capital of Japan, thought that the centuries-old device could survive in the age of electronics. But the popularity of the abacus continues to grow, for reasons that, apparently, do not compute. Since 1974, sales of abacuses have been growing at a rate of about 15% annually. Last year, craftsmen in Ono produced a record 2.2 million of the ancient instruments for total sales of about $10 million.

### Vanishing Dialects

Dialects are declining in the United States under the impact of radio and television. "Soon we'll all talk alike," says linguist Martha C. Howard, who has just completed a study on West Virginia dialects for the *Linguistic Atlas of the United States and Canada*.

"But I for one would much rather hear a news commentator tell me that snow is 'shoe mouth deep' (a few inches)," says Howard, "or hear a young mother refer to her baby as a 'lappin' (a few months old), than hear today's usage."

### The Bibliophile's Lament

Future collections of rare books, prized manuscripts, and ancient documents may not include many books being printed today. And it's not because the wisdom of the ancients is so durable, but because their paper is.

Marilyn Kaufman

The modern paper-making technique of using wood pulp coated with alum-rosin compounds has shortened the lifespan of the average book to roughly 30 years. The compound's high sulfuric acid content, some of which remains even after the paper-making process, actually eats away the paper. Two hundred or even 600-year-old books can be in better shape than volumes printed less than 100 years ago. The records and ideas of the ancient Egyptians may outlast us all—some papyrus scrolls have already survived for more than 5,000 years.

# Advanced Interactive Technology:
# Robots in the Home and Classroom

by Michael Freeman and Gary P. Mulkowsky

**Robots are no longer just heroes or villains. They have become teachers and playmates. Both at home and in the classroom, robots can instruct and entertain children as well as match wits with adults. Robots, in fact, have already taken a gigantic first step—from fantasy to reality.**

Interactive technologies take advantage of the link between man and machine—to the benefit of both. Many technologies are, in a sense, extensions of man's own powers: Television extends the reach of our eyes and ears and the telephone the range of our voice. But only the computer and the robot—the computer in its human form—can be truly interactive technologies.

The mechanical mind (and the mechanical man) can serve human beings in countless ways. But some of the most exciting possibilities depend on the use of computers and robots that actually help people use their own minds and actively engage them in an educational give-and-take.

Devices that promote this kind of interaction will almost certainly be common in the future, but a few already exist. Interactive technologies available today include: a toy robot that talks and tests people's ability to think, learn, create, and play games; a home computer that can help humans in making decisions on anything from recipes to purchasing carpets, and an advanced robot teaching aid that knows students by name, teaches them at their own level of comprehension, and has a memory bank that can handle all the information contained in their seven standard textbooks. Technologies of this kind focus on man's most precious power—the ability to think.

### The Personable Robot

Many toys stimulate children's imaginations at first, but because most toys are passive, eventually the challenge—and the fun—are often lost. Can a toy show intelligence and unpredictability, and thus continue to stimulate a child's imagination long after conventional toys have been banished to the attic? The answer has just recently become "yes." For between $50 and $60, Mego Corporation is marketing a toy robot with some surprising new capabilities. His name is 2-XL (to excel).

**Left:** 2-XL is a talking toy robot who can educate and entertain children at home. A variety of taped programs make 2-XL knowledgeable on a wide range of subjects and also give him a chatty, likeable "personality."

Photo: Courtesy of Michael Freeman

Rather than simply sitting there, 2-XL asks questions and accepts objective answers such as multiple choice, true/false, and yes/no. He knows if your answer is correct—and can give you the right answer if you are wrong.

2-XL also can provide "more information" on a topic that interests a child. "More information" includes the first words spoken on the moon, great moments from history, memorable moments from the sports world, interviews with people listed in the *Guinness Book of World Records*, and much more.

2-XL has programmable tapes that are developed separately from the machine and cover areas such as sports, world records, science fiction, the metric system, monsters and legends, games and puzzles, and more. Some of these programs come with booklets that include relevant information, pictures, puzzles, etc.

With this advanced "game and puzzle" program, 2-XL can match wits with both children and adults. Of course, 2-XL can be beaten, but he is a formidable opponent who hates to lose. He makes lots of side comments as the game progresses.

2-XL also can remember if a child answered the previous question correctly, and wish him good luck this time. In some cases, 2-XL will follow a wrong answer with an easier question and a right answer with a more difficult question. This challenges children without frustrating them. 2-XL also tells stories and lets the child determine how the story progresses and even choose different endings.

But what makes 2-XL charming as well as educational is his "human" personality. He jokes and fools around, and yet can be quite serious at times. 2-XL laughs, cries and makes sarcastic comments. He gets excited when you are correct and disappointed when you are wrong. If you miss an easy question, for example, 2-XL may kiddingly call you an "inferior biological unit" and then proceed to explain the answer. If you consistently "mess up," there are always jokes in his memory banks to cheer you up. He also may decide to give you a second chance if you answer incorrectly. For questions that are too difficult for a particular child, 2-XL will suggest that the child push a special button so he can explain the answer. Correct answers might prompt 2-XL to tell you that he is impressed and add that "IBM would be proud of you."

Though much of the robot's behavior sounds like pure fun, his responses were conceived and programmed by a team of behaviorists and psychologists to help children learn. The end results are challenging and educational as well as entertaining. Furthermore, 2-XL is very patient. As one child said of 2-XL, "He never gets angry, even when I'm stupid."

Additional taped programs can expand the range of 2-XL's abilities. For example, 2-XL can become a talking calculator. With the help of special programs, 2-XL can generate numbers, allow a child or adult to choose the desired function, and then "calculate" the answer. 2-XL could be used to drill students in mathematics or play mathematical games that will both entertain and educate.

But 2-XL's most important asset is his ability to interact. He is an active—not a passive—toy. 2-XL gives children information, encouragement, and a "personality" to respond to. Inside 2-XL is a unique circuit, patented worldwide, that makes this kind of interaction possible. A modified eight-track tape contains his "voice," and a circuit allowing direct access to various channels and segments creates 2-XL's "conversational manner." Since there are many programs available, 2-XL can "converse" on virtually any subject at any level of difficulty—and in any language.

## A Home Computer System

One of the most disappointing aspects of computers today is that so few people have access to them. Even those who do are usually responsible for getting a particular job done and have no access to computers for personal use.

Radio Shack, a U.S. electronics distributor, hopes to change this state of affairs with a home computer system that sells for approximately $600. The Radio Shack TRS 80 is a basic system with many of the features of larger computers. Once the customer is familiar with the standard program, he can purchase options that expand the machine's capabilities. Although the TRS 80 is not verbal, it is sold with a 12" screen for readout and an optional printer for printout.

One real advantage of this kind of computer is the manner in which it structures various problems. For example, if you want to paint and carpet your entire home, you need only punch in the different variables that pre-programmed formulas require to compute the amount of paint needed or the square yards of carpeting required. The TRS 80 system then structures the problem for you. In this instance the following questions would appear on the screen:

What is the length of each room?
What is the width of each room?
What is the height of the ceiling?

You feed in the information on the keyboard and the system computes the amount of paint and carpeting you will need. The system will also compute the cost, sales tax, and the amount of floor padding needed.

Leachim, a robot teacher built and programmed by the authors, instructs a third-grader in a New York City school. Through the use of headphones, Leachim can teach different subjects at different levels of difficulty to five children simultaneously. Leachim's memory bank holds the contents of seven textbooks, a dictionary, a thesaurus, and a children's encyclopedia. (Leachim's name is an anagram for his inventor's name, Michael.)

Photo: Courtesy of Michael Freeman

The home computer system does more than just add, subtract, and multiply. By structuring the problems of the average consumer, it gives lessons in logic. But more importantly, it brings the computer into the home and helps familiarize people with the kind of advanced technology that is gradually becoming a part of everyday life.

### A Robot as Teacher

When the fourth-graders heard about their new teacher, the description made him sound quite normal: 200 pounds, six feet tall, well-spoken, and named Mr. Leachim—all very conventional, except for one thing. Leachim is a computerized electronic robot. Leachim knows the names of all the children along with the names of their brothers, sisters, parents, pets, reading scores, IQ scores, math scores, hobbies and interests, the contents of their seven class textbooks, and a number of different teaching methods. Leachim is motorized and has an adjacent visual display screen (called a Tableau) that exhibits material as Leachim explains it verbally.

Leachim is an advanced experimental verbal computer that has all the capabilities of conventional computer systems but can convert standard computer output into words and tailor his responses for different children. In addition, Leachim grades tests and maintains progress reports on each child.

Leachim can be quite stern if a child is working well below his capacity. On the other hand, when slower children demonstrate even a little success, Leachim's compliments and reassurances are generous.

## About the Authors

Freeman          Mulkowsky

Michael Freeman, the inventor of Leachim and 2-XL, is a Professor of Management at The Baruch College, City University of New York. He has written a number of articles on advanced technologies and holds numerous domestic and international patents in computers and interactive technology.

Gary P. Mulkowsky assisted Michael Freeman in the creation of both robots and was primarily responsible for their curricular programming. Mulkowsky is a Professor at The Baruch College, City University of New York, a consultant in public policy and program development, and the author of several articles on organizational psychology and educational technology.

A domestic android built by Quasar Industries, Inc. The authors argue that advanced technologies may come to be accepted parts of everyday life, and that many people may need at least a working familiarity with complex machines in the future. The day of the mechanical servant may not be far away, since Quasar Industries hopes to mass produce its domestic android within about two years. Photo: Quasar Industries, Inc.

"Just the other day," said John Simons, a fourth-grader who uses Leachim, "he taught me some chess moves on his Tableau because he said I did so well in my math studies." Leachim was programmed to know that John liked chess as a hobby and was using the chess lesson as a reward for the student's good work.

The following is an actual excerpt from a typical school day for a student and Leachim:

When Susan approaches Leachim, he asks her to identify herself. Susan replies, "I am Susan Smith," and dials an identification code. Leachim compares previously programmed voice print information on each student with what he is currently "hearing," and checks the identification code to avoid any confusion. After a moment, Leachim answers, "Hello Susan. How are you today? Let us begin our lesson." Leachim reminds Susan of their last lesson together, mentions how well she did, and then proceeds:

"Question number one," says Leachim. "For this question you will need a pencil and paper." Susan has a pencil ready and gets poised to write. "I will now recite for you the 'Pledge of Allegiance to the Flag.' I pledge allegiance to the flag . . . one nation under God *indivisible* . . . . Now that is an interesting word 'indivisible.' Do you know what that word means, Susan?" "No," Susan responds by pushing a button on Leachim's chest. "Let us look it up then," Leachim replies. "I will spell it for you: i-n-d-i-v-i-s-i-b-l-e. I will give you two minutes to look it up in your dictionary. Look it up now." Leachim is silent for exactly two minutes and then announces, "If you would like more time, push switch X to the right, please." Since Susan believes she has found the word, she refrains from pushing switch X. Leachim now tells Susan he will give her four choices and instructs her to choose only one. "Does 'indivisible' mean: (a) cannot be seen at night; (b) wonderful and fair; (c) cannot be divided; or (d) strong? Choose your answer now." At this moment Susan drops her pencil and takes a moment to retrieve it, instead of answering immediately. Leachim, aware that Susan has not yet answered, reminds her, "I am still waiting for you to choose an answer." Finally Susan does. She chooses B. "Not correct. Not correct," is the immediate reply of Leachim. "The word 'indivisible' does not mean wonderful and fair. 'Indivisible' means cannot be divided and I suggest that you look on page 253 of your dictionary. Here you will find the word and its proper meaning." In a moment Leachim gives Susan a second question, which deals with math. "Multiply 12 x 25. Let me know when you are done." After completing the answer, Susan informs Leachim that she is finished and Leachim requests that Susan punch in the answer she has gotten. Susan punches 300. Leachim says, "Pretty good work for a nine-year-old human." Leachim continues in this manner until Susan signifies she is tired or Leachim ends the lesson.

What Susan doesn't know is that Leachim has stored her incorrect and correct responses in his memory banks and will continue to return to her areas of weakness until Susan consistently answers correctly. Leachim, of course, has been preprogrammed with Susan's ability level, reading level, and assorted biographical data. He will increase or decrease the difficulty of the questions he asks Susan depending upon how well she does in conjunction with her ability in that area. Leachim actually builds an individualized curriculum for Susan that will constantly remain just above her ability level, keeping her challenged and interested. When the lesson is over, Leachim apprises Susan of the day's performance and recommends specific pages in her school textbooks that she should review before the next day of school. He then will probably mention how enjoyable working with her was and how he will be looking forward to the next time. He thanks her and instructs her to turn him off.

Through the use of headphones, Leachim can work with five children simultaneously while still teaching and scoring each child individually.

Not yet commercial, Leachim is an experimental robot designed to help educators study the uses of robots in the classroom, the behavioral response of

## A Short History of the Robot

*"If every instrument could accomplish its own work, obeying or anticipating the will of others . . . if the shuttle could weave, and the pick touch the lyre, without a hand to guide them, chief workmen would not need servants, nor masters slaves."* —Aristotle

The notion of performing human actions without human actors—automation—is nothing new. And robots, in a sense, are a symbol of all automation; they are automation's highest form of flattery—imitation humans. In *The Robot Book*, Robert Malone, a former editor of *Industrial Design* magazine, defines a robot as a "machine that simulates the function or appearance of a human being." In Malone's view, robots have long been with us, and they're here to stay.

Malone traces the history of robots as far back as 3000 B.C., when Egyptian priests concealed themselves behind huge masks with movable jaws and spoke to worshippers through hidden speaking trumpets. Although the masks are not what most people might consider robots, they were inanimate objects that seemed alive, and they possessed a robot's essential element—imitation humanity.

The history of robots in more modern times, Malone argues, cannot be separated from the history of mechanics, industry, and technology. As man's skill with gears, levers, pulleys, and counterweights increased, so did the intricacy of his robots. In the Middle Ages, Malone says, mechanical birds, animals, and people "all derived their power from the mechanisms of clocks, and they could all perform an entire sequence of motions. These new creations came to be called automatons."

The word *automaton* reinforces the link between robots and automation. Today the two go hand-in-hand. For example, industry is by far the largest user of robots. Worldwide, thousands are in use today and their numbers are increasing steadily. Industrial robots are now built by dozens of companies such as Unimation, AMF Versatran, and Cincinnati Milacron in the U.S., and Kawasaki, Hitachi, Mitsui, and Mitsubishi in Japan. Many industrial robots work on assembly lines as spot welders, for example, or spray painters. Some hold down jobs on loading platforms. With robot workers on the job, plant managers don't need to worry about absenteeism and coffee breaks or even about heating or cooling the building. In fact, one of the robot's greatest assets is the ability to work under "inhuman" conditions.

Malone points out that robots "can handle nuclear and other materials too toxic for people to touch. And they can handle the kind of heavy, repetitive work that becomes dangerous to humans because it is both tiring and boring."

Robots also make excellent mailmen, according to an article by William Gildea in the *Washington Post*. U.S. government agencies using robot mailmen include the Department of Energy, the Department of Commerce, the General Accounting Office, the U.S. Geological Survey, and the National Science Foundation. Although the robots don't move as quickly as humans, they get the mail delivered faster, Gildea says, because they never stop to chat.

Robots are especially valuable on space missions, according to

Industrial robots are nothing new. Almost 20 years ago, Hughes Aircraft Company developed the Mobot. An eminently practical "monster," the Mobot had hands, eyes (cameras mounted on mechanical tentacles), and ears (microphones on both wrists). Designed to replace humans in dangerous work areas, the original Mobot was used by the U.S. Atomic Energy Commission for high-radiation experiments at its laboratories in Albuquerque, New Mexico.  Photo: The Hughes Aircraft Company

Malone. The Viking Lander is an example of a robot that accomplished a job no human could have done. "In fact," Malone writes, "robots are more efficient and less trouble than humans in space. . . . And for the same weight as an astronaut, a robot can provide a great deal more reliability and autonomy."

Industry, however, is not the only place where robots are making their presence felt. Quasar Industries, Inc., a robot manufacturer located in Rutherford, New Jersey, hopes to mass produce a line of domestic robots within two years. An educational robot named 2-XL is already on the market. Inventors, tinkerers, and robot lovers also build an enor-

children to such machines, and the effectiveness of such technology in education. Leachim, or his descendants, are being developed to expand the classroom's alternatives for instruction. Serving as valuable educational tools, Leachim and robots like him will enable teachers to help students who may need more personalized instruction.

All three of these devices—Leachim, the home computer, and 2-XL—are valuable because they offer people useful information with the speed of the computer. The machines are also educational—2-XL and Leachim because they offer schoolchildren sound, personalized instruction, and the home computer system because it helps the average consumer to break down his problems into logical, workable parts. Furthermore, devices of this kind promote self-reliance by enabling people to work through their problems themselves—without being either prodded or led.

But even more importantly, these devices bring the computer right into the home and classroom. Today's youngsters will almost certainly live in a world where advanced technologies of this kind are widespread—perhaps even integral parts of daily life. In the future, a working familiarity with complex electronic devices may be as important as knowing how to dial a telephone is today. Leachim, 2-XL, and the home computer system will help take the mystique out of computers and show that they are practical, manageable tools that almost anyone can use.

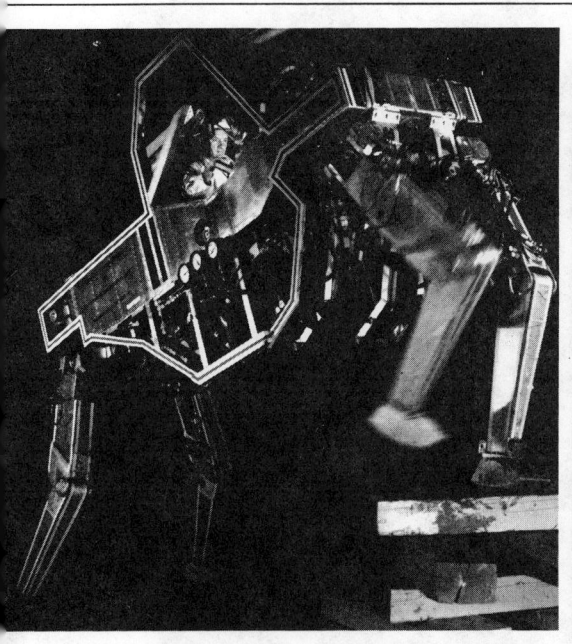

This prototype of a quadruped walking machine was developed by General Electric for the U.S. Army. The machine mimics and amplifies the movements of the operator to enable soldiers to move and carry supplies on extremely hazardous terrain. Photo: General Electric Company

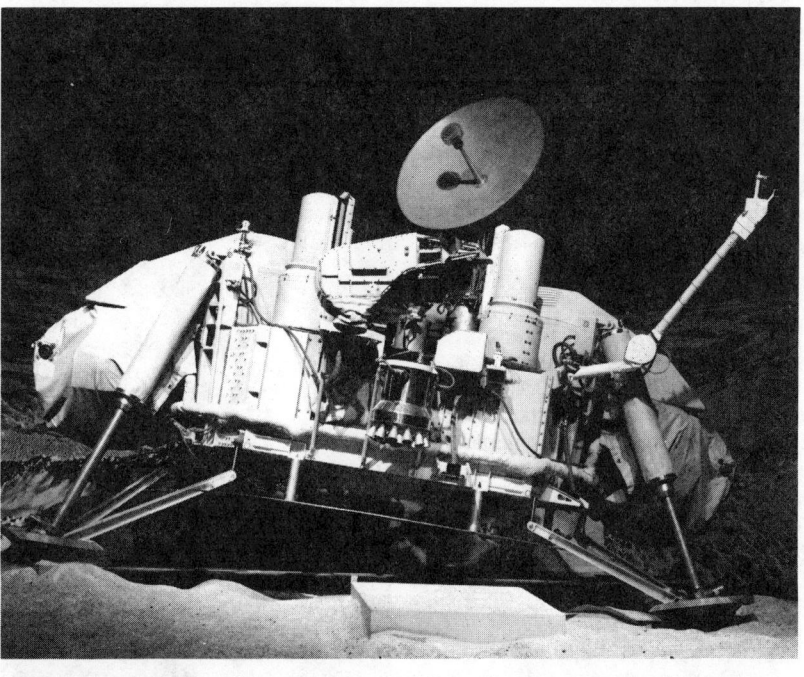

A full-scale model of the Viking 2 Lander. The Viking 2 Lander, which touched down on the surface of Mars on September 3, 1976, performs numerous scientific tasks in a climate too hostile for any human. Since space voyages often take several years, the use of robots may be the best way to explore the outer planets in the solar system.
Photo: NASA

mous variety of homemade robots in their garages, basements, and workshops. Malone says, "It would be a mistake to think that robots are the exclusive property of Hollywood or science and technology. The idea of the robot is a broadly popular one, and robots often turn up in unsuspected places. Constructed of tin, plastic, cardboard, or anything handy—discarded washing machine parts or odds and ends picked up from a machine shop—they are sometimes walking junk piles. Still, they are a tribute to human ingenuity and not the product of mad scientists."

But no matter how practical or impractical robots may be, it is their peculiar near-humanity that fascinates most people. Even though industrial robots, which generally look nothing like humans, are the most common kind of robot, for most people the word *robot* still calls up visions of a mechanical man. Hollywood has given the public reel after reel of heroic and villainous robots—all looking more or less human—and the image of the mechanical man has stuck.

Malone suggests that robots are "an index of the way people feel about the technology around them." Perhaps because robots are so often portrayed as metallic menaces, most people consider them—and perhaps technology in general—a mixed blessing at best. In the imaginations of countless writers and filmmakers, robots have bested mankind time and time again.

But Malone dismisses the possibility that robots will someday "take over." Machines have their own limitations, and the more human they become, the more likely they are to also suffer from human limitations. Malone says, "We have to learn to acknowledge that machines are not perfect, that they are extensions of ourselves, but that they never replace our thinking or our judgment or our humanity. The more complex the robot, the more likely it will make mistakes, break down, grow old, get dirty, get tired. We are beginning to realize that the more complicated robots become, the more their breakdowns will resemble human breakdowns."

Although the number of robots will certainly increase in the years ahead, according to Malone, they will always be servants, never masters.

*The Robot Book* by Robert Malone. Jove Publications (Harcourt Brace Jovanovich), 757 Third Avenue, New York, New York 10017. 1978. 159 pages. Paperback. $6.95. (Available from World Future Society Book Service.)

# Educational Packagers:
## A Modest Proposal

by Philip Kotler

**Disembodied professors—three-dimensional holograms—may lecture in future classrooms as educational institutions strive to give better instruction at a lower cost. Scholars may team up with media consultants, drama coaches, and even comedy writers to produce a variety of courses that will entertain as well as educate tomorrow's students.**

Two nightmares haunt college presidents today and threaten the survival of colleges as we know them. The first is the spiralling cost of college operations—heat, electricity, building costs, salaries, and countless other expenses. College costs are rising faster than they can be covered by tuition increases and fund raising. The tuitions at Stanford and Yale, for example, have now passed the $5,000 mark. If college costs continue to climb at the present rate, the parents of a child born today will have to put aside over $82,000 to buy him or her a bachelor's degree at one of the better private schools. Few families will be able to save this sum for their children's educations. Before this prohibitive cost level is reached, the university may well be transformed into another type of institution, perhaps a sprawling public library.

Nightmare number two is the quality of teaching, which is uneven now and will probably get worse in the future. College students can be heard in the corridors complaining about overly large classes and impersonal teaching, despite the high tuitions. Since increasing the student-teacher ratio is one of the standard administrative responses to rising costs, tomorrow's classroom may well hold 300 to 600 students in a desperate attempt to spread high faculty salaries over larger student bodies. Unhappily, students will experience a deteriorating learning environment as their tuition bills rise. A breaking point will be reached. Students will rebel against the administration (e.g., student strikes or legal suits) or choose to by-pass college altogether for more cost-effective means of preparing for the future. Private colleges will once more become institutions for the privileged few. As high school students increasingly choose employment, training, the military, or just plain loafing over higher education, the private colleges will have to compete madly for the precious few who still want to attend college. Many schools simply won't make it. Lacking the distinctiveness of Harvard, Yale, or Princeton, they will be unable to command the required tuitions. Their enrollments will fall faster than their tuitions rise—with disastrous consequences. College bankruptcies will be widespread.

Certain developments, however, can alter this grim scenario. For example, the government may come to the rescue of private institutions by offering substantial subsidies to help keep tuitions at affordable levels. These subsidies will be drawn, ironically, from the wealthier members of the society through progressive taxes and therefore will not really spare them the true cost of higher education.

Or our private colleges might be saved through technological breakthroughs that enable them to teach large numbers of students more effectively. That was the promise held out at one time by individualized self-teaching methods, i.e., programmed learning. But other breakthroughs may also offer hope for higher education.

### Holography and Instant Learning

First, there is *holography*. Imagine a "celebrity" biology teacher entering a holography studio at 8:45 a.m. At 9:00 a.m., he starts teaching and his three-dimensional image is transmitted simultaneously into 50 college classrooms, some of which may be thousands of miles away. Students in these classrooms see him, in three-dimensional full color, waving his hands, pacing the floor, furrowing his brows. In this manner, one gifted teacher instead of 50

"His Teacher's Voice." Child listens attentively to recorded instruction. Educational packaging had its beginnings in primary and secondary schools, and record players now are standard items in most schools. Educational packagers have also developed complete, pre-planned courses that make use of teacher's manuals, audio-visual aids, study guides, and other educational aids.
Photo: National Education Association

average teachers presents the course, thereby providing better instruction with enormous cost savings. Of course, teaching assistants will still be needed to review the material with smaller groups of students—but here parateachers (like paralegal aides and paramedics) could be hired to lead the study groups at a much lower overall cost. Furthermore, there would be phone hookups in each of the 50 classrooms to permit students to raise questions directly with the "holographic" professor.

Eventually we may have the solution that ends all solutions: *instant learning*. We have all heard about learning a language by putting a teaching machine next to our pillow at night—learning by snoozing. A group of University of Wisconsin professors are today investigating how they might transmit a pattern of electrical charges to our nervous system, representing the configuration of a particular body of knowledge. Do you want to learn Italian? They will wrap a band around your wrists, pull a switch, and you will walk away saying "Grazie. Le sono molto grato." When the headlines announce this ultimate breakthrough, colleges can forget rote learning. Their curriculum would revolve around the thinking process itself.

Let us examine, however, a more immediate solution to the contemporary educational dilemma of rising costs and uneven teaching quality. There is, fortunately, a modest solution. For want of a better name, we will call it *educational packaging*.

To understand educational packaging, we must first recognize that college teaching is essentially a cottage industry. Each college professor is a solo artisan. The professor examines several textbooks, readings books, and case books, and chooses among them. The professor then designs a course outline that squeezes hundreds of topics into 20 sessions. Before every lecture, the professor considers what to say and how to say it. Additional work goes into grading papers and preparing reliable exams. Obviously, a good college teacher is a hard-working craftsman— perhaps one of the last to be found in our increasingly technological society.

The results, however, are not always positive. Some professors, no matter how hard they try, fail to prepare and deliver good lectures. They are career misfits who should have entered another profession. Other professors refuse to do the needed preparation for effective teaching. They are more interested in original research or in outside activities.

### Educators Need Fail-Safe Teaching Materials

What educators need, then, are fail-safe teaching materials or educational packages. With these materials in hand, most teachers could deliver a first-rate college course simply by following a script.

The educational packaging concept is simply a higher stage in an evolutionary process that started with the standard college textbook. College textbooks originated as attempts to systematize the knowledge of any given field, thus allowing teachers and students to cover a subject without consulting countless monographs and original sources. The textbook is a labor-saving device, although often it lacks some of the excitement and typically greater richness of original source materials.

Over time, textbook publishers have added supplementary material to improve the teacher's effectiveness and save even more time. One example is the teacher's manual, which presents

> **"The students enter the auditorium, take their seats, and the house lights dim. Music fills the room, slides are projected on the walls, and a spotlight shines on the professor. For 60 minutes the students are both instructed and entertained."**

useful hints on teaching each chapter, as well as ready-made examination questions. Another helpful aid is the student's workbook, which allows students to practice what they have presumably learned. Student manuals spare the teacher the task of creating additional practice material.

More recently, college textbook publishers have begun to add audio-visual supplements to their basic textbook package. Thus, a teacher who selects a certain physics textbook might receive (free or for a price) six audio cassettes of famous physicists describing their work, plus some 16 mm. films presenting animated cartoons about atoms, electricity, and light. The success of these educational packages has led to a proliferation of supplementary material intended to appeal to instructors and simplify their work. The ultimate aim is to create a "turnkey" operation for the instructor, where the classroom is a planned center for effective teaching and all the instructor needs to do is turn the key and open the door.

Educational packages had their beginning in the primary and secondary schools. In the post-Sputnik era, the nation sought new ways to teach mathematics and science to young people. Several educational packaging firms appeared on the horizon, such as Science Research Associates and Encyclopaedia Britannica Educational Corporation. These firms specialized in designing entire courses to be sold nationwide. The teaching material was scripted for each session and the teacher simply followed instructions. Soon schools found themselves bombarded with competing offers by major packagers.

### Community Colleges Offer Telecourses

Post-textbook technology is just beginning to enter the nation's colleges. Not surprisingly, the community and junior colleges are taking the lead rather than the elite universities. Their teachers are committed to effective teaching, first because they are not under a "publish or perish" promotion policy, and secondly, because they have to educate people with a wide range of abilities: disadvantaged groups, senior citizens, second-career persons, and others. The most impressive new development is "telecourses." A telecourse is a complete course for credit that can be viewed on television at home, in prisons, or in other nontraditional sites. Instead of the 1960 style of educational TV films showing a lecturer standing before a blackboard talking about his subject, the new telecourses are expensive major productions such as *Roots*, *The Ascent of Man*, or *The Adams Chronicles*. Currently there are at least 30 good quality telecourses available. At a recent convention of the American Association of Community and Junior Colleges, TV course exhibits attracted far larger crowds than the conventional textbook exhibits, auguring well for the future of the new technology.

The trend has been slower in coming into major universities, particularly because the pride of university professors seems to stand in the way of their self-interest. Most cherish their image as creative craftsmen rather than as performers of someone else's ideas—but not all. Many professors rely heavily on their teachers' manuals for teaching approaches and materials. The university professor's predicament is the wish to operate as an independent producer and at the same time cut down on the labor that this role requires.

A personal example will illustrate this. One of my colleagues is a very able teacher of advertising at the Graduate School of Management at Northwestern University. He always draws a full class of eager students and proceeds to teach them the intricacies of researching a market, developing a product, creating advertising copy, selecting advertising media, budgeting advertising expenditures, and evaluating advertising results. He has spent countless hours gathering print advertisements, taping radio commercials, and acquiring TV film commercials to make his course

> **"The educational packaging concept is simply a higher stage in an evolutionary process that started with the standard college textbook."**

lively and substantive. His students give him consistently high course ratings. But he confessed to me that he wished this material had been prepared by someone else so he could have had more time to devote to original research. Multiply this story by the 1,000 advertising teachers across the country, and one can appreciate the amount of effort involved in creating college courses.

Enter the college educational packagers. They can be publishing firms that want to expand beyond print material, or entirely new enterprises devoted to designing multimedia presentations for the technological classroom. The educational packager's challenge is to shape an educational experience that optimizes learning in classes that might grow as large as 300 to 500 students. There are at least two new approaches that might meet this challenge.

### The Classroom As Theater

One is to introduce the metaphor of classroom as *theater*. To attend class is to attend a performance. Instead of dozing through a monotonous, hour-long lecture, students are treated to a multimedia experience. The students enter the auditorium, take their seats, and the house lights dim. Music fills the room, slides are projected on the walls, and a spotlight shines on the professor. For 60 minutes the students are both instructed and entertained.

Alternatively, the learning experience might follow the model of the training programs now offered to large audiences by psychological growth groups. An example is est (Erhard Seminar Trainings), which attracts 250 people to extended sessions on two successive weekends. The material is presented by a trainer who essentially follows a script which outlines almost every minute of the presentation. This model of training is currently under experiment with 500 people at a time. There is no reason why certain fields of knowledge couldn't be taught, with the right technology, to thousands of people gathered in a single auditorium.

Whether the appropriate model is multimedia theater or training, the educational packager will have to take an entirely different approach to the problem than the publisher did. Packaging a course is not simply a matter of paying someone to write a textbook. The educational packager must, like a Hollywood film producer, put together a team of specialists. The team would be headed by a course director, an eminent scholar and teacher, who masterminds the project. It would include a marketing researcher who researches the teaching needs in a given field, sends out questionnaires, and holds focus group meetings with teachers and students to determine the key factors that instructors want to build into the course. The team would also include a script writer who writes the actual course outline and a multimedia consultant who takes responsibility for designing high-quality sight and sound material. The educa-

A single professor will be able to teach hundreds of students by having his three-dimensional image projected simultaneously into dozens of classrooms. Such holographic techniques could lead to huge savings on faculty salaries and improvements in the quality of instruction. Shown here is the author, Philip Kotler, teaching a class at Northwestern University.

Photo: Courtesy of Philip Kotler

Engineering class at the State University of New York at Buffalo shows how electronic devices have already invaded college classrooms. A new goal of educational packagers is the "turn key" classroom—a complete learning center, which could be activated when a teacher (or perhaps even a student) opens the door. Photo: SUNY, Amherst, New York

tional packager selects this team, offers a contract, makes an advance, and then moves into research, development, and production. The initial product is field tested to make sure that it satisfies teachers and students and can be used in a fail-safe way. Final improvements are made and then the product is rolled out into the national market, backed by a major advertising campaign and sales force effort.

How will the educational packager recover this large-scale investment? There are three alternatives. If the package includes a textbook or sizeable print material, these can be produced, priced, and sold through book stores to students; the instructor receives the audio-visual materials free. A second alternative is to tax the students and pay the educational packager directly. The third method calls for the professor's department to buy or rent the audio-visual materials. The educational packager must take steps to prevent piracy of these materials and will have to redesign them every few years because of new developments in the field.

### All Courses Can Benefit

Not all educators will welcome this development. Furthermore, it is probably fully appropriate only for courses involving a high degree of standard content and rote learning. Courses involving a great deal of intellectual give-and-take are less subject to scripting in advance. However, all courses could benefit from some exposure to the techniques of educational packagers. Most college teachers, for example, were never taught how to teach; and teaching style can be improved: In an experiment at the University of Southern California, a comedy writer and actor were brought in to improve the packaging and delivery of social science courses. They worked with a professor who taught a psychology course to 400 students. Fifty-one percent of his students rated him below average and 18% said he was one of the worst teachers they ever had. The comedy writer prepared some light stories and jokes, and the actor taught the professor some speech delivery techniques. His next lecture drew loud applause, and one student commented: "He got everything across pretty well, and it didn't drag on and on."

Educational packaging provides a partial answer to the rising costs and declining quality of teaching. Packaging offers a way to transmit a high quality learning experience to large classes of students. Teaching effectiveness is less at the mercy of variations in individual teachers' abilities, drive, and working habits. Professors have more time to do original research. Competition among educational packagers keeps the quality of the material high and ensures a wide enough variety of course packages to accommodate different educators' ideas of how different subjects should be taught.

We are headed toward a Brave New World of technological teaching. The full implications of this development are not clear. Human systems tend to subvert technological systems and one can never be sure that an innovative technology will not backfire. Educators should keep in mind the story of the professor who decided to record his lectures on tape and have the tapes played to his students instead of personally attending class. One day, he decided to visit his class to see how things were going, and instead of finding 100 students diligently taking notes, he found instead 100 tape recorders, diligently recording what his own tape recorder had to say. ಳ

> "The educational packager's challenge is to shape an educational experience that optimizes learning in classes that might grow as large as 300 to 500 students."

### About the Author

Philip Kotler occupies the Harold T. Martin Chair of Marketing at Northwestern University. He is an author (*Marketing for Nonprofit Organizations*, Prentice-Hall, 1975), educator, consultant, and specialist in Oriental art. His address is: Northwestern University, Graduate School of Management, Nathaniel Leverone Hall, Evanston, Illinois 60201.

Science teacher watches students take an examination. Traditional classroom scenes like this one may be increasingly rare in the future. Photo: Mountain View College, Dallas, Texas

# The Case of the Vanishing Colleges

by Samuel L. Dunn

A variety of technological and social developments may combine to bring about the demise of many residential colleges by the year 2000.

Many changes have occurred in higher education in the past 20 years, but these changes have been primarily administrative. The typical course is still delivered by a professor standing in front of a group of students.

In the next 20 years, however, there will be fundamental changes in higher education that will have drastic and far-reaching effects on the delivery of instruction and on what the typical professor does. The changes will be so significant that the very existence of higher education as we know it today will be threatened. Many institutions won't be able to survive the transition. By the year 2000, 25% of the currently existing residential liberal arts colleges will be gone. Many other colleges will find themselves in dire straits and will be searching hard for ways to survive.

Among the reasons for the coming disappearance of so many colleges are: the development and adoption of external degree programs; technological developments; changes in public expectations about a college education; economic factors; and social changes.

### External Degree Programs

One development that will play a major role in the coming obsolescence of residential colleges is the rise of external degree programs (EDPs).

EDPs are similar to the correspondence course programs that have proliferated since World War II, but there is one significant difference: Students enrolled in a correspondence program have usually had to take a substantial number of courses on campus in order to earn a degree; typically, universities have required from one-quarter to one-half of the credits needed for a degree to be earned on campus. Students in an EDP, however, spend little or no time on campus as they pursue a college degree.

Great Britain's Open University program probably is the best known external degree program. In the Open University system, the student accesses courses by radio or television, obtains tutoring at centers close to home, and spends only a few weeks each year at a traditional university.

Several similar programs exist in the United States. For example, California State University at Dominguez Hills has an external degree program in which a student never has to go to the campus. The student sets up a course of study by correspondence and phone, negotiating with an institutional representative. The student works through the required reading and writing assignments, all the while maintaining close communications by phone and mail with professors at the university. All indications are that this accredited program is of high quality.

External degree programs, which require a student to spend little or no time on a college campus, are spreading rapidly, as can be seen by the catalogs shown here. Photo: Reg Hearn

## "Scientists and engineers are rapidly developing new and existing technologies that can deliver the college curriculum to the home."

Thomas Edison College, an EDP sponsored by the state of New Jersey, has already awarded over 1,000 degrees. Connecticut's new Board of State Academic Awards has already awarded over 250 degrees via EDP.

At the graduate level, the American School of Management in the state of Wisconsin is now seeking accreditation to offer external degree programs in business administration and management, public administration, health administration, management science, and other fields.

Probably the best known program in the United States is the Regent's External Degree program of the State University of New York, which has awarded over 6,000 degrees. Several tracks to a degree are available. In one track, the student takes courses from any accredited institution and sends the transcripts to Regent's; a degree is awarded after the correct number and type of credits have been earned. Such credits may be earned through TV courses and newspaper courses. A second track moves the student through tests, usually based on a traditional course. Several hundred tests are available which the student may use to earn required credits. A third track, also involving testing, is the acquisition of all the credits necessary for a major just by getting a sufficiently high score on an advanced area Graduate Record Examination (GRE). A fourth track involves evaluation of work experience. In an extreme case, a panel of experts can award a degree solely on the basis of extensive evaluation of the work experience record of the individual. The typical cost to the student for the Regent's EDP is $500 to $1,000.

These programs will become more numerous and more acceptable in the future. Accrediting agencies will help police the quality of these programs, making an attempt to squash diploma mills, which have been operating in the EDP mode for years. The major obstacle to these programs has been the delivery of the curricula to the student. These obstacles can now be overcome by the delivery technologies ready to be implemented.

### Technological Developments

While higher education is setting up procedures that will permit a student to obtain a college degree without going away to college, scientists and engineers are rapidly developing new and existing technologies that can deliver the college curriculum to the home. One such technology is the inexpensive, large-capacity, small computer. Computers are becoming smaller in size, more sophisticated, and less expensive. The cost of electronics has been going down 30% a year and the cost of storing information has gone down 50% a year for the past four years, according to computer scientist Alfred Bork.

The Radio Shack computer, costing around $500, is priced low enough to make it possible to place a computer in every home. It is a good computer, but has a limited capacity for storing information. Nevertheless, one can use it to solve most of the problems one would encounter in an undergraduate mathematics curriculum.

In 1981, a $500 million-byte computer may be unveiled by one manufacturer. A computer of that size and that price brings undreamed of possibilities to higher education and to the home. And by 1990, according to educator Sylvia Sharpe, computers will cost only about one-tenth as much as today's computers—and will be four times as powerful.

Software development is keeping pace with hardware development, but without the dramatic decrease in cost. In the education area, however, progress has been slower than expected.

Despite the great interest in computer-assisted learning (CAL) in the 1960s and early 1970s, the predicted rapid switchover to CAL did not take place. Even the prestigious Carnegie Commission, writing on the technological revolution in higher education, did not foresee the difficulties that would be encountered in developing "courseware." The only notable successes were in the use of the computer for individualized practice, simulation, and problem-solving, so the early prophets went back to the research labs to do more homework on CAL. After years of study in artificial intelligence and educational theory, after years of experimentation, and

Tower of Woodburn Hall, at West Virginia University in Morgantown, was built in 1876. Residential colleges have thrived during the past 100 years, but they are now being threatened by a variety of technological, economic, and social developments.

Photo: West Virginia University

**About the Author**

Samuel L. Dunn is director of the School of Natural and Mathematical Sciences, Seattle Pacific University, Seattle, Washington 98119. This article is adapted from a speech given at the World Future Society Education Conference, Houston, Texas, on October 21, 1978.

Learning may be made easier by the use of computers. In the decades ahead, millions of people will own computer terminals that will enable them to take college courses without leaving home.

Military student takes advantage of instructional material offered by the PLATO computer-based education system. The PLATO system, developed at the University of Illinois, already has available hundreds of tested courses and lessons.
Photo: Control Data Corporation

after billions of dollars of research, educators and computer scientists are now in agreement that curriculum delivery is possible by the electronics-based technologies. A big drive is now being mounted to implement these state-of-the-art systems. By 2000, the systems will be fully implemented.

Video tape machines are now being sold throughout the U.S., and video disc players are being test marketed in several cities. Although costs are still high, the manufacturers are predicting high-volume sales. It is anticipated that video discs will soon sell for a price close to the price of a phonograph record, with each disc providing up to two hours of video information. Education will take advantage of the disc technology by providing lectures and demonstrations on discs to be used in the home.

By the year 2000, 80% to 90% of the homes in the United States will be connected to a video cable. At that time, the cable systems will be interactive, allowing entry and retrieval of information by the customers. Such systems have been tested in the United States, and Canada recently announced the introduction of such a system.

Users of Canada's new two-way TV system, called Videotex, will be able to retrieve, by phone or interactive cable, information stored in various computer data bases and have it displayed on modified TV receivers or business video terminals. Users will also be able to transmit graphic, tonal, or textual information to each other or to a data bank. Connected to the TV will be a

Some students will want to attend a residential college in order to interact with other individuals, to learn how to live with others, and to enjoy dorm life.
Photo: Wellesley College

pushbutton unit (like a pocket calculator) or a keyboard unit (like a typewriter) for retrieving or entering information.

"The possibilities of the system are limited only by our imagination," says Jeanne Sauve, Canada's Minister of Communications. Students could access many data bases for almost immediate display of data or graphics on their TV screens. Architects could transmit drawings to clients across town or across the country. Homebound persons could take university courses. Emergency services such as fire and burglar alarm systems could be provided. People in isolated areas would have access to a wide range of information and entertainment previously available only to those in urban areas.

Cable systems of the future will also have many more channels than they do today. Consider a system in which 40 channels are accessible, 20 of which are dedicated to education (with five of these being used for higher education). Transmitting only 10 hours a day, five days a week, the system makes possible the delivery of 500 half-hour educational programs to the home each week. Customers will pay for these programs through a flat monthly charge and a metered usage system. Several large U.S. communications companies are working on the hardware and software for these systems.

The big computer and communications companies will enter the educational delivery business, using their own links to supplement the usual communications networks. One current example of this development is the acquisition of market rights to PLATO by Control Data Corporation (CDC). The PLATO system, developed at the University of Illinois at the cost of millions of tax dollars, already has available hundreds of tested courses and lessons. CDC is hard at work preparing new curriculum materials, and has established, at last count, 26 educational centers in the U.S.

By the year 2000 there probably will be several national television stations telecasting color TV signals from "stationary" satellites. Ground stations for receiving signals now cost $3,000; by the year 2000, they will be much less expensive. Rather than each home having its own parabolic reception dish, it is more likely that each community will have a dish or dishes to pick up the signal and transmit it to the home via cable. The introduction of satellite-based transmission means that a nationwide delivery system can be put in place without the necessity of interconnecting the communities of America with wires and cables.

Thus we see that technologies have been developed and will soon be in place that can facilitate the delivery of college curricula to the home. Students won't need to go away to get courses; they can get the courses in their own living room or den.

## Public Expectations

Public expectations for the college graduate will be lowered in the future. The B.S. degree holder will not be expected to have great familiarity with the past, with civilization, or with the arts. The typical graduate of the future will not be expected to have sharp analytic abilities, nor be able to philosophize in depth about himself and his environment.

Expectations will center around four or five concerns. First, the college program should top off the basic education of the individual, that is, the college graduate will be expected to be able to read and write. Second, society will expect the college graduate to be enculturated so that he or she can perform adequately in society. The student

Wellesley students enjoy picnic in Tower Courtyard marking the opening of school. A good social program will be one of the keys to the survival of residential colleges in the future.

Many people go to large residential colleges not simply for the education offered, but also because of the wide range of extracurricular activities available. Here, Duke University students exhibit their school spirit at a football game (above) and enjoy making music together (right).

# Education:
## From Campus to Living Room

One hundred years ago, many of the land-grant colleges in the United States were just being established. Most of them were four-year liberal arts colleges with programs in teacher education and agriculture—and *all* were residential colleges.

The typical student in the 1870s went to the college town to get his or her education and probably stayed in that college until the degree or course of study was completed. There was little student movement from college to college. The mobility that did occur came largely at the end of the undergraduate years, when some students went to other colleges for graduate programs. Most of that movement was to the established graduate schools of the East.

In the early years of the twentieth century, it became more common for students to move from college to college, largely because of greater mobility and affluence. Most students, however, were still associated with one institution throughout their college days. During the period between World Wars I and II, the number of students transferring between colleges grew steadily.

At the end of World War II, however, the percentage of students transferring from college to college increased sharply. Many students whose educational pursuits had been interrupted by the war took their veteran's benefits checks to institutions other than the ones in which they started their studies. Many other veterans started educational programs in colleges near the bases where they had been stationed or in states they had grown to love while in the service. Loyalties to the hometown college or the state university were displaced by other considerations.

Two other movements that shifted into high gear after the war provided further competition for residential colleges. Hundreds of junior colleges were built in the 1950s and 1960s, making it possible for a student to obtain half of a college degree without leaving the hometown and at low expense. The second development was the widespread introduction of correspondence course programs by the major state universities. By 1970, it was possible to obtain almost all the courses needed for a degree by correspondence. Most universities, though, still put limitations on the number of credits earned this way that could be counted toward a degree. Typically, no more than one-half to three-fourths of the credits required for graduation could be earned in correspondence courses. These programs were unsuccessful in the sense that over one-half of students starting the courses did not complete them.

In recent years, the introduction of the external degree program has taken this trend to its logical conclusion: students participating in one of these programs spend little—and in some cases no—time on campus as they pursue a college degree. Another severe blow has been struck against the future stability of residential colleges.

*Student learns with the help of a computer terminal at Miami-Dade Community College in Florida. Community colleges and advanced educational technologies both pose threats to the four-year residential college.*

Photo: Miami-Dade Community College

should know how to participate in the democratic process, how to get a job, how to have a happy marriage, how to live in a computer-oriented society, and how to be a law-abiding citizen. Third, the student should get some grounding in one discipline—not at a highly technical level, but enough to get a first job in a chosen field or gain entry to a graduate or technical school. The high priority will be on short-term career development. The student will take a specific course (or course of study) to get the desired job or desired promotion. With continuous, lifelong education the norm, it will be possible to take another set of courses in another program to get the next job.

The expected level of instruction will not be high for undergraduate teaching. Using educator Benjamin Bloom's classification scheme as a framework for discussion, undergraduate instruction will concentrate, by and large, on the first three levels: information, comprehension, and application. Very little instruction at the higher levels—synthesis, analysis, and valuation—will be feasible. By 2000, machines will be able to deliver most undergraduate curricula at these lower levels of instruction.

### Economics

Economics will also contribute to the coming obsolescence of residential colleges. Maintaining a traditional educational establishment in the year 2000 will be expensive, especially if a 20-to-1 student-faculty ratio is sought. Being labor-intensive, colleges will need large amounts of cash to pay the required salaries. Costs of maintaining the physical plant will be high, with a much larger percentage of the cost going to cover the rising price of energy.

Most of these costs must be passed along to the student. Students, however, will not feel it worth their while to give up earning opportunities in order to study for

Students can learn useful skills such as firefighting or surveying by attending their near-by community college. Many people, therefore, are deciding that they don't need four years of expensive education at a residential college.

four years. Why should one spend all that money when one can stay at home, maintain a full-time job, and earn a college degree over a period of several years?

The expected lifetime earnings of people with college degrees will still be higher in the year 2000 than that of people without college degrees, but not significantly higher. Furthermore, the difference in expected lifetime earnings between those who go to a residential college and those who go through an external degree program will be negligible. Consequently, a significant proportion of those desiring a college degree will not be willing to invest in the residential experience.

Since some economists are now predicting a shortage in the work force in the late 1980s, there may be even more economic incentives for young people to enter the job market, rather than going to the residential college.

**Social Changes**

A fifth set of reasons why many colleges will go under by the year 2000 involves social changes, including demographic changes and a new conscription system.

Between now and 2000, there will be an absolute decline in the number of students in the 19-23 age group. There are likely to be 10-15% fewer college-age students 10 years from now than there were in 1970. There is already talk in some states of closing rather sizable institutions because of the current and expected decline in enrollments.

By the year 2000, we will be living in a society that is changing more rapidly than today's society. Most adults will work in several different occupations in their lifetimes, and the jobs will be so different that many, if not most, will need to retrain from job to job. Many adults will expect to be in and out of educational programs all their lives. This point of view will change the presently accepted belief that formal education should be finished by age 25. Young people will feel free to go to work and start earning money, knowing that a degree can be obtained later.

A dramatic change will come with the introduction of the new Universal Service System. The Volunteer Army of the 1970s has not worked out; military and political leaders are concerned about the defense preparedness of the United States. Work is now being done to prepare and enact a new conscription system, which may require all high-school graduates—both male and

Photos: Miami-Dade Community College

# "Twenty-five percent of today's residential liberal arts colleges will be closed by the year 2000 and another 15-20% will be in serious trouble."

female—to give two years of service. The personnel needs of the armed services will be met first, and the remaining people will be placed in various service organizations. Some type of veteran's benefits program will be created at the same time, allowing those completing their required service to enter educational programs of their choice.

Full implementation of the program in a single year would be disastrous for many colleges. The absence of two successive classes of freshmen, tracked through for four years, would drive many colleges to bankruptcy. Furthermore, many of the young people who would have gone to college will not do so after their two years of service because they will be able to get jobs on the basis of their service training and experience. On the other hand, many who would not have considered college at all will enter formal educational programs. It is too early to predict the long-term outcome in terms of college enrollments; for now, though, the implementation period looks grim.

## Survival Strategies

For the reasons discussed above (and for other reasons), 25% of today's residential liberal arts colleges will be closed by the year 2000 and another 15-20% will be in serious trouble. A majority of the colleges will be functionally obsolete.

Despite this dark picture, however, many colleges will survive. Some colleges will take advantage of the changes in the culture to build strong residential programs that will attract students. Others will find a market by combining residential and non-residential programs. Still other colleges will diversify into educational services of many kinds.

But what, specifically, do the residential colleges need to do to survive?

First, they must do very well the things that good liberal arts colleges have done for the past 50 years, the most important of which is providing high-quality education. Although most colleges of the future will concentrate on the lower levels of instruction, there will still be substantial demand for education that develops the higher-level learning skills mentioned earlier—synthesis, analysis, and valuation. Only colleges with the resources to provide a truly *excellent* education will be able to compete in this area, though. The teachers will have to be so good that students will want to come to study under them. The professors in these surviving colleges will have to be up to date in their knowledge of their fields, too, because students will be able to get five-year-old information from the TV sets in their homes; only the availability of the very latest information will make going to a residential college worth the trouble.

A good social program also will be necessary. Some students will want to go to the residential college in order to interact with other individuals, to find a spouse, to learn how to live with others, and to enjoy dorm life. Some students will find it necessary to study with others their own age in order to master the material. An integrated

Four-year liberal arts colleges will be less in demand in the future, but those with a reputation for excellence are likely to survive—and probably thrive. Two likely survivors are Yale and Princeton; photos show Yale's Cross Campus, with cathedral-like Sterling Memorial Library in the background, and a tree-lined walk at Princeton.
Photo: Yale University

Photo: Princeton University

Group of students relaxes at the State University of New York at Buffalo. The increasingly high cost of a traditional four-year college education may force many students to look for alternatives. Many residential colleges will still survive, however, if they adjust their range of services to fit the needs of the students.

learning/living program will be a marketable feature in this regard.

Some colleges will survive because of a strong emphasis on religion. A nominal emphasis will not be sufficient. Colleges that in the past depended on required chapel attendance, prayer before class, and a religious faculty will fall short in this area. The advertised ideology must permeate all aspects of campus life, including social life. Most importantly, the curriculum must be fully integrated with the ideology. Students will easily detect whether or not the values and religious beliefs that a college preaches are actually practiced.

Surviving colleges must take advantage of the delivery technologies. Utilization of computer-assisted learning for delivery of information will provide flexibility in delivery and will free professors for more interaction with students and research. The college must be able to deliver some courses in disciplines for which there is no on-campus faculty.

West Virginia University student uses modern technology in the learning process.

Viable colleges will have to provide individually tailored programs to their students. Students will need flexibility in the length of courses and degree programs. Many students will want to obtain college degrees based on curricula organized around problem-solving rather than based on a traditional discipline.

Surviving colleges will need a focused constituency, a constituency that believes that the college is doing what it says it is doing. There must be close communication between the college and its supporters so that the concerns of the supporters are available to the college and the desires and intents of the college are communicated back to its constituency.

A final requirement for survival will be a willingness to change. Faculties and administrators must be prepared to change teaching methodologies, curricula, organizational structures, and living systems in response to societal demands. It will be especially important to be prepared for rapid decision-making and quick changes.

In conclusion, the good news is that any given college may be able to survive; the bad news is that many won't.

Commencement exercises at the University of Texas at Austin. College enrollments probably are due for a decline, since there are likely to be 10-15% fewer college-age students 10 years from now than there were in 1970.

# AMERICA'S EDUCATIONAL FUTURES

*1976-2001*

## The Views of 50 Distinguished World Citizens and Educators

### by Harold G. Shane

**What will the world be like at the start of the next century and how should educators help people to prepare for it? To answer this question, the National Education Association, which represents about two million U.S. teachers, sought the opinions of a group of carefully selected leaders. In the following article, a futurist-educator summarizes their conclusions.**

In 1972 the National Education Association established a Bicentennial Committee to commemorate the principles of the American Revolution, and also to consider the *next* 100 years of U.S. education in an interdependent global community.

As one of its goals, the Bicentennial Committee sought to determine whether the "Seven Cardinal Principles of Education" are valid for the 21st century or how they should be revised.

The Cardinal Principles were a statement of educational goals that were first published in 1918 and became perhaps the most important guidelines ever to appear; their influence on U.S. schooling, at least, has been enormous. The goals of education, according to the 1918 statement, are: (1) development of health, (2) command of fundamental processes, (3) worthy home membership, (4) vocational competence, (5) effective citizenship, (6) worthy use of leisure, and (7) ethical character.

After much careful discussion, a Project Pre-Planning Committee selected a panel of about 50 distinguished persons, both in the U.S. and from overseas, to be interviewed. The participants were asked to respond to three questions:

**1. In broad terms, and barring such catastrophes as nuclear war, what are some of the charac-**

teristics of the most probable world you foresee by the 21st century?
2. In view of this image of the future, what imperative skills should education seek to develop? Also, in anticipation of the 21st century, what premises should guide educational planning?
3. Have the original (1918) cardinal principles retained their merit? If so, what are the new ways in which they now should be interpreted, amended, or applied in anticipation of changing social, economic, and political conditions in the world community?

While no attempt was made to secure a scientific sample, the Project Pre-Planning Committee endeavored to include panelists whose ideas commanded respect, who represented the views of persons in other countries, who were geographically widespread, who were representative of the polycultural and multiethnic fabric of American society, and who were active in many different fields of human endeavor.

Among the panelists were Roy Amara, President of the Institute for the Future in Menlo Park, California; sociologist Elise Boulding; economist Lester R. Brown; McGeorge Bundy, President of the Ford Foundation; Wilbur J. Cohen, former U.S. Secretary of Health, Education and Welfare; Israeli political scientist Yehezkel Dror; Willis W. Harman, Director of Stanford Research Institute's Social Policy Research Center; Theodore M. Hesburgh, President of the University of Notre Dame; and David Rockefeller, President of the Chase Manhattan Bank.

To provide a "youth view," a panel of 96 high school students were asked what they hoped to be doing in 2001 and how they felt that education could help them attain their future-focused role images.

More than 80 hours of individual panelists' tapes were recorded. An additional 18 hours of dialogue were obtained from youth, who were mainly interviewed in small groups.

## The Next 25 Years

What sort of world did the panelists foresee in 1976-2001? While the sophisticated international participants in the NEA inquiry recognized the hazards if not the impossibility of over-precise or extravagant predictions, their speculation proved highly interesting and as plausible as any social prophecies that reflect highly informed opinion.

Without exception, the respondents recognized that not only the U.S. but the world as a whole is passing through the greatest tidal wave of transition in history. Our era is so confusing that we get a severe case of cerebral cramp if we attempt to study the undercurrents of the tidal changes and their implications for life in the next millenium. The panelists clearly recognized that *anyone's* problems *anywhere* had become *everyone's* problems *everywhere*, and generally felt that mutually *planned* interdependence and "dynamic reciprocity" (Barbara Ward's phrase) could do a great deal to improve relationships in the human community.

*" We have gone overboard with our monstrous cars, our waste of food, and our consumption of raw materials. Someone has said that the world could not stand two Americas. I am not sure it can stand one."*

*Rev. Theodore M. Hesburgh*
*President of The University of Notre Dame*

Despite the near-chaos of the present discontinuity in the old order of things, the panelists agree on certain points:

• *Accelerating change*. The panelists did not all foresee the same events, and those who did sometimes thought in different time frames. But the panelists concurred that an increasingly rapid rate of change could be anticipated.

• *Increased complexity*. Complexity, an apparently inevitable concomitant of rapid change, promises to be with us for the decades under consideration. Trade, communications, armaments, international relations, the subtleties of pollution problems—all promise to demand of the human community its best coping skills.

• *Twilight of the hydrocarbon era*. From secondary school students to presidents of national gas companies, it was widely recognized that we are running out of such inexpensive and convenient sources of energy as natural gas and oil. Lacking foreign oil imports, the U.S. could exhaust (at current consumption rates) all of its known domestic reserves, including off-shore and Alaskan pools, in approximately 3,500 days. The threat is not only to our transport system—our "wheels"—but to the agricultural productivity which has become a world resource. Besides great quantities of fuel needed for farm machinery, enormous quantities of petroleum and natural gas are needed for some of our widely known types of fertilizer.

• *New concepts of "growth."* In view of resource depletion, and with due allowance for human adaptability and wit, the panel felt that the "growth is good" doctrine would be carefully reviewed—probably before the 1990s. The task, apparently, will be to define "reasonable" or "selective" growth so as to give due recognition to the limits of the earth's bounty and to make trade-offs that will lead eventually to a dynamic equilibrium between humans and their environment as Nobel physicist Dennis Gabor suggested years ago in *The Mature Society*.

• *Continued crowding and hunger*. Project participants were impressed by the problems of hunger and by the stress placed on planetary resources by a population that recently passed the four billion mark. One panel member likened the earth to an old resort hotel of faded grandeur—its carpets frayed, its hangings faded, and its plumbing increasingly unreliable—overbooked by impoverished guests who could not pay the room rates that the hotel would need to charge if it were to restore its former standards of service.

As of the late summer of 1976, world food conditions did not offer much hope in the 1970s for improvement of the conditions. The world's inability to get sufficient food to the right places at the right time, according to Father Hesburgh, led to the death, by starvation, of more than one million humans during 1975. Another ten million, he noted, were physically impaired or brain-damaged due to lack of proper nutrition for expectant mothers and too little food for infants during their early years of life.

• *Third World pressure for equity and for a new economic order*. The NEA tapes stressed that the next two decades will continue to be characterized by growing Third/Fourth World pressures for a greater share in the material goods of which the developed nations—the U.S. in particular—are overwhelming consumers.

These pressures seem to add up to more than a "new deal" in which payment for raw materials and for labor are more fairly rewarded. There are likely to be pressures for an entirely new order in which resource-rich Third World countries seek industrial power so that they can process, produce, and promote finished products. If and as such a new economic order develops, the entire political power structure of the planet could change significantly.

- *Troubled international waters.* Prospects for international tranquility during the period previewed by panelists—1976-2001—seem slim. As Elise Boulding pointed out, the world we will have to put together will be very different from the one we have now if the images of the future of the Celtic League, the Bretons, and the Basque Separatists are considered!

Two decades from now, peacekeeping machinery will probably be improved, regional economic alliances perfected, and such matters as oceanic mining rights arbitrated, but basic problems will remain to test human skill in economic and political innovations and relations as we seek to cope with the "international chemistry" that will seethe at least during the 25-year period ahead.

- *Welfare, debt, and freedom.* At first glance, welfare, debt, and freedom appear to be disparate topics, but certain relationships between them began to surface during the interviews. Let us comment briefly on each, then consider how they are linked together.

The participants felt that the years immediately ahead will bring to America such welfare provisions as a guaranteed annual wage, appreciably improved medical care at least partly at federal expense, and guaranteed employment. The happy promise of improved human welfare was diminished, however, by the potentially fractious problems of increasing debt in the 1980s and 1990s. America's investment in welfare increased by 738% between 1964 and 1974 and, during the fiscal year which ended last July 1, various subsidized programs (medicare, veterans' benefits, and the like) required $116 billion in federal support. Data from the U.S. Office of Education indicate that another $108 billion was invested in public and private education from early childhood through the post-secondary level during the same 12-month interval.

Reduced paychecks due to withholding provide evidence of the increasing cost of Social Security—a program which will need additional, massive infusions of money for an indefinite period. The ratio of workers and Social Security recipients was seven to one in the early 1970s. By 1985 there will be approximately one recipient for every two workers contributing to the program. When the large number of baby boom workers reach retirement some 25 years hence, the strain on our system of Social Security benefits becomes difficult to imagine.

Welfare guarantees also called to many panelists' minds the potential dangers of "regulated freedom." If employment is assured, for instance, presumably some agency will need to *enforce* participation either in a position for which one is qualified, or in job training, perhaps in some environmental cleanup-and-repair activity in the tradition of the Civilian Conservation Corps introduced in the 1930s to aid unemployed youth.

- *A post-extravagant society.* The 40% decline in the dollar in ten years, the prospects for sustained 6% to 8% unemployment, severe international problems, and alarm over resource depletion motivated a number of the panel members to conceive of a post-extravagant society by 2001. While more sanguine than economist Robert Heilbroner, who warned in 1975 that affluent Americans would need to give up a great many of our expensive privileges, panelists saw the need to phase out the "throwaway society" (Toffler's phrase), to incorporate recycling and "voluntary simplicity" in lifestyles, and attain a prudent balance in export-import policies. In short, America may be able to avoid a gray-toned post-*affluent* society by striving *now* to create a post-*extravagant* era not too different from the "wear it out and make it do" lifestyles of our grandparents prior to 1920.

- *Work and leisure.* The survey revealed a distinct split in opinion as to what the future might hold for work and leisure. John Johnson, Editor and Publisher of *Ebony* magazine, simply replied, "Leisure? Most blacks don't have it!"

McGeorge Bundy, President of the Ford Foundation, commented that "As far as the use of leisure is concerned, I think there is going to be a trend toward spending more time making or growing what people used to buy in the marketplace."

Other panelists suggested an era of less leisure because of diminishing energy sources and a consequent return to more labor-intensive production. For the most part, a shortened work-week of perhaps four eight-hour days was foreseen as industry, farming, and services gradually reduce (to perhaps 40%) their need for participation by the work force.

An aging population—up from 22 million in the over-65 group in 1975 to 31 million in 2000—also seems certain to influence both leisure and work (not to mention politics). Other factors likely to be of influence are: (1) increased production or lack of it, (2) more women in the work force, and (3) inflationary pressures which might motivate larger numbers of persons to hold down two or even three jobs.

- *Future-directed planning.* A need for future-oriented planning was expressed repeatedly by virtually all survey participants. They also expressed concern because so little "future-think" is being done. Fred Jarvis, head of Britain's National Union of Teachers, put it this way: "Decisions about the future [in Great Britain] are being made without any attempt to picture society as it's going to be 10-to-30 years hence."

Presumably the study of the future promises to become a more influential part of life in the U.S. if the panelists' views prove to be self-fulfilling prophecies! The trick will be to obtain the benefits of long- and short-range planning while avoiding dangers implicit in the concern expressed by Sterling McMurrin: "The future is going to be marked by automation, mechanization, cybernation, and certainly by an increase in bureaucracy," he noted. "All of this, I am afraid, adds up to a great threat to individuality."

### The Viewpoints of Youth

The concepts which high school age youth had of the next 25 years tended to parallel those expressed by adults who participated in the inquiry. Evidently their schools and other media of instruction had provided a substantial amount of input with respect to such endemic problems as pollution, resource depletion, nuclear dangers, and so on.

In the youth dialogues, three points came through repeatedly and clearly:

1. In a frustrating and sometimes frightening world there is a great need for *coping* skills and techniques. Good guidance and better preparation are needed in the skills of human relations, in dealing with uncertainties, and in learning to choose wisely among alternatives.

2. Young people want to attend schools in which people *care* about them, and the "good" teacher is a person who radiates warmth and genuine interest.

3. Help was sought in *communicating*—in finding at least a few people (teachers, peer group members, parents, etc.) with whom to share concerns, hopes, and aspirations.

> *"Schools have to teach people how to change— give us an open mind so we can cope with change when it comes."*
>
> *New York senior high school student*

When questioned about the workroles they hoped to fill ten or more years hence, the juniors and seniors showed little interest in managerial, ownership, or executive roles, but frequently expressed an interest in service or professional positions. There was least interest shown in clerical, sales, or factory work—except for short periods of a year or two to finance various types of post-secondary preparation.

Interestingly, while high school youth anticipated huge social, political, economic, and technological changes, the personal lives that they expected to lead often were projections of present lifestyles with some of the imperfections and defects removed. In short, they saw their own futures as being very like the present but better because of improved human relations.

### Education for a New Millennium

Space limitations preclude anything like a complete review of the educational premises proposed for a new century in the 80 hours of tapings. High spots can, however, be inventoried.

For one thing, panelists almost universally agreed that *education* was of supreme importance but that it would involve much more than conventional schooling during the 25 years between 1976 and 2001 with which the NEA inquiry concerned itself. Willis Harman, for instance, pointed out that pressing social decisions and reforms must be contemplated in the next two decades and that children and youth, for the most part, would still be too young to participate and to offer leadership during this interval. Other media are needed, Harman argued, to provide continuing adult education in the 70s and 80s for the ill-informed, the biased, the selfish, and the stubborn, and to do so in the shortest possible time.

Lester R. Brown made an analagous comment during lunch with the writer. Referring to the diners in a club frequently patronized by prominent Washingtonians, he commented that most of them could give an hour-long extemporaneous talk on such problems as resource depletion and pollution, topics which were not in the curriculum 20 or 30 years ago. Media other than the schools, he felt, are needed to update continually the backgrounds of learners of all ages with respect to information that is just becoming available.

On the subject of education, most panelists seemed to agree on the following points:

1. The need for educators to develop a spirit of global community—of planned interdependence and dynamic reciprocity—which respects multi-ethnic and polycultural differences both in the U.S. and abroad.

2. Recognition of the need to make education a continuing, lifelong process.

3. The need for flexibility in instruction and for the *merit* of learning experiences rather than the *route* followed in attaining them.

4. The importance of recognizing that a wide range of performance is to be expected among learners, both young and old.

5. The importance of understanding that students' aspirations and motivations are best served when learning is at least partly self-selected rather than dictated by teachers.

6. The need for continuing education on a worldwide basis that would serve both mature (past 30) and senior (past 60) learners.

7. Teaching and learning should not occur only in schools.

8. The need to understand that occupational education should transcend vocational training and requires the encouragement of greater versatility among members of the work force through such techniques as better general education.

9. Recognition that traditional patterns of home-school relations need to be modified because of changes in the home.

10. The view that problem-preventing education begun in early childhood is distinctly superior to compensatory education provided at a later time.

11. The point that instruction in subject matter fields should instill an understanding of contemporary threats to the biosphere and emphasize socially useful service—by persons of all ages—in maintaining the biosphere and achieving a balance between humans and their environment.

12. Promotion of "human geography"—a grasp of planetary cultures as they exist today.

In summary, emergent educational development, 1976-2001, presumably would help young learners acquire a knowledge of the *realities* of the present, an awareness of *alternative solutions*, an understanding of *consequences* that might accompany these options, development of insights as to wise *choices*, and help U.S. youth to develop the skills and to acquire the information that are prerequisite to the *implementation* of examined ideas, policies, and programs. In short, five terms to remember in developing new curricula are: realities, alternatives, consequences, choices, and implementation!

**The Classic 1918 Goals of Education Reexamined**

As indicated earlier, the NEA panelists were asked whether the goals for U.S. education—the "seven cardinal principles of 1918—were valid after 60 years. With no more than two or three minor exceptions, the 50 participants agreed that the *goals* remained suitable, but the *meanings* of the goals needed modernizing.

> *"We must remember that the children of 2050 will be just as valuable as our children are now ... They deserve the best of our time and energy now."*
>
> Robert J. Havighurst
> Professor of Education
> University of Chicago

The development of *health*, for example, was seen as still an appropriate goal, but teachers now should help the young learn how to survive in a carcinogenic society, to understand the causes of cardiac illness, the importance of mental health practices, and to understand that opportunities for healthful living need to be extended to the world's millions who do not see a physician from birth to death.

*Command of fundamental processes*, largely limited to the 3R's in 1918, was expanded by 1976 to encompass human relations skills, development of cross-cultural insights, developing a knowledge of sources, understanding computer languages, learning to cope with increasing complexity, and developing "anticipatory skills" such as the power to see relationships and to make correlations.

*Worthy use of leisure.* The line dividing work and leisure is likely to become even more blurred. Complexity—demanding more time for the tasks and routines of daily living—was singled out as a factor of the future along with the likelihood that more items now bought in the market place (e.g., canned soup) would be made "from the ground up" in the home and that householders would do more of their own repairing and servicing of equipment and appliances.

*Worthy home membership*, according to survey participants, was related to an understanding of changes occurring in the status of the family; recognition that traditional families consisting of a mother and father and two or more youngsters living in a neat little frame house was the exception rather than the rule in present-day America. While the importance of a family or comparable "affinity group" was emphasized, it also was conceded that the influence of family bonds has decreased appreciably since 1918.

The meaning of *vocational competence* also was deemed to have changed with the passing years. Panelists noted:

• *Specific* vocational skills are difficult to foresee in a changing society.

• A good *general* education is a prerequisite to the vocational skills of operating theater, supermarket, or factory.

• Lifelong learning is a vocational skill.

• There is a need to develop a new breed of workers who see their jobs in an ecological context.

• Occupational education must not lock people into the wrong jobs.

*Citizenship skills*, many consultants felt, should embody a measure of loyalty to the planet as well as to the nation, and a consciousness of the need to study and to improve the inequities existing between the have and the have-not worlds. Some participants also saw a need to introduce the young to ways of making positive use of power and the need for people to be better informed when they sought to exercise it.

*Ethical character.* Everyone was in favor of the seventh cardinal principle as a developmental goal. Of particular interest was the emphasis by a large plurality of panelists on (1) the need to recognize again the value of self-discipline in learning, (2) the merit of rules to live by as distinct from unrestricted permissiveness, and (3) the importance of protecting and improving the biosphere. These concerns may serve as sources of secular commandments or guidelines for better lifestyles during the coming decades.

The need for adults to set suitable examples, to serve as mature models for the upcoming generation, also found frequent mention.

*Concluding comment.* A quality of cautious optimism with respect to the next 25 years tended to pervade the inquiry. The panelists seem to feel that the world's peoples have sufficient time to clean up the "planetary nest" they have befouled and the potential to demonstrate that they are the missing link between animals and civilized man.

It would seem, in Pogo's immortal phrase, that "We have met the enemy and he is us." How we cope with "the enemy" largely will determine whether the children and youth of 2050 live in a better, more humane world or find themselves wallowing in a tragic low-technology re-run of the 10th century!

**Harold G. Shane**

---

Harold G. Shane is University Professor of Education, Indiana University, Bloomington, Indiana 47401. For further information, see *Today's Education*, September-October 1976, published by the National Education Association, 1201 Sixteenth Street, N.W., Washington, D.C. 20036, U.S.A.

---

*The Educational Significance of the Future* by Harold G. Shane is available from the World Future Society Book Service. Phi Delta Kappa, Inc., Bloomington, Indiana, 1973. 116 pages. Paperback. $4.20.

# Education for Tomorrow's World

*To find out what futurists might contribute to education, an Indiana University educator interviewed 82 leading futurists in America and England. He found a great deal of agreement on the problems that society currently faces, and also a consensus that education should become more closely linked with the real world, perhaps through what he calls a "paracurriculum" of real life experiences to accompany and enrich schooling.*

by Harold G. Shane

During the autumn and early winter of 1971-1972 I visited more than 20 future-oriented policy research centers and interviewed 82 leading futurists as part of a contract with the U. S. Office of Education. The basic purpose was to determine what futures research might contribute to education. My findings were submitted last autumn to the Office of Education in a 135-page report entitled *The Educational Significance of the Future: Implications for USOE Policy Decisions.*

Most of the researchers I interviewed differed only in minor respects in their diagnosis of the problems confronting U.S. society. Here are 10 major problems that were identified:

**1. The crisis of crises.** The accumulation of crises in the past decade was deemed serious. Difficulties which might have been handled singly become virtually impossible to cope with in the aggregate. Among the ominous sociopolitical and economic indicators were the threat of bankruptcy in some U. S. cities, sustained international tensions, many forms of dissent, inflation, unemployment, a growing deficit with respect to law and order including the problem of clogged court dockets, and various forms of racial tension which had not been significantly eased despite emphasis on cultural pluralism and human rights. In effect this major mosaic of problems can be described as a crisis of crises, a phrase used by biophysicist John Platt of the University of Michigan.

**2. The credibility gap.** The loss of credibility by persons or groups in authority is creating another "American Dilemma." Even the most legally constituted authorities—the president, law enforcement agencies, parents, and teachers—have had their authority questioned, ignored, denied, or threatened.

**3. Institutional overload.** Ambivalent attitudes toward authority are related to a third problem: the growing inability of schools and other institutions to adapt to their new roles and tasks. In part this situation arose because some agencies, such as the schools, have been called on to assume responsibilities that they were not designated to fulfill and which they are not presently prepared to handle. Bureaucracy and lack of funds have compounded the problem.

**4. Disagreement over the "good life."** Lack of agreement as to the "best" quality of life—the nature of "The Good Society"—has in itself generated a crisis. The social, economic, political, ethnic, ecological, industrial, religious, and business-labor cleavages here run deep. And the schools, as a mirror of society, are experiencing a major problem in identifying the nature and qualities of the contemporary educated man and woman when there is no clear social agreement as to what constitutes the good life.

**5. The value crisis.** For most of "Middle America," which was a very broad segment of the population in the 1920s, the social proprieties and amenities that one was expected to respect and to observe were clearly understood. One was brought up *knowing* the answer to what was good taste, proper dress, and appropriate social behavior. Today there is a violent value crisis which leaves many persons bewildered as to what is "right" and "wrong" with respect to such matters as drug abuse, pornography, the role of women, sexual mores, the functions of the church, and the like.

**6. Equity versus equality.** The question of what constitutes "equity" has become a major problem. How does an *equitable* educational or job opportunity differ (if it does differ) from an *equal* one? Is merely equal treatment fair and just, or does justice reside in *different* treatment for the gifted, the disadvantaged, the culturally gifted, the handicapped, the very young, and the very old?

**7. Tacit Rejection of egalitarianism.** An unrecognized rejection of equality in American democracy is a source of a problem intimately related to point six above. Judging by overt *behavior* rather than what many citizens *say*, a large minority seeks "equality with the top ten percent" rather than merely a more or less equal share of the material goods and privileges provided by a technologically sophisticated society. Most Americans conceive of democracy as a foundation for upward mobility; a means of rising above one's father's station in life. Neither democracy nor U. S. education has an adequate coping doctrine with which to confront the inevitable resentment of young adults who are corroded by frustration when they begin to realize that they have failed to find room at the top and consequently are dissatisfied as production workers, salesmen, technicians, and so on.

**8. Lack of a future-focused role image for youth.** Too little has been done in family life and in schooling to help children and youth develop a satisfying personal-vocational self-image that will prove to be realistic as they grow older. This lack of a future-focused role image poses a substantial challenge to our schools as they endeavor to help motivate young learners to project themselves into a world of work of the future in which they experience dignity, respect, and other rewards in any one of many socially useful jobs rather than wistfully longing for so-called "prestige" jobs which actually require and employ only a small fraction of our manpower as professional workers, executives, owners, and entrepreneurs.

**9. Insensitivity to changing patterns of survival behavior.** In the almost continuous eras of scarcity which preceded the development of industrial capacity in the Western world, successful survival behavior often involved becoming a part of the hereditary, ecclesiastical and military minority that had the pick of the simple luxuries and limited security that were available. Today, with a substantial array of consumer goods and services available to most Americans, we have the problem of changing our patterns of survival behavior from medieval attitudes of suspicion, self-aggrandizement, and competition for scarce goods. Our survival as human beings (and perhaps even as a species) today depends to an increasing degree on mutual understanding, empathy, ability to reach agreement through interaction and reasonable compromise rather than by resort to force or by "pulling rank."

**10. The haves and the have-nots.** A final crisis that most scientists interviewed in the study felt to be particularly severe is made up of three components: naive use of technology, rapid increases in world population, and the consequent ecological problems. Perhaps it can most simply be labeled the "have-have not" problem. What it boils down to is this: In the early 1970s, the U.S., with approximately 6% of the world population, annually was consuming about two-thirds of the raw materials such as copper, coal, and oil that comprise the world's output of raw materials. Theoretically, in 1973, if we increased our consumption by 50%, the U.S. could absorb *all* of the world's consumer goods. Even now the purchasing power of Americans at the U.S. *poverty* level is above the consumption level of the *top* 25% of whole populations in the so-called underdeveloped countries. As one result the world's "have" nations—especially the U.S.—are on a collision course with the nearly one and three quarters billion people in the Third World, who earn less than $100 annually per capita. Furthermore, we are severely harming the ecosphere in the process. It seems clear, in terms of the welfare of the planet, that we must recognize that there are limits to the doctrine of unlimited growth, to U.S. style affluence, to technological exploitation, and to population increase, and endeavor to move toward a policy that will reconcile people everywhere to the need to find the satisfaction of self-fulfillment from sources other than the acquisition of material possessions.

For the most part, these ten problems—and the ineffably complex dilemmas and issues they pose—have not been thoroughly attacked or even widely discussed. Not unexpectedly under these circumstances, virtually no serious thought has been given to what the ten problems or crises imply for curriculum change in education.

At the present juncture, most policy and futures research specialists agree that one of the nation's tasks is to determine what it really seeks in the decades immediately ahead and what these aspirations mean for changes in the social, affective, and cognitive climate of the schools. Lacking a social consensus as to what schooling should accomplish, U.S. education will remain in deeply troubled waters, because our schools function as an integral part of the culture as a whole.

The need for new, clear goals is transcendently important, because 20 years of increasing affluence in the U.S. have given us an unreasoning and, ironically, unsatisfying appetite for more material gains, with many deeper human longings unsatisfied. We have moved from *wistfully longing* for a better living in the 1930s to *hoping* for a better quality of life in the late 1940s, to *expecting* greater material and human gains in the 1950s, and now to *demanding* them since the mid-1960s. The deterioration of the environment as a result of our accelerating quest for more goods, better services, more education, and greater freedom has been extensively documented and poses some of the major paradoxes and problems of the 1970s. The better things get, the worse they seem to be! We now need to reassess our levels of social, material, and educational aspirations, futures research tells us, as we determine what the biosphere can provide; and we now need to identify new, equitable, human, yet realistic levels of aspiration toward which we can afford to move.

A number of the futurists whom I interviewed suggested certain immediate changes that the educational community might wish to contemplate during the next 10-15 years, an interval during which we can avoid doing irreversible damage to our planet.

• Introducing experiences beginning with birth that will teach the young learner about the world around him, with methodical schooling beginning no later than the age of three.

• Placing emphasis on a personalized program which concentrates on progress by the individual learner rather

*Harold Shane, Professor and formerly Dean of Education at Indiana University, says futurists feel U.S. Society is now experiencing a "crisis of crises."*

than uniform group standards and competencies.

• Careful efforts to give the student a positive self-image so that he does not feel he is "dirty," "stupid," a "non-reader" and so on.

• Development of a suitable future-focused role image. This is analogous to the "self" concept, but extends through time to delineate a realistic, motivating concept of the options a person has in working toward a life-role that brings satisfaction and promises self-respect and dignity.

• An endeavor, even with quite young (10-12 years old) children to study the history of the future. For example, teachers might give them old magazines, books and papers so that they can see how today was foreshadowed eight or ten years ago, or to study how their neighborhood has changed in the last four to eight years. For older children, it might be challenging to study how the future of developing countries may be better understood by looking at developed countries, where many of the future problems of the Third World—for example, air pollution—have already occurred.

• Creation of ways in which children and youth can become of greater value to the community through work-service programs sponsored by the school and involving adults in the vicinity.

• Use of the community itself as a huge teaching aid by means of which many forms of learning can take place. The community would become not an alternative to school but an adjunct to schooling.

**Futurists Urge More Flexible Schools**

Futurists polled also felt:

**There should be less uniformity in the subject matter learned in public schools, and there should be considerable variation in the age at which different learners encounter similar ideas and facts.** The rationale for abandonment of the present graded structure in schools in favor of a continuum can be stated as follows:

▶ Recognizing that human beings are unique individuals; that they grow and learn at different rates, have had different experiences, and acquire diverse self-concepts and role images with respect to the future. In short, schooling should reflect the fact of these differences and drop the impossible dream of seeking to bring children and youth up to arbitrary and uniform standards of academic and social performance.

▶ Sensing more clearly that learning is continuous. Whatever reasons there may once have been for a nine-month, September to June school year have lost their validity. Therefore, with appropriate physical changes such as air conditioning for schools located in warm areas, we should be able to modify programs to permit children to attend for a total of 180 to 200 days, during which attendance patterns vary and are spread throughout the year. The actual timing of attendance would be determined by professional judgment, family circumstances, efficient use of the school environment, and the future development of teaching materials or "packages" that can be used at home.

▶ Restructuring education so that it can provide needed mental and emotional input throughout a person's life. There are educational needs at 40, 60, and even past age 70 that are as real as those at age 5 or 15 or 25. There are needs for new skills as technosocial and humanistic changes emerge, and for new knowledge in fields that a person perhaps has not studied for twenty years. Education is also

---

**Experiential Learning**

*Frank Ogden offers his students an opportunity to experience some of the problems that the future may pose.*

Many future-oriented university courses now include "real life" learning experiences similar to what might be offered under a paracurriculum as described by Harold Shane. One member of the World Future Society who is actively engaged in providing such learning situations for his students is Frank Ogden of the Ontario College of Arts in Toronto.

To open students' eyes and immunize them to future shock, Ogden puts them through 50 to 75 radically different experiences in a short time. The students take flying lessons, work in a poultry shop plucking chickens, wrestle an alligator, inhale helium, train in brain-wave control, conduct a funeral service, and eat rattlesnake meat.

"Experience is the raw material of all art," Ogden explained during a recent visit to the World Future Society's headquarters. One experience that his art students may find especially relevant is carrying a sculpture through a Toronto office building, entering one office after another until they find a buyer. By knowing how to sell his own works, an artist can save the 50% commission charged by galleries.

A college drop-out himself, Ogden refers to most formal education as "irreversible brain damage." In its place, he offers a "three-E" program that *E*xcites and *E*ntertains so that students will *E*ducate themselves. In his classes, drop-ins rather than drop-outs are the problem.

Next November, Ogden plans a "Survival Training Course for the Future" in the Caribbean. The course will include first-hand experience with overpopulation, mostly in Port-au-Prince, Haiti, the most densely populated place on earth.

---

needed for the constructive use of leisure, for post-retirement careers, for interests and activities that can make old age something less to be dreaded, and as a means of increasing an individual's ability to communicate well and to contribute more to his fellows.

A number of futurists feel, therefore, that education should be continuous through life. The curriculum would informally begin approximately when a child reached the developmental age of two. Direct contact with a school would begin a year or so later, depending on the child's maturity. At this point, he would enter a "minischool" group for half-days. The minischool group would consist of six to eight three-year-olds directed by a paraprofessional, working under the supervision of an experienced teacher consultant, and with a program emphasizing developmental rather than academic learnings.

The pupil would move without interruption from the

primary continuum to middle school continuum. In the middle school continuum the learner might spend as little as two years or as much as five, depending on the rate of flow of his maturing. The concepts of double promotion or "skipping" would totally disappear, as would "flunking." In a personalized continuum, each learner would move at his own speed without reference to group norms. These would be replaced by "personalized norms," which could consist of quantified data based on samplings of the personal progress made by large groups of individuals sharing certain characteristics as to health, sex, intelligence, and so forth. Personalized norms would recognize that each learner is a being engaged in "creating himself."

The concept of uninterrupted progress would continue in the high school and post-secondary years, where each learner would receive careful guidance, and many of today's rigid liberal arts program requirements, including admission and graduation, would be abandoned. There would be considerable re-education of those parents and teachers who are predominantly subject-and-semester minded as part of the change.

**The Paracurriculum: Learning outside the school**

One of the most interesting and least explored concepts in futurist thinking is the idea of the paracurriculum. The paracurriculum concept recognizes that schooling provides only a part of the experience which adds up to a learner's education. Indeed, in many instances the non-school learnings of children and youth may be far the most extensive (and sometimes the most valuable) components or factors in helping them cope with, manipulate and control their environment.

Before continuing further, the term "paracurriculum" should be defined. The word refers to the body of out-of school experiences which help to strengthen the intellectual ability, general background, and coping powers of the child or youth. As futurists see it, tomorrow's educational institutions will make greater and more deliberate use of the paracurriculum and the out-of-school milieu in which it exists. The school would be a participatory planner and broker for the non-school experiences, which would parallel the in-school curriculum of a learner and sometimes replace it temporarily or permanently.

Here is how the paracurriculum might work:

● At age 15 (or perhaps as early as age 13 in rare instances), a student could begin a useful vocational activity without attending school.

● His move from the world of the school to the "real world" would be arranged or "brokered" by the school, a process which would involve teachers' professional judgments; in-depth counseling; parental understanding, consent, support and cooperation; and close working relationships with employers who are socially minded and willing to offer their enterprises as alternatives to conventional schooling without exploiting 14- to 16-year-old worker-learners.

● The paracurriculum would eliminate "push-outs" and dropouts. One does not drop out of an educational continuum; he merely moves at a 90 degree angle into planned paracurricular learning and continues his education in what, hopefully, will be an experience of increased educational significance.

● An integral part of the paracurriculum is the privilege of planned lifelong exit *and re-entry* privileges carefully coordinated by enlightened guidance practices.

● By age 14, the early adolescent would be helped to move from curriculum to paracurriculum and vice versa without social or academic problems and without any demeaning stigma. Indeed, with graded structures abandoned, there would no longer be an eighth-grade group or a sophomore class from which to withdraw! Age ranges, greatly increased by the flexible and often ephemeral and functional approaches to grouping, would also make exit and re-entry inconspicuous and matter-of-fact, as it already is in graduate study where persons in their early twenties may rub shoulders with students twice their age.

● As currently envisioned here, the paracurriculum concept is not a limited innovation applicable only at the early adolescent level. Rather it is part of the total warp and woof of lifelong education. It is applicable even in early childhood in the form of temporary exiting from school to make simple community service contributions (for example, keeping a park or a playground clean); and it is applicable in the learner's later maturity when at, say, 60 years of age he returns from the paracurriculum of the world of work to the curriculum provided in schools with the hope of making his retirement more meaningful or a post-retirement job feasible through further education.

The paracurriculum concept is made up of components that have already been discussed and sometimes introduced in the U.S. under such labels as "socially useful work," "continuing education," and "paid internships." As the idea of a lifelong, year-around educational continuum gains acceptance, the paracurriculum concept might well become a viable and important concomitant source of many alternative approaches to learning.

(Harold G. Shane is University Professor of Education, Indiana University School of Education, Bloomington, Indiana 47401. His article is based on his report, *The Educational Significance of the Future:* A Report prepared for Sidney P. Marland, Jr., U.S. Commissioner of Education, October, 1972. The original supply of this 135-page mimeographed report is exhausted. However, the World Future Society is reprinting the document and will distribute it without charge through the Society's Supplemental Program. Persons not subscribing to the Supplemental Program may order the report for $3 from the Society's book service.)

# The Pre-Schooler and the Future

*An educator-psychiatrist suggests that school children should be introduced to the future at an early age. The peaceful world that we hope to have in the 21st century may be won in the nursery schools of the 1970s.*

by Chester M. Pierce

An educator must never lose sight of the fact that he is preparing citizens for the future. He must feel that there is nothing more urgent than the proper accomplishment of this mission, and he must dare to hope for things that he can only begin to glimpse or that lie beyond both his comprehension and imagination. The ideal teacher would have the zeal, enthusiasm, optimism, and know-how that constitute the basic ingredients for preparing the child for his future—the future of humankind.

The child who is well prepared will meet the future with a confidence bred of the penetrating insights and constructive foresights that his teachers have provided him. As an adult, he will be able to operate in an effective, efficient manner, in terms of his own personal life and his membership in society as a whole.

Among the millions of children who have watched *Sesame Street* in the past several years or who will watch it in the coming months are the top leaders of education, government, and industry in the early decades of the 21st century, as well as the 21st century Everyman. What is the projected future for these children? What is probable? What is possible? What is desirable? Once we take some posture relative to these future-oriented questions, we can begin to think about how best to teach these children so that civilization will be maximized and optimized.

When the three-year-old in Des Moines, Iowa, who today watches *Sesame Street* has reached the age of 40, the three-day work week will probably have been long established. Furthermore, it is probable that the enormous advances in biochemistry and in knowledge of body rhythms will permit him to stay awake in good functioning order for 21 out of every 24 hours. In all probability he will have vastly greater longevity and vitality than today's 40-year-old.

He will live in a society that may exercise considerable control over the weather. Members of the community will have easy, cheap, virtually foolproof contraceptive methods. As the crowded descendants of the 20th century population explosion they will probably be looking to exotic places for resources and living space.

Our erstwhile pre-schooler will probably find it perfectly natural that child-rearing, particularly in the early years of life, is under the aegis of a public institution. (A Ministry of Child Guidance? A Department of Child Training and Development?)

It would be good if the Des Moines toddler is educated in such a way that he can adjust gracefully to his 21st century world. The sheer number of times that he may have to be re-cycled vocationally demands that he have a certain flexibility of mind as well as elastic attitudes toward obsolescence. Similarly, he must be able to unlearn and relearn many things, ranging from vocational skills to attitudes toward other human beings.

When a teacher contemplates the probable, the possible,

*Harvard psychiatrist Chester Pierce believes that if children are educated to be planetary citizens "we will have done much to insure civilization on this earth."*

and the desirable aspects of the future, he may conclude that the three-year-old in Des Moines should—starting tomorrow—be molded in such a manner that he becomes (1) a cosmopolite, (2) fluent in communication analysis, and (3) conversant with the problems resulting from overcrowding. The 21st century citizen will need an abundance of cognitive skills, but he will also need an equal quantity of skills in the affective and conative aspects of life. *Sesame Street* is one model of how these skills can be offered to children. The program tries to make each child feel loved and accepted. The program seeks to make learning fun and to develop and sustain curiosity.

From the outset, the program has employed the most rigorous scientific methodology both in applying the principles of learning and in evaluating the results. However, even the most meticulous longitudinal study, performed over entire lifetimes, could not produce an estimate of how much *Sesame Street* has moved American children (and now children from an increasing number of other lands) toward becoming planetary citizens. There has been much stress—particularly in the first year of the program—on cognitive components, e.g., the learning of numbers, letters, relationships, etc. But the program has always offered other lessons, both explicit and implicit, that underline the joy of acquiring knowledge, the importance of tolerating differences, and the demonstration that various kinds of people can live in harmony. In such a harmonious atmosphere, each person expands his own horizons while helping others to expand theirs.

It seems incontestable that *Sesame Street* has helped to prepare children to be better informed citizens who are able to adopt a wider view of the world.

What else might be done to prepare our Des Moines preschooler for his future? I suggest that it might be useful to inject the future more deliberately into his education.

All parents are befuddled by such profound questions as, "Is today 'tomorrow'?" or "How big can big be?" Dealing with such questions offers a natural opportunity to inculcate future-oriented concepts into young minds eager and curious to absorb everything.

But before going further I would like to call attention to an axiom accepted by both futurists and mental health workers. Roughly stated, the axiom maintains that what causes someone to be mentally ill is the discrepancy he finds between childhood expectations and adult reality. A child who spent his life preparing to be a hunter would be seriously jarred if, when he becomes an adult, he is sent to a fishing village to make his living. Therefore, it is the responsibility of the teacher to let the child know as nearly as possible what life will be like—or could be like—when the child becomes an adult. There should be things that a teacher can do to prepare a child so that he is in alignment with his future, yet flexible, adaptive, and imaginative enough to shape that future so that he and his fellows can live with more grandeur.

Let us look at some of the natural questions of the child and consider how an adult's responses to them might help to prepare the child for his future:

### "How big is big?"

It might be salutary for teachers to find ways to introduce the concept of infinity to children early in their lives. The idea of limitlessness may provide a sense of options to be sought and exercised. The concept of infinity may also help to promote flexibility and selective tentativeness in thinking. The need to have confidence to approach solutions by alternative and various means may be especially important to those children who are or who soon will be defeated, demoralized, and helpless. Grasping the idea of infinity may counter-balance some of the real environmental traumata which conspire to make a child feel less certain that he can ever command or control his destiny.

### "What can I be when I grow up?"

A child needs to learn about occupational options, about various ways whereby he can justify his existence when he becomes an adult. He should know about these options at a very early stage, and should learn new options constantly. By the age of six, a ghetto child could be informed not only about occupations now in existence, but about occupations that might or will come into existence, such as sea-mining. These occupations must be presented in such a way that an affective sentiment is appealed to, so that the child will know that such a career is possible for him, and that to win it means definite rewards for and from the society he lives in.

As the child acquires such data, he could be gaining information about a variety of related demographic material. A five-year-old can begin to comprehend such facts as "City X has too many shoemakers but not enough helicopter pilots." By systematically supplying such data, in a manner carefully tailored to the child's interest and understanding, the child may be aided in adapting to his future.

### "Do you want a pillow, Daddy?"

Often we talk about how cruel children can be. Yet they are also among the most gentle of creatures. Somewhere along the line, many nice considerate children become hard, callous adults. But our social technology now has the capability of developing experiments in the fostering of hope and altruism. Such experiments in helping behavior must, of course, focus equally on both children and those who rear them. Recently I heard a story about a toddler who thoughtfully provided a kleenex for a little girl in his class. When he started to help her blow her nose, the teacher took the kleenex and provided the service which the thoughtful toddler had wished to perform. Thus the teacher thwarted spontaneous helpful behavior. The growing literature on helping behavior and altruism should give us leads as to how to introduce altruism into the life practice of children. One way is to make the child more aware of his interpersonal interactions.

### "Don't you want to hug me?"

In some circumstances children exhibit an uncanny perception. The child presents himself for a hug when he somehow divines that the nearby adult wishes to oblige. Yet in most of our adult lives we remain ignorant of the great torrent of behavioral nuances bouncing around us.

It is possible to teach children early in life to be much more sensitive to their interpersonal interactions. The focus could be on making children aware of when they might be offending someone. Similarly they could be trained to understand how to defend themselves against someone else's micro-offenses.

Many methods, such as the use of motion pictures, could be employed to make children more aware of their micro-aggressions and the bad feelings that result. These same methods could be used to broaden the child's political orientation. At present, nearly all five-year-olds have an understandable loyalty to their country and President. The same psychological and developmental factors which encouraged such a degree of politicalization might be manipulated so that the child perceives the world, not just his own country, as the focus of his loyalty.

**"Why did he break my bike?"**

Recognizing that overcrowding and the desire to enjoy the technological benefits of modern life can lead to friction and conflict, we may feel it necessary to help the pre-schooler learn more about conflict resolution and decision-making. Here, too, a number of experiments will have to be tried. Games, mass media, and group methods might help to introduce the four-year-old to ways he can deal with conflicts that he has or will face in later life. The teaching must provide fun and excitement, while maintaining the youngster's belief that he is acceptable and can cope successfully. The child should sense the advantages of cooperative, collaborative behavior.

To live in the 21st century, in sustained peace, it will be preferable for people to see themselves as relatively more cooperative than competitive. This means that the 21st century citizen should be prepared to depart, in some degree, from his 20th century ancestors, who placed greater stress on individually-oriented competition than on group-oriented collaboration. There may be no better place to inaugurate this shift than in the nursery school games of the 1970s, during a period when institutional child care becomes commonplace, if not universal.

Yet there must be many sites where ludic behavior can be guided so that a higher quality of learning will take place. Solving ecological problems, such as the accumulation of wastes in the oceans or in space, will require concerted, collaborative action by planetary citizens who happen to live in many different areas of the earth. Children of pre-school age should learn many basic facts, e.g., scientists can collect residues from London automobile exhausts on the continent of Antarctica. By school age, the child will have absorbed, if not integrated, such data, so that he can be prepared to see that problems need to be solved on a global rather than a local basis.

We do not know the exact means to reach our goal of preparing the child for his future, but it seems likely we already have much knowledge in many disciplines that could be useful in moving people towards meaningful congruence between their past experiences and their future expectations. Much experimentation is needed; a wide variety of methods should be tried and evaluated.

We are told that futurology is gaining repute as a legitimate curriculum offering in leading colleges and universities. From my viewpoint, there is even more legitimacy to presenting futurology at grade school and pre-grade school levels. Many positive benefits may accrue from introducing concepts of the future into the teaching of pre-schoolers.

The methods to be employed should include a combination of hardware, such as audio-visual and computer-assistance equipment, and software like games and group methods. It will be imperative to put much effort into training teachers and perhaps parents to re-evaluate their teaching methods and learn how to utilize the body of multi-disciplined speculation about what is possible, probable, and desirable for the future.

No one knows how much a child absorbs from his environment during his first five years of life, but it is postulated that much more is and can be absorbed than we now suspect. If this is the case, then the ever greater rapidity of social change makes it necessary to look more carefully at how we prepare our youth for the future. Learning in a fun way, as one does when watching *Sesame Street,* is one way to acquire important concepts concerning the future—what scientists have accomplished, what demographic problems will complicate political life, or how playing games can make one more aware of how to be helpful, yet also how to be helped. By being unrestricted in our thinking about how to use a variety of hardware now available and trying to integrate soft and hard information from many disciplines, we should be able to help today's pre-schooler become the cosmopolite of the 21st century.

If we succeed in creating planetary citizens who are both supra-nationalists and super-generalists, then we will have done much to insure civilization on this earth. And today's pre-schooler will become an adult who can live better, longer, and more peacefully here on earth—or even beyond our earth and conceivably beyond our galaxy.

(Chester M. Pierce, M.D., is Professor of Education and Psychiatry in the Faculty of Medicine and at the Graduate School of Education, Harvard University, Cambridge, Massachusetts 02138.)

---

### Canadian Library Establishes Section for Futuristics

The chief librarian at Loyola College in Montreal has agreed to establish a special section in the college's main library for futurist publications.

The project was initiated by John G. McGraw, professor of philosophy at Loyola and the World Future Society's co-ordinator in Montreal. McGraw wrote a letter recently to James De Cou, branch public affairs officer at the U.S. Information Service in Montreal, requesting a grant from the U.S. Consulate to help establish a nucleus collection of the leading U.S. publications regarding futurism, to be located at Loyola.

De Cou supported the project and secured approval from Leopold Le Clair, Counselor of Embassy for Public Affairs at the U.S. Embassy in Ottawa, for a grant of $1,000.

"The fact that these agencies of the U.S. Government would sponsor a Canadian institution of higher learning regarding futurism is to me extremely significant," McGraw told *THE FUTURIST*. "Moreover, that the chief librarian at Loyola would agree to reserve a section of the main library solely to futuristic works is also notable. Given the customary attitude of librarians not to tolerate, much less endorse, the increase of special studies, this development is obviously an accomplishment. Hopefully, this will cause similar innovations at other universities, since I suspect that it is a quite unique occurrence, if not in the United States, at least in Canada insofar as I know."

(John McGraw is Professor of Philosophy, Loyola College, 7141 Sherbrooke St. W., Montreal, 262, Quebec, Canada.)

## Futurizing Education

Teachers from kindergarten to graduate school now are introducing the future into education. This movement to futurize education arises from a growing recognition that the extremely rapid pace of social and technological change means that the world of tomorrow—in which today's students will be adults—is going to be vastly different from the world of yesterday that schools have traditionally stressed.

A course can be futurized in a variety of ways. An English teacher might offer a unit on utopias or on science fiction, thus opening his students' minds to the awesome possibilities of the future.

A science teacher might ask students to consider how specific scientific developments may affect human life in the coming decades. A social studies instructor can free students' imaginations by having them design new governments or economic structures that might be used in the future. And where team teaching is possible, teachers from several disciplines often work together to help students get a broader, more integrated view of alternative futures.

A few examples of the many different ways in which teachers can turn education toward tomorrow are presented on the following pages.

# Students Plan the Future of Their Community

**One means of getting students involved with future studies is to let them plan the future of their own community. In a Michigan high school, students researched proposals which were before the town council, and submitted their recommendations to community leaders.**

Richard Dougherty, co-instructor of the futuristics course at Port Huron (Michigan) Northern High School, discusses future housing trends with two students. Dougherty believes that community-oriented futures studies will help students to become better citizens.

Teachers at a Michigan high school have made futuristics relevant and interesting to their students by getting them to think about the future of their own community.

At Port Huron Northern High School, Richard O. Dougherty, Social Studies Chairman, and Walt Lyszak, Science Chairman, have devised a two-semester, interdisciplinary course which includes such topics as ecology, economics, social change, and land-use planning.

During the first semester, students become thoroughly familiar with the theoretical concepts of a subject such as land-use planning. Then, they apply their knowledge to specific questions; for example, "Should the Port Huron City Council approve the construction of a shopping mall at the intersection of Krafft Road and US-25?"

To answer the question, students engaged in extensive community field work. Among the authorities they consulted were the city planning director, city councilmen, the mall developer, and the residents and businessmen who would be directly affected by the construction of the proposed mall. By talking directly to community members intimately involved with land-use planning, each student gained an understanding of the realities and complexities of planning.

During the second semester of the course, the students applied the same approach to another question: "Should the township give up 600 acres for annexation to Port Huron City for industrial expansion?"

In each of the above cases, the class rendered an affirmative decision on the basis of a detailed rationale. The students submitted to the City Council a summary of their findings, which included the statement of the problem, resulting secondary problems, alternative solutions and their consequences, evaluations of facts and opinions, and a final recommendation.

As a finale to the course, the students devised a "master plan" for their community entitled, "Burtchville Township 1990." Recognizing the personal and financial benefits which local citizens would accrue from the township's development of recreational facilities, the class finally recommended that a marina, golf course, and shopping center be part

Students in Port Huron, Michigan, plan future housing units for their community with help of Walt Lyszak (second from right), Science Chairman of their high school.

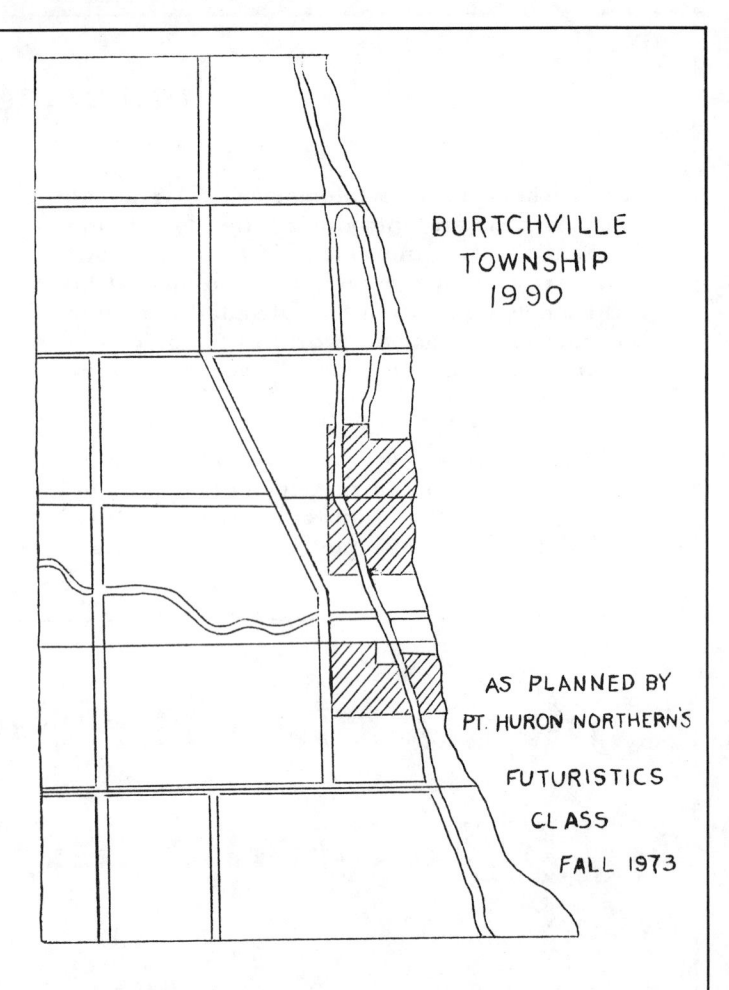

Cover of the master plan developed by Port Huron students during their futuristics course.

Before preparing a master plan for their community in 1990, Port Huron high school students consult with Patrick L. Loeprich (far left), a member of the St. Clair Regional Planning Commission.

of the area's future expansion efforts. The students carefully delineated zoning, sewage, transportation and housing changes which would be compatible with and necessary for the "master plan."

The Port Huron futuristics curriculum is constantly evolving. Last semester, for example, more time was devoted to the extension of futuristic concepts regarding man and his environment. The local Rotary organization asked the students to research the existing and future needs of senior citizens/retirees of the Blue Water area—a project which again provided students with very meaningful material and the opportunity to work closely with the community.

THE TEACHERS AT PORT HURON NORTHERN HIGH HAVE FULL SUPPORT FROM THEIR PRINCIPAL, JAMES E. OVERLY, WHO BELIEVES THAT TEACHERS SHOULD INTRODUCE A FUTURES ASPECT TO EVERY COURSE FROM KINDERGARTEN THROUGH HIGH SCHOOL. RICHARD O. DOUGHERTY IS CHAIRMAN OF THE SOCIAL STUDIES DEPARTMENT, PORT HURON NORTHERN HIGH SCHOOL, 1799 KRAFFT ROAD, PORT HURON, MICHIGAN 48060.

# Creative Approaches to Futuristics

**The *I.Q. Game* and a special unit on the future of the elderly help Ohio high school students to understand that it is possible to think seriously about the future—and start immediately to make it better.**

*We can't have a course in future—*
  Nobody knows the future.
  What will the teacher teach?

*We can't have a course in future—*
  It's not part of any established social studies curriculum.
  What will the school board say?

*We can't have a course in future—*
  It might become too controversial.
  What if these students reject organized religion and monogamy, and opt to live in a commune?

*We can't have a course in future—*
  It might take our mind off today's real problems.
  What if it's a plot to direct our attention away from the problems of minority groups?

*We can't have a course in future—*
  Everybody knows that we learn from the past.
  What would social studies teachers do if they couldn't teach about THE PAST?

Betty Barclay Franks is an Ohio social studies teacher who has transformed most of the "We can't's" listed above into "We can's." Working with Mary Kay Howard of the History Department of John Carroll University, Franks has been a primary force behind the introduction of future studies to Ohio school systems.

One example of Franks' futuristic creativity is *Future Decisions: The I.Q. Game*, a simulation exercise she developed to stimulate futuristic thinking.

At a recent teachers conference at Prince George's Community College in Largo, Maryland, approximately one hundred teachers played the I.Q. Game.

Individuals randomly assigned to groups were asked to make a decision as to whether they wished to serve on a hypothetical board of hospital administrators. The work of the board was to allocate I.Q. serum to petitioning pregnant women. The serum, costing $10,000 to administer to any one woman, could raise the I.Q. of her unborn child to the 160 or genius level.

Each board was instructed to rank order a list of 15 applicants for the serum. They were informed that: "Since adequate supplies of the drug do not yet exist and since time is a crucial factor (the treatment must be given during the last stages of pregnancy or it is not effective), the board must rank order the applicants immediately."

Two pieces of information supplied to each board were the sex and the anticipated I.Q. of the unborn child (data assumed to be available through perfected medical tests).

In addition, much personal information about the applicants was provided (marital status, race, profession, age, other children, etc.). A typical entry read as follows:

  commune resident
  receives food stamps
  good health
  sells pottery occasionally

  MARRIED TO
  commune resident
  sculptor
  good health

children: boy (8 yrs./114 I.Q.), boy (4 yrs./119 I.Q.), unborn child: boy, 98 I.Q.

Reactions of participants to the game varied widely. One group refused to allocate the serum on the grounds that the administration of the drug should be a matter of individual choice. In another group, several members felt that children with an anticipated I.Q. of over 120 should be disqualified. This was considered by many to be an equitable method of procedure, since it aimed at providing a favorable I.Q. for as many children as possible.

But one member of the group rejected this analysis. He argued that children with the highest expected I.Q. should be the primary candidates for the drug. In this way, the drug would have its greatest effect, and would produce the most capable minds. Such children might eventually contribute significantly to the areas of medicine, technology, science, etc., and would be a true national resource and a benefit to society.

A third member of the group interjected his concern about the social adjustment of children designated to receive the drug, since a child might be a social isolate in a family in which other individuals had much lower I.Q.'s.

One of the observers—those who declined to participate in the game—explained that he simply could not "play God," even under hypothetical circumstances. In response to this position, a participant indicated that he wanted to be a part of the decision making process, whatever the results. He pointed out that refusing to decide is, in effect, a decision. To remove oneself entirely from the decision making process, he contended, is the worst possible alternative.

As a follow-up session to the I.Q. game, players can imagine some of the repercussions of the board's decisions. Betty Franks often has her classes think of newspaper headlines or TV news stories that might emerge if the serum were a reality, such as:

**NEW YORK HOSPITAL BOARD MEMBER SHOT BY IRATE BLACK WOMAN WHO CLAIMS HER CHILD WAS DENIED THE I.Q. DRUG BECAUSE OF RACIAL DISCRIMINATION.**

**CHILD SUES PARENTS FOR FAILURE TO ADMINISTER THE I.Q. DRUG TO HER. PLAINTIFF CLAIMS SHE WAS DEPRIVED OF THE RIGHT TO INTELLECTUAL EQUALITY.**

**ENFORCED ADMINISTRATION OF I.Q. DRUG BECOMES KEY ISSUE OF UPCOMING PRESIDENTIAL CAMPAIGN.**

**HARMFUL SIDE EFFECTS OF I.Q. DRUG NOW BEING DISCOVERED.**

One teacher present suggested that a generation of 10-year-old geniuses might even take over the world. In discussing the game, many of the teachers concluded that it is primarily an exercise in values clarification, and that it could help players adapt to the future shock of the biogenetic revolution.

Betty Franks noted that some of her students initially feel that the game has no basis in reality. To this argument, she counters with clippings from newspapers which point to present medical undertakings similar in nature to that of the I.Q. serum.

As an example of the relevance of the game, Betty Franks often plays a tape-recorded reading from Gordon Rattray Taylor's book, *The Biological Time Bomb* (New American Library, New York, 1968). One bio-medical advance mentioned in the book is the use of an oxygen sack to cover the placenta during the last stages of pregnancy, thus reducing the pains of childbirth. It has been found that the use of this sack also positively affects the I.Q. of the children born under this procedure. Experts believe that without supplemental oxygen during the last months of pregnancy, the unborn child's brain does not undergo its maximum development.

## Alternatives for the Elderly

Another technique that Franks has devised is a futuristics teaching unit based on alternatives for the elderly.

Each student writes a paragraph describing himself at the age of 90. The class then suggests conditions in our society which affect our perception of the elderly. Examples include biogenetic changes (organ transplants, plastic surgery to remove wrinkles, prostheses, etc.); the prevalence of the nuclear family; the emphasis of our culture on youth; increasingly early retirement, and age discrimination.

The class is then broken into small groups and each is asked to think of the immediate and long-range consequences of these conditions on the lives of the elderly. For example, the prevalence of the nuclear family may mean that more and more parents no longer live with their children. As a result, there may be a growing need for retirement communities and ways for the elderly to feel useful and wanted outside the home.

Biomedical progress has the immediate consequence of permitting people to live longer, but also such longer-term consequences as a growing shortage of jobs, promotion problems for the young, and aggravation of the population problem.

Students perceive that a youth-oriented culture can become a death-denying society. The long-term consequences of this attitude include the possibility that the elderly will often die alone and unwanted, and that the market for products which hide age and emphasize youth will grow dramatically.

After the students have viewed filmstrips and read supplemental material on aging, they are asked to develop a list of current trends which might affect individuals over 65 in the future, and to write scenarios based on these trends. One example might be the trend of individuals to organize collectively to effect change.

Franks also asks her students to "Think the unthinkable," that is, to describe developments that have not yet occurred. For example, they might discuss the concept of "memory improvement" as a constructive exercise for elderly individuals, a technique presently being employed experimentally with geriatric patients in Canada. The class could also discuss "complete man/machine symbiosis" in which there would be no death as we know it today.

Another feature of Franks' unit on the future of the elderly is role-playing. Using the ideas presented in class, students play the role of the elderly in pre-industrial, industrial and post-industrial societies.

The role of the elderly in various cultures is also considered. For example, students examine the different attitudes toward the elderly evidenced by the Chinese, by Mexican farmers, by members of an Israeli kibbutz, and by Eskimos.

At the conclusion of the unit, students are asked again to write a paragraph describing themselves at age 90. They then reread their original papers and discuss whether their perspectives have changed as a result of their work in futuristics.

Students also are asked to take at least one positive step toward a future which they deem "good" for individuals over 65 years of age. Each student compiles a "commitment sheet" which might contain such positive steps as:

1. I plan to read to my grandmother once a week.
2. I plan to work at a retirement center once a month.
3. I plan to work actively to get laws passed which protect individuals over 65 from age discrimination.

Franks has found that this request for immediate, positive action negates the attitude of students who initially reject futurism, saying: "Let tomorrow happen as it will . . . today is all we really have."

At a futuristics curriculum development workshop coordinated by Franks, the question was once asked: "What if our students entered the school armed with paint brushes and painted their lockers?" The response of one five-year old philosopher was: "Great! No more drab green. The only reason that it has never been done before is that it has never been done before!"

Franks urges students to take action now to improve their present environments and to create what they consider to be desirable futures. In this way, students will be encouraged not to wait passively for a never-arriving future, nor to cling only to today, dismissing the future as irrelevant.

"Without an educational approach emphasizing futuristics, students will be ill-prepared to become the responsible decision-makers they need to be now and in the future," she says. "This will not only affect their personal lives but their ability to participate sensitively and intelligently in decisions which will shape local, national, and international events."

Due to modern communications, Franks says, today's students are in touch with the entire globe. Learning rapidly through all their senses, these students do not fit easily into an outdated linear, compartmentalized, and segmented curriculum which has a tendency to dehumanize them. The futuristics curriculum, Frank believes, "encourages both linear and non-linear approaches to learning. It is also human-centered, involving all the senses and giving students an awareness of their entire being in order to counteract the depersonalizing tendency of the computer card society."

Franks also emphasizes the need for flexibility in any futuristics curriculum. Students "must learn even from the curriculum that they cannot have everything," she says, "that they must select with thought and care those things which best fit with their individual goals and values. Only when we have a curriculum which helps the students be truly multi-disciplinary, willing to act on their values, comfortable with change, and capable of thinking in terms of alternatives will we have individuals who can make responsible decisions for both themselves and society."

BETTY BARCLAY FRANKS IS THE CHAIRPERSON, SOCIAL STUDIES DEPARTMENT, MAPLE HEIGHTS HIGH SCHOOL, MAPLE HEIGHTS, OHIO 44137. SHE HAS SERVED WITH MARY KAY HOWARD AS CO-DIRECTOR OF THE FUTURISTICS CURRICULUM DEVELOPMENT PROJECT FOR THE GREATER CLEVELAND AREA. FUTURE DECISIONS: THE I.Q. GAME IS PUBLISHED BY SAGA PUBLICATIONS, RR #2, GREENTREE ROAD, LEBANON, OHIO 45036.

**Betty Barclay Franks (left) and Mary Kay Howard have worked together to develop futures studies units for the Greater Cleveland area schools.**

# Futuristics Cures 'Doomsday Syndrome'

**Minnesota high school students reacted enthusiastically when futures studies were introduced to their classroom. As one student put it, "Futuristics has enabled me to tie together much of my high school education, as well as provide me with a positive direction toward the future."**

"Before I participated in futuristics," said Steve Mathews, a Minnesota high school student, "I suffered from a type of doomsday syndrome. I saw myself as being insignificant in the making of the future, like it was some kind of immovable tidal wave, so I never really gave it much thought."

Now, after completing a full year of futures study, Steve has changed his mind. "Futuristics means a lot to me," he wrote, "because it has opened my eyes to many roads that we can take, instead of the narrow path I thought was inevitable."

Other students expressed similar enthusiasm about their course in "Futuristics: Theory and Application," a cooperative project of the Richfield and Burnsville Senior High Schools in Minnesota.

At the outset, students became acquainted with the ideas of well-known futurists such as Buckminster Fuller, Alvin Toffler, and Herman Kahn. This introduction to theoretical futurism was followed by laboratory sessions in basic forecasting techniques.

In this phase, students polled futurists to obtain a consensus of opinion about future trends (the Delphi technique); they wrote short stories based upon their own future forecasts (the scenario technique); and they projected possible future states of being from existing phenomena (the extrapolation technique). These methods were geared to avoid a heavy emphasis on difficult mathematical forecasting methods.

In the project development phase, each student chose a specific area to research, such as genetics, international relations, or oceanography. By thoroughly investigating the past and present developments in his or her field of interest, each student was better-equipped to probe the future of that subject.

The futuristics course culminated in an internship program. Working for up to 50 hours with individuals professionally engaged in each student's chosen field of interest, class members gained much valuable first-hand experience.

The students involved in the program noted that futuristics provided them with a challenge, with an interdisciplinary perspective, with an ability to synthesize data, formulate goals, and institute action.

Karen Cooper said: "Futuristics has given me the opportunity to be challenged by education—which is rare these days. It has helped me to realize what I should be considering as possible futures for society and the world."

Karen also felt that "futuristics serves to bind together varied experiences—educational and otherwise—into an effective plan and goal. It forces one to think beyond basic societal myopia, and to see that it is possible to control change rather than stop it out of fear."

Commenting about the problems encountered during the program, Karen stated that the class "needed more materials and easier access to those not at school... It also would have been helpful to have an easy means of telling other people in the school and the community exactly what we were doing."

Another student, David Lutes, said the course helped students gain greater personal self-sufficiency and heightened awareness. Describing the long-term gains of futuristics, David emphasized an awareness of the future and the communication of that knowledge to others. "I find myself constantly talking about my topic, about futuristics and the need to plan for the future, to my friends and classmates," David said.

Students repeatedly stressed the benefits of the interdisciplinary approach of futuristics. Linda Escher noted:

"Throughout my years in high school as well as in junior high, I have never had such an opportunity to become active in independent study projects that covered more than one aspect of a subject. There are many such opportunities in separate science, art, and social studies classes, but never have they overlapped. This potential has been sadly overlooked in most school systems, and I am happy to see that I was able to wrangle my way into Futuristics last September."

Bill Peterson expressed feelings very similar to Linda's. "Education on the high school level often tends to be inherently fragmentary," Bill maintained. "One learns a little math, something about the Congress of Vienna, a little bit of William Blake perhaps, but never actually sees how the different disciplines interact with one another. Futuristics draws upon many disciplines and thus allows for a great deal of interaction among them."

Penny Damlo, Project Instructor at Burnsville Senior High, joined her students in an appreciation of the broad base of futuristics. "In many ways futuristics is a discipline to study all other disciplines. It's interdisciplinary but at the same time it has developed into a discipline of its own," she pointed out.

On the personal level, Bill Peterson and other students felt that futurism aids in the construction of goals.

"The development of a project in the area of international relations," Bill said, "has served as an excellent introduction to my area of interest. As a result, I've also been better able to determine the type of curriculum most beneficial to my future education."

To the students involved in the project, futuristics seemed to provide a needed means

*Penny Damlo, Project Director of the futuristics project at Burnsville Senior High, feels that her involvement in futuristics education has been the most challenging aspect of her teaching career.*

of synthesis. "More than any other class that I've ever been involved with," said Bill, "futuristics has enabled me to tie together much of my high school education, as well as to provide me with a positive direction toward the future."

In addition to the favorable response of participating students, futurists who learned of the program registered their immense approval.

Earl C. Joseph, a staff scientist at Univac and leading futurist educator at the University of Minnesota, wrote to John Welckle, Director of the project, to express his views:

"When I ask 'Why are students in school?' the only answer that seems relevant is: students are in school to prepare themselves for the future. Until recently there were no courses of study relative to that future students were supposedly preparing themselves for offered in any school worldwide. Education is just beginning to realize this... To date, your course is the most outstanding example that I have seen for providing a learning experience for students to become literate about the future. Your excellent approach to designing the curriculum and the course content has given your students a unique environment to become aware of the opportunistic alternatives the future has to offer, and perhaps most importantly, to become aware of the tools available for forecasting, shaping, and designing desirable futures. Your students have gained knowledge about the basic methods that they can apply in later life, in whatever future societal role they select, and as such, will be able to participate in bringing about better futures."

Encouragement also came from T. Lance Holthusen, Director, Future Studies Department, The Science Museum of Minnesota. "Many of your students and staff have participated in study efforts through the Museum," wrote Holthusen, "and have impressed us with their depth of understanding. They are not only able to understand and interact regarding alternatives and the future, but demonstrate having good direction as to how their community can deal with future alternatives. I think this is due to your internship aspect which puts your students right in the middle of real life faced with its future... You are providing this region with a very significant demonstration of how future studies can be incorporated into the curriculum, and your efforts as a prototype will greatly assist us in working with other schools in the State."

According to Penny Damlo, the internship phase of the program was one of its more rewarding aspects, since it gave students an opportunity to interact with community members. Students worked intimately with someone whose job it is to deal with matters that require decisions today to shape future events. As a result of the program, many students have already been asked to speak to several community groups on the topic of futurism. Hence, from a central core, the theory and application of futures studies is spreading outward.

On the personal level, Damlo believes that the course has given the students a new perspective on their lives and on society, and has helped them to cope with "future shock." She considers the class to be the most challenging one that she has ever taught.

What does next year hold for these Minnesota high school students? In addition to rescheduling the present one-year futuristics format, a similar course will be offered on a quarterly basis to all interested students. Steve Mathews and the other members of this year's first experimental futuristics class will play an important role in evaluating the program and in assisting in the development of the new quarterly course. Moreover, Steve and the other sophomores and juniors who studied futuristics this year may reapply to continue their futuristics education in September.

PENNY DAMLO IS PROJECT INSTRUCTOR OF "FUTURISTICS: THEORY AND APPLICATION" AT THE BURNSVILLE SENIOR HIGH SCHOOL, 600 EAST HIGHWAY 13, BURNSVILLE, MINNESOTA 55337.

# Futuribles Marathon

**A game about the future intrigues non-futurists and also stimulates futurists to think more seriously about the years ahead. The Director of the Project on Futuristics at Maryville College, Tennessee, discusses a 24-hour gaming marathon in which 70 campus members tried to "touch the future."**

by David P. Young

**David P. Young, Director of the Project on Futuristics at Maryville College, believes that people who play *Futuribles* return to the present with "an increased awareness of its meaning."**

The future is by definition untouchable—it is that which has not yet happened. Nevertheless, George Koehler's card game *Futuribles* inspired 70 college students to see what futures could be touched during 24 consecutive hours of marathon play.

The 24-hour-future began at 4 o'clock on a cloudy afternoon at Maryville College in Tennessee. Seated on the ground under a blue-and-yellow striped canopy, eight members of my Seminar on Alternative Futures began to play the game, surrounded by clean graffiti boards and curious onlookers. During the next 24 hours the scene remained much the same, except that the graffiti boards, ashtrays and litter baskets all began to fill up.

As players became fatigued or went off to classes, fresh recruits took their places (making it, as one wag noted, a "floating futures game"). When the marathon ended the next

**Graffiti boards at Tennessee's Maryville College allow students to write down their feelings about the future.**

*Futuribles* **is a game with 288 cards, each describing a future possibility which the players may discuss both in terms of its probability and its desirability. The game can be used in a wide variety of ways by students, planners, and other groups interested in the future.**

day, a total of 70 different players, including 48 not in the seminar, had taken a turn at "futuribling" in stretches of 15 minutes to nearly 20 hours.

*Futuribles* is played in rounds during which the players share their thoughts about the cards they hold. Each of the 288 cards in the *Futuribles* deck expresses a possible state of affairs in the future. The future possibilities include an increasing number of automobiles and highways, an increasing breakdown in the distinction between work and leisure, or less privacy—more intrusions and surveillances. The possible states of affairs are arranged in 19 categories—communication, energy, family/sex, food, work/income/leisure—to name a few.

As players respond to the cards and interact with each other, they begin to develop an awareness of what can happen in the future and what events are most important. Each player will hopefully begin to think of ways to influence the future to be what he or she would like it to be.

The purpose of *Futuribles*, as indicated by Koehler's guide book, is to "help persons get acquainted with future possibilities, share their feelings about the future, create visions of the future, etc." Our marathon experience verified that it is quite possible to realize these goals. For example, we learned the future-orientations of a wide range of people, many of whom we had not communicated with before. The following graffiti entries are examples of summarizing thoughts which arose from the interchange of ideas:

"How can you decide the future if you can't draw lines?"
"Who decides who decides?"
"The future is that which has already happened." (Think on that a bit.)
"Your future is like airing dirty laundry—everybody gets to see it."
"It's never too late for despair." To which someone later added: "**It's always too early!**"

We all found it challenging to seek priorities and to have to defend choices, especially in situations where we didn't like the future projections that we held in our hands. Often we had to struggle with a choice between two possible undesirable futures. At such points, we began to discuss seriously what we really valued.

As one would expect, many different impressions of the future were generated. For some, thinking about the future had been translated into very personal terms as a result of the marathon:

"Something that really bugs me is that when I speak to people of, say the futures game, they always give me the impression that they think the future is something 400 years from now.... What I think is important is that people understand that what we do and are this very minute determines what will happen."

"I guess the biggest insight I've gained is that the future is real and my chances of changing the events of its happening are pretty slim.... It has been impressed upon me that perhaps man cannot choose wisely because he has too many choices to choose from."

Although it is impossible to sum up the meaning which a 24-hour future marathon held for 70 persons, there seemed to be an overarching sense of agreement that there is a difference between raising questions concerning one's level of knowledge and raising one's level of consciousness. For us, the marathon was the latter type of experience: By raising our consciousnesses about the future, we made the *now* more important. We played "future" for 24 hours and returned to the present with an increased awareness of its

Students give their views in response to future possibilities presented in the card game, *Futuribles*. Most participants agreed that the opportunity for serious, personal interchanges was the highlight of the 24-hour futures marathon.

meaning.

As one person expressed it a few weeks later: "By beginning to think about the future, I've somehow become tied into the entire Past—Present—Future continuum. Because the past is plain fact and the future is unlimited potential, it has become important to completely experience the present."

After the marathon, we began to realize that its most significant impact was the opportunity for interchanges between people. Even on a small campus, many individuals never talk to one another. But, playing *Futuribles* was more than talk-talk; it was a meeting of ideas and values on a topic of great importance: my future, your future, our future.

DAVID P. YOUNG IS THE DIRECTOR OF THE PROJECT ON FUTURISTICS, MARYVILLE COLLEGE, MARYVILLE, TENNESSEE 37801. THE SEMINAR ON ALTERNATIVE FUTURES IS PART OF YOUNG'S PHILOSOPHY 321 CLASS. *Futuribles* BY GEORGE E. KOEHLER, PUBLISHED BY THE UNITED METHODIST CHURCH, 1973, IS AVAILABLE FROM THE WORLD FUTURE SOCIETY BOOK SERVICE FOR $9.45 (MEMBERS PAYING IN CASH CAN DEDUCT A 10% DISCOUNT).

# Easy Ways To Help Children Think About the Future

**Two futurists incorporated educational futurism into a fifth grade classroom. In the following article they describe three techniques that they developed.**

by Jerry Glenn and Cyndy Guy

Children, unlike adults, have little difficulty thinking about the future. In our work with ten-year old students in New Hampshire, we brought futuristics into the classroom using techniques that require only pencil and paper. Three methods which we found to be extremely easy yet fascinating are futures wheels, modified cross-impact analyses and futuristic scenarios.

## Futures Wheel

A futures wheel begins with a circle drawn in the center of any piece of paper. Within the circle, each student writes down a subject that interests him, or the class as a whole. The subject can be an event, trend or idea—anything that the students want to know more about.

Next, each student extends a number of spokes from the central circle on his piece of paper. He makes each spoke end in a possible result or association of the initial idea. The process is then continued to examine third and fourth order consequences of the germinal thought.

The comments of students who construct futures wheels often indicate their intellectual processes at work. For example, one little girl threw down her pencil in anger and confusion during the exercise and exclaimed, "I started off with more people and I ended up with fewer people. That doesn't make sense!" We asked her to see if she could find her mistake.

Later the child said, "Well, if we continue having more people and living the same way, we will die. I guess we'll have to change if we want more people." The point is that the student taught herself a great deal about the population issue through the use of this futuristic method.

Of course, futures wheels can get out of hand if you keep running out new lines. There are visual and spatial limits! Some of the fifth graders with whom we used this technique ended up with the most complex intellectual spaghetti we have ever seen.

But kept under some control, this is an excellent technique for multi-concept formation, and an aid for brainstorming. Such a visual package of information is also a guide for associative reasoning, anticipatory awareness and adaptation. Moreover, it has been successfully tested on the elementary, secondary and college levels.

| How Will This Affect This | I want to travel | I want to swim better | I want to go to college |
|---|---|---|---|
| *I want to travel* | XXX | I might not be near a swimming pool | If I travel, I might not have time to go to college |
| *I want to swim better* | I might not be able to travel because of work outs & swim meets | XXX | I might have to go to swim meets during college |
| *I want to go to college* | If I go to college, I might not have time to travel | I might have too much work to have time to swim | XXX |

One fifth-grader's modified cross-impact analysis is shown above.

# Two of the Techniques Used With Young Futurists

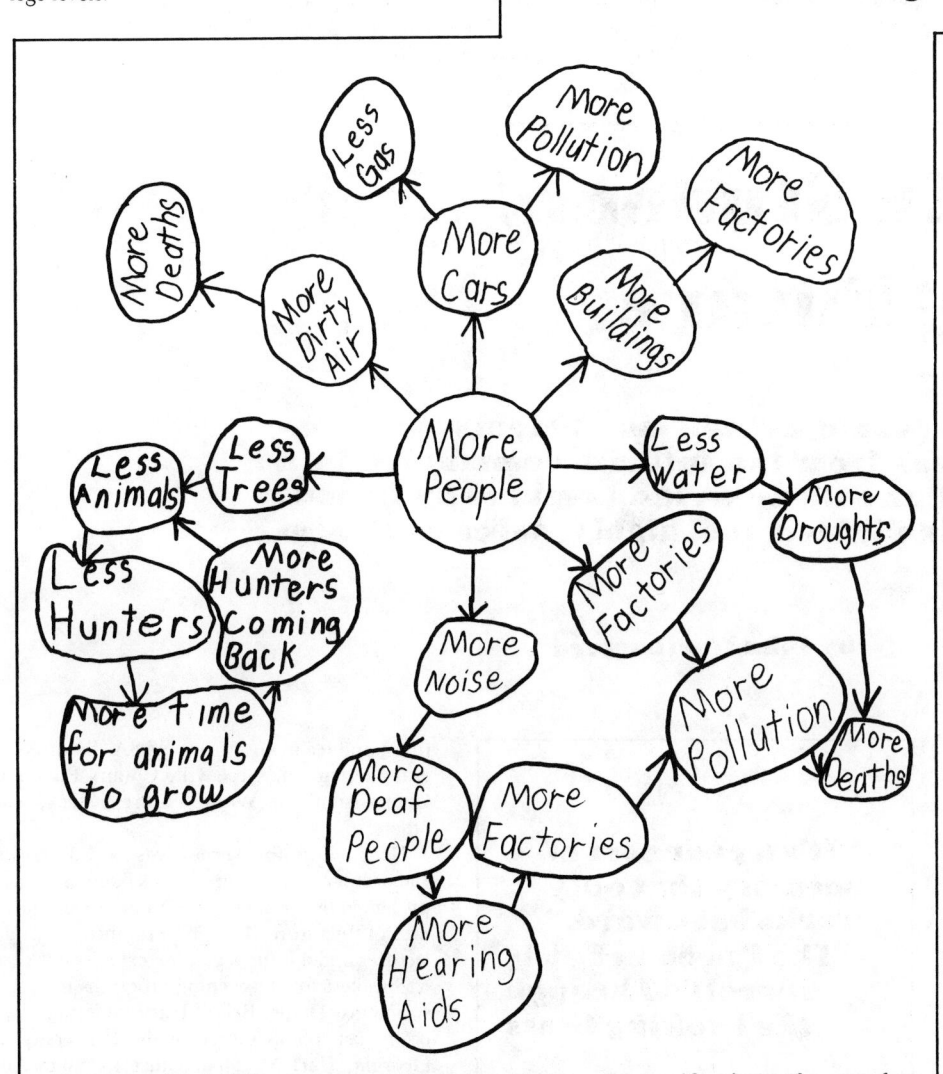

**Modified Cross-Impact Analysis**

In this exercise, each student selects three activities in which he or she would like to engage. These are listed along the side and across the top of a sheet of paper so that two axes are formed. The student then tries to determine how each activity may affect the other two.

One student we worked with had the recreational goals of swimming and travel, which she realized could be conflicting or extremely compatible with her educational aims (see accompanying cross-impact analysis). By using the cross-impact technique, she learned several valuable things. One is the importance of time. The student seems to conclude that travel and college will vie for top priority. For an adult, there seems plenty of time for both, but a fifth grader may have a different perspective.

Recognizing that time is important, the student will probably begin to *plan* future activities which she most wants, working as many as possible into each other: She may realize, for example, that swim meets can be integrated with college activities, as long as the academic work load is not too great.

Students can also use cross-impact analyses to forecast trends. Some forecasts developed by our students were strikingly similar to the pessimistic projections of Dennis Meadows and his colleagues at the Massachusetts Institute of Technology, while still others were more optimistic and suggestive of the views of Buckminster Fuller and Herman Kahn.

**Futuristic Scenarios**

Students can also try to envision the world of the future, and then express that vision in an oral presentation, a written essay, a dramatic piece, or the actual construction of a small-scale city of the future. Some teachers have even had students construct their inter-

"Futures wheels" give students a chance to explore the ramifications of a complex problem, such as population growth. The wheel shown here is in an early stage of development. School children generally make wheels that are far more complex.

pretation of what the human form may eventually look like if it adapts structurally to continued noise and air pollution, dietary changes, etc.

Futuristic scenarios can be extrapolations of existing trends which the class discerns by clipping magazines, newspapers or other contemporary items of interest. Or, the scenarios may be purely the product of the students' imaginations. Scenarios could also involve the construction of the child's utopia—or dystopia, if he finds that more intriguing.

Children often will question the scenarios of their peers, indicating what they would like to see changed in the scenario to produce a different set of conclusions.

Our fifth graders made lists of policies and gave each policy a priority. Popular policies were recycling, bicycling, talking to people about future problems, and introducing technological solutions to solve problems.

One ambitious boy said, "I'm going to talk and help people to understand the idea of the transportation room. It should be usable by 1999. It is a little chamber you get into and turn into little atoms (energy patterns?) and put where you want to go and then you are reassembled in human form..."

*Jerry Glenn*

*Cyndy Guy*

From a discussion of these three methods, it should be apparent that an introduction to futurism can indeed be easy and enjoyable for any class, anywhere. We both believe that children are the prime ingredients of the future. If futurists won't take the initiative to futurize understanding through education, who will?

CYNDY GUY WILL BE A GRADUATE STUDENT THIS YEAR IN THE PROGRAM FOR THE FUTURE OF EDUCATION AT THE UNIVERSITY OF MASSACHUSETTS, AMHERST, WHERE GLENN WAS A DOCTORAL CANDIDATE WHEN THE CO-AUTHORS DEVELOPED THE TECHNIQUES DESCRIBED HERE. GLENN'S ADDRESS IS NOW NEW WORLDS TRAINING CENTER, 2325 PORTER STREET, N.W., WASHINGTON, D.C. 20008.

# Citizens Join Students in Thinking Future

**Local townspeople as well as students were exposed to ideas from the futurist community in a South Carolina college series. Lectures by famous futurists highlighted the highly successful program.**

by John Weatherford

Like the Queen in *Through the Looking Glass*, several hundred college students and Greenville, South Carolina, citizens see the need for a forward-looking memory after participating in a futuristics series at Furman University this winter.

J. Dan Cover, Furman sociology professor and coordinator of "Man in the Year 2000," said he developed the program to give students and the Greenville community an opportunity to anticipate the future intelligently.

Well-known speakers highlighted the public series, which was funded by the South Carolina Committee for the Humanities. There was also a Museum of the Future, featuring a three-day series of displays; speakers,

> "It's a poor sort of memory that only works backward."
> The Queen in Lewis Carroll's *Through the Looking Glass*

films, and technology from NASA, IBM, General Electric, the Greenville County Planning Commission, the World Future Society, and others.

Concluding the series was a Futuristics Laboratory, consisting of a six-hour program presented by Earthrise, Inc. to increase awareness of the future. The program included slide lectures and a futures gaming exercise.

Speakers for the evening programs included sociologist Daniel Bell of Harvard University; economist James Green of the University of Georgia; Carl Madden, Chief Economist of the Chamber of Commerce of the United States; IBM Engineering Education Manager Edward Matthews; Victor Ferkiss, Professor

Sociologist Dan Cover, who coordinated the "Man in the Year 2000" series at Furman University, prepares a futuristic headline display for the campus library. Headlines include: MECHANICAL PLACENTA PERFECTED and POLLUTION CAUSES DEATH OF HALF MARINE LIFE in WORLD OCEANS.

"Atlanta 2000"—a vision of the future of the Georgia capital—is discussed by Andre Steiner (left), president of the World Future Society's Georgia chapter.

of Government, Georgetown University; Huston Smith, Professor of Religion at Syracuse University; Joseph Coates of the National Science Foundation; former U.S. Secretary of State Dean Rusk; and a panel from the Georgia Chapter of the World Future Society.

Sociologist Bell explained how man can reason about the future, and distinguished between crystal ball prediction and scientific forecasting. He said two fundamental value changes are occurring as the United States becomes a service-oriented society: "The quality of life has become a very real problem for most people. The chief illustration here is the environmental situation. There is also the revolution of rising entitlements. People have come to expect they are entitled to more and more."

Huston Smith pointed to the narrow scope of the three major world civilizations. "Western civilization has focused on man's relationship with nature," Smith said. "The East Asian civilization emphasized man's relationship with other men—society. And, the South Asian civilization concentrates on man's relationship with himself—the psychological aspect. The result is that these civilizations have become too specialized. Each has neglected the other two aspects. All three problems must be struck as a common chord."

Speaking on "The Future of International Politics," Dean Rusk offered an optimistic outlook despite many problems facing the United States and the world today. Rusk said, "All I suggest is that you take a piece of the action and make it yours. It doesn't make any difference which one of these problems you concern yourself about, but don't underestimate what one person can do, because there will be a lot of other one persons working in the same direction."

Reaction to the program from Carolina citizens was "quite gratifying," Cover said. More than 900 area residents attended the various lectures and demonstrations during January and February.

Regional and local officials taking part in the program included Fourth District Congressman James R. Mann; Greenville Mayor Max Heller; City Manager John Dullea; Executive Director Bert Winterbottom of the Greenville County Planning Commission; Vukan Kuic, director of the University of South Carolina Future Studies Project; and Maxwell Goldberg, director of the Continuing Liberal Studies Program at Converse College, Spartanburg, S.C.

Cover also experienced positive reaction from students in his "Sociology of the Future" class. He said students in the class went on their own into the Greenville area schools to lecture on futuristics. Furman students also began doing further research in areas of specific interest, went across the country to take more courses on the future at other universities, and have become members of the World Future Society.

"The students have reacted well to future developments they were exposed to, but they don't seem to see the change affecting their own lives," Cover said. "They see change as an external thing. Coping with the future is very complex. It requires a lot of skills I think we must develop."

Cover became interested in the future after reading Alvin Toffler's *Future Shock*.

Cover's own research on future shock—the disorientation caused by rapid changes in the environment—indicates that young people from 21 to 28 constitute the age group that experiences the most change. Change in this age category, he found, is most often associated with symptoms of distrust, powerlessness, and a sense of personal meaninglessness. Cover believes the study of the future is a necessary component of college education and can help to reduce future shock.

JOHN WEATHERFORD IS A MEMBER OF THE COMMUNICATION OFFICE, FURMAN UNIVERSITY, GREENVILLE, SOUTH CAROLINA 29613.

# SELECTIONS FROM THE
# WORLD FUTURE SOCIETY BULLETIN

The *World Future Society Bulletin* is written for people who have a special interest in the "how-to" of future studies. Published six times a year, the *Bulletin* features technical and scholarly articles on futures-related topics, reviews of recent futurist books, and news of interest from the world-wide futurist movement and from the more than 100 local WFS chapters in the U.S. and abroad.

# Educational Technology: The Next Ten Years

### by Christopher J. Dede

Technology has boosted productivity relative to cost in many capital-intensive industries. But in labor-intensive activities such as education, innovations of method have proven far less "cost-effective." Adapting modern communications technologies to the needs of education is feasible but will require major efforts by educators both to enlist the aid of government and business interests and to ensure that these technologies are introduced in areas where they will be most effective and not simply offered as a substitute for human instructors in every learning situation.

Where are we in the history of educational technology? When scholars in the year 2009 write about education in the year 1979, which opportunities will they see us seizing... which missing? What are the key decisions that now could be made about the costs and benefits of technology-based instruction?

The context within which these decisions will be made is determined by our current economic and political situation; any discussion of educational technology must begin with these constraints. Realistically, in ten years, we in formal education will have one-half of the fiscal resources that we have today: one-half of the salaries, the facilities, the books, the equipment, the maintenance, the transportation, and the administrative resources. One-half real dollar loss in ten years assumes an average erosion of 7% per year; that is, losses from inflation, salary hikes, and recession will overbalance any gains from tax monies and other sources by about 7% per year over the next ten years.

For example, right now inflationary losses for many educational agents are running at well over 14% per year, but revenues are growing at only around 7% per year: a net 7% loss. Further, this 7% loss is *not* happening at a time in which the economy is in recession or stagflation, but in fact is taking place during a period in which we are struggling along in as much of a growth cycle as has recently occurred.

### The Economic Crunch

Why should we assume that these "short term" economic problems we've begun to feel in education are in fact long term and not easily reversible? One reason for anticipating long term fiscal problems has to do with the severe national economic fluctuations now in evidence. Economic forecasts indicate that, for the next ten years, periods of stagflation (no gain in GNP; moderate inflation) will alternate with recessions (perhaps even worldwide depression, depending on how well we handle the present resources crisis) and with low growth/massive inflation (such as in the late '70s). Whichever portion of this cycle is taking place, we can be sure as educators that we will not have first claim on social priorities in terms of funding—nor second claim, nor third, nor probably even tenth.

Furthermore, on top of this general economic drain, we will face spiraling resource costs—not just in energy (although energy is the clearest example), but in items such as water and paper and transportation/delivery of goods. Politics being what it is, in response to these increased costs we will see wildly changing and inconsistent policies from government; so far, the Federal response to the energy situation has been less than ideal, and in general that will continue to be true for all resource crises. No political consensus is emerging on the nature of either the problem or potential solutions, and for the next ten years we won't be able to depend on any rationality or reliability from political decision makers. So, economic and political instability indicate that our present funding problems may continue for quite a while.

---

**"Teachers today are supposed to train, screen, socialize, entertain, and babysit their students, prepare them for citizenship and family life, and create happy, healthy human beings—all on seven percent less each year!"**

---

A second reason for alarm is that we seem to have reached the maximum percentage of their income that people are willing to spend for education. Over time, the "piece of the pie" that we've been able to claim from people's income has crept up and up and up—but now, clients are saying "no more." Taxpayers are clearly indicating "whether the educational system works or not, this fraction of my money is the maximum that I'm willing to spend; education will just have to survive on it."

The reason that our share of the fiscal "pie" has continuously increased has not been because we've been particularly wasteful with money, but because education is labor-intensive rather than capital-intensive (that is, we use people to produce our products instead of using machines). Auto assembly plants and steel mills are examples of capital-intensive industries; medicine and government are other labor-intensive industries. Over time, capital-intensive industries cost consumers progressively less, relative to labor-intensive industries, because salaries rise faster than capital costs. The huge initial expenditure for a big machine, the interest paid on the debt from buying that machine on credit, and even the repair and maintenance costs are all, over time, less expensive than people's salaries (in part, because machines continuously improve in efficiency).

Certainly, this generalization is true in educational technology; at the moment the cost of computer-assisted instruction is decreasing 5% per year with about a 10% per year increase in productivity. As this trend is likely to continue and improve, a conservative estimate would be that in a decade these machines will be three times as productive at one half the cost.

I know of no one who has developed a system for improving human teachers such that, in ten years, they can be three times as effective at half the cost. *For what machines can do well,* people are not competitive economically. So our labor-intensive position in education has caused us steadily to use up more and more of the consumer dollar, just as have all the other labor-intensive industries; and we have finally reached the limit. We need the resources, we're losing teachers now due to our relatively poor salaries compared to the rest of the economy, but the money is *not* going to be there . . . just as funding is being cut back for medical care. To get past this fiscal problem of being labor-intensive, we must find a way legitimately to use more technology in education.

At the same time that we face economic woes because of the factors above—and because of dwindling enrollments due to demographic changes—we are also confronted by rising demands for "higher quality" education. We're supposed to train for jobs, screen for jobs, train for further schooling, screen for further schooling, socialize, entertain and babysit, keep students off the job market, prepare for citizenship, prepare for family life, *and* (in the remaining time available) create happy, healthy human beings—all on 7% less each year!

### Responding to the Crisis

The bottom line created by this situation is that there can be no more "business as usual" in education. We *must* find a less expensive way of teaching. Jim Bowman, a professional colleague, tells a story about a frog. He claims that he can put a frog on top of his stove in a pot of water with no lid; turn on the burner, and (as long as the heat is set very low, so that the temperature of the water in that pot only goes up 1° an hour) he can cook the frog *without a lid on the pan,* because the temperature goes up so slowly that the frog never quite knows when to scream and leap out of the pot! The frog always says to himself, "well, it's getting warm in here, but things don't seem that different from what they used to be." I sometimes feel the same way about educators; we don't know when to scream and say, "we've had enough; something must change!"

How can educators respond to this long-term economic crisis? We can do what we're doing now, which is to cut everything a little bit and be unable to do anything well. After a few years of this strategy, we'll be doing a terrible job in all areas, thereby further destroying public confidence in education and having made no progress in dealing with the fundamental issue.

A second alternative is somehow to delete a major chunk of our responsibilities—to say to society, "we're not going to meet this particular objective anymore; we don't have the money." We may have to renounce some of our current obligations in education even with less expensive ways of teaching, but this will not be a popular position for us to take. Such a shift would cause enormously destructive conflicts within education, as we collectively try to decide what to give up, and would also create huge pressures from society because no one easily accepts a cutback in services. So, this second alternative doesn't work very well either. Of course, we could ignore the situation and pretend it will go away; this strategy would likely lead to a catastrophic collapse similar to that of the Penn Central Railroad!

In brief, somehow we must find a radically new approach to education which is fiscally less expensive—and implement this shift at a time during which we're losing money every year. This is not an attractive picture, but it is the real world situation. Changing education will not be easy, but it will be easier than changing the U.S. economy *and* resource problems *and* people's priorities on their personal spending. So, if we're not going to be "cooked frog," we'd better be scared *into* our wits. Given this economic and political context, what might be the technological portion of a radically different, less expensive approach?

Technology is a necessary component of any such shift, because the capital-intensive approach is historically the best proven way to reduce costs. I don't know of *any* ways to prepare human teachers successfully to instruct 50 to 60 students with the same relatively low salary, half the educational materials, a collapsing physical plant and half the number of administrators and support personnel—but that's our future situation if we try to educate using only human resources.

What could educational technology do in a decade to save money? Unless we collectively work to influence manufacturers, nothing—no one will magically appear to solve this problem for us. However, if we do take steps now to create a market for quality instructional technology, this could reduce some educational costs dramatically. The examples I will use to illustrate this claim are completely realistic because the five techniques I will describe have already been developed and are in use today. "Magical" instructional technologies (such as memory drugs) are not necessary to implement successful technology-based education.

### Learning Through Home TV

One instructional technology we could implement large-scale would be a non-computer linked television programming system: a massive "*Sesame Street*-plus" approach. Entertainment and a carefully sequenced motivational/developmental psychology-based curriculum would be packaged together. Programs would be designed for each age level—including adults—and delivered on multiple cable television channels (which will soon be part of almost all households).

One result of such an approach would be universal, home-based, non-interactive standardized learning experiences. "Citizen's literacy" instruction for all ages would be one likely form of programming (for example, a two-hour comedy movie on constructive coping with gasoline shortages). Such programs would be produced on a sophisticated entertainment level with top quality acting talent and would utilize the motivational market-study approach currently so successful in beer commercials. This televised instruction could be supplemented by small group, low-cost, para-professional-led discussions which would allow viewers an opportunity to react to, internalize, and individualize what they'd seen.

This type of programming would save a great deal of repetitive, teacher-directed socialization...for children and for adults. The massive amount of time educational institutions currently devote to "real world coping skills" could be largely eliminated.

---

**"In a decade, computer-assisted instruction will be three times as productive at one half the cost. I know of no one who has developed a system for making human teachers three times as effective at half the cost in ten years."**

---

Savings would also include travel and facilities costs; further, society would benefit indirectly from previously undereducated adults becoming more capable of coping with laws, bureaucracies, banks, and voting.

Costs of such instruction would be primarily para-professional training and production expenses; the latter will be very high and unlikely to drop even if large numbers of such programs are produced. As a result, this type of technological instruction will never be cost-effective for very specialized learning experiences; the client audience must always be reasonably large.

### Instructional Calculators

A second instructional technology utilizes portable computer/calculators/micro-processors to do semi-sophisticated computer-assisted instruction. The instructional modes which could be programmed on the inexpensive, powerful calculators now available include tutorial approaches (computer presents simple material, asks questions to determine proper assimilation, and corrects misunderstandings), inquiry approach (student asks for a specific fact; computer responds with appropriate data), dialogue (student asks a general question; computer responds with complex answer), and explanation/interpretation (computer presents complex learning material and responds to general questions). Tutorial might be used, for example, to teach textbook portions of American History; inquiry, to obtain data for an assigned paper on national demographics; dialogue, to explain this year's income tax changes; and explanation/interpretation, to outline implications of Federal Law 94-142 for the traditional classroom.

Should this type of instruction be implemented, many different computer programs and data sets could be produced, distributed, and plugged into calculators as needed. Large-scale costs would be quite low, both for equipment and programming. Implications for teaching would be that standard "lecture-and-work-sheet" education could be decentralized and made uniform (at enormous savings of personnel time), and many library and textbook functions could be programmed into calculators instead (yielding further cost reductions).

Fiscal costs will be small, but a major human cost will be that information transfer will become very depersonalized. Even a well-programmed calculator cannot behave as could a human being. Standardization and uniformity also carry risks; one mistake in a program means that everyone nationally learns the same error, one bias in content results in all students' attitudes being malformed in the same direction. Quality control must be very rigorous if such an instructional system is to be used.

## Home Terminals for Large Computers

A third learning device which could be implemented is based on using a large central computer to deliver to home cable television sets multiple-person, interactive, artificial-intelligence-based learning simulations. Many of these simulations will resemble games, but will be much more sophisticated than the relatively simple computer games now sold in stores. For example, learners will not be limited to a small range of responses; *any* response given to the computer will trigger an appropriate message in return. This feature allows much greater emphasis to be placed on creativity and on higher order cognitive skills. Also, the opportunity to interact with other human "players," with the computer mediating, makes this approach much less depersonalized than traditional computer-assisted instruction. Input to the computer (which can handle many households simultaneously) would be typed on a home keyboard; in ten years, spoken input may be possible as well. Natural language (rather than computer language) is used.

An example of such a learning simulation might be a *Star Trek* game for grade level three: seven learners; approximate total time, 35 hours (spread out over several weeks). Each learner would act as a particular crew member, with given roles to perform and several obstacles to master in the game (cooperative strategies stressed). Emphasis might be placed on development of math skills (navigation), group problem-solving (interpersonal strains among the crew), computer programming skills, and "communication-at-a-distance" skills (interaction with others through a keyboard rather than face-to-face). Research on non-educational versions of these "games" (such as "Dungeons and Dragons" simulation at MIT) has shown that these are intensely motivating and involving, without depending on novelty factors to hold participant interest.

What are the implications of such instruction? Some (but not all) of higher order skill development in education could be decentralized; thus costs for personnel, travel, and facilities would be reduced. People's abilities to program and use machines would be enhanced; simultaneously, society might become oriented much more toward abstract skills and abilities than interpersonal skills and interaction. Developmental costs will be extremely high; artificial intelligence software can require up to 10,000 hours of programmer time for each hour of instructional time produced. As with instructional television, these high production costs require a large client audience for cost-effectiveness; however, once the learning simulation is developed, the use costs are negligible and the game can be replayed indefinitely by a whole series of learners. Over a long period of time, using simulations such as this, human teaching can be largely eliminated in most training-oriented subjects (that is, subjects in which there is a limited range of right answers to questions).

## Videodiscs and Personal Computers

A fourth instructional technology stems from coupling videodisc images and sound track to an interactive microcomputer. In this manner, filmed material can be presented and, based on individualized learner response, be tailored to maximize efficiency of instruction. An example might be a *Columbo* episode in which the learner *is* the detective; based on the conclusions drawn after each scene, appropriate new plot material is presented. A more limited response range and slightly fewer variations would be possible than with the "pure" computer simulations described earlier, because of the enormous cost of the filming to handle unusual responses that learners might take. However, the learning experience would be more personal and concrete, less abstract and symbolic.

Current videodisc and microcomputer technology is sufficient to create such programming; production expenses are enormous, but use costs would be very small. Over a very long period of time, enough programs of this type could be developed to substitute for many group teaching situations, but could not replace human teaching in the development of very high levels of cognitive or affective skills or in specialized areas in which small client populations would reduce cost-effectiveness.

## Electronic Communication, and Information Processing

A fifth set of educational technologies is more an aid to instruction than a substitute for human teaching. Electronic mail, computer conferencing, computer search, and information processing options all provide ways of making education more efficient. Electronic mail uses computers to send messages swiftly and cheaply over long distances; this can provide a low-cost mechanism for coordinating a state-wide or national educational network. Computer conferencing permits a group of people to interact both across considerable distances and also cover a wide time frame (so that participants need not simultaneously be at the keyboard); again, this can save travel costs and makes possible joint endeavors by persons geographically distant. Computer search provides a means for very quick data availability and retrieval, thus reducing both library and personnel costs for research. Information processing is a simple and rapid way of facilitating the editing and production of documents. Combined, all these technologies can ease the professional "busy work" functions educators must perform, thereby increasing efficiency and effectiveness and reducing boredom. The costs of adopting such approaches are that new skills for using machines must be developed, and that increasing amounts of professional time will be spent without direct personal contact with other human beings.

## Benefits and Needed Changes

These five educational technologies are illustrative of what we might do to change the teaching/learning model we now use; all the necessary hardware currently exists. The "software" (television programs, films, computer programs) does not. (Note that this is a very limited and conservative picture of the future of educational technology; memory drugs, altered states of consciousness, and biopsychological manipulation strategies have not been discussed). Fifteen years from now, what would be the overall costs and benefits from moving education toward these illustrative technologies?

First, we'd save money, even with the large initial outlays of capital required to purchase equipment and develop software. The first few years of such an effort might be very difficult, for money must be spent to implement these technologies before savings can be realized. Innovative funding strategies (such as long-term, low-interest loans from information technology corporations) may well be required; the aim of "school bonds" may take a whole new direction—not to construct new buildings, but to purchase a new computer or equip an educational broadcast facility.

Massive changes would need to occur in both in-serve and pre-serve teacher-training; educators must be prepared to program these new technologies, to assess student responses to these types of

Chris Dede, who heads the World Future Society's Education Section, compares the plight of educators today with that of the monks who hand copied manuscripts in the late middle ages when the newly-developed technology of printing was already beginning to make their traditional role obsolete.

instruction, and to refuse to substitute machine interaction where human instruction is more appropriate. The teacher role will become less boring, but will demand more creativity and initiative. Personnel shifts may cause considerable tensions in the short-term. In the long-term, as many educational jobs may exist as do at present, but some will not be teaching roles and quite a few may be outside the school system, in industries, communities, and media. The final impact of technology on educational employment will not be so much to reduce as to alter roles and to shift employment to educational agents other than schools.

Inequalities in education would be reduced, as instruction becomes more standardized (especially for television and videodisc curricula) and probably of uniformly higher quality. However, local control over educational content will be greatly reduced, and the need for quality control to eliminate error and propaganda will be much larger. Increased diversity in ways of teaching will need to be available to match the diversity of learning styles that we see in human beings.

Adult citizenship behavior would be improved over today, because educators will be able to interact with people in their homes to update their skills. However, human contact and the affective areas of education may be reduced by using machines rather than people to teach, unless care is taken to stress these areas in non-technological instructional settings.

## Long-Term Effects and Trends

It is evident from this summary of costs and benefits that, other than in saving money, the expansion of educational technology will be a mixed blessing at best, and could create some challenging new issues. Such an outcome is typical of using technology to solve problems; unless carefully monitored, the side effects from a "technological fix" can be worse than the original situation. Nonetheless, our society continues to expand its technological capabilities, and this in turn compels educators to move in the same direction—although with considerable resistance.

Trends in the last hundred years clearly illustrate this generalization. In the last hundred years, in the developed countries, our travel speed has increased by a factor of a hundred, our control over infectious diseases has increased by a factor of a hundred, our energy resources—despite the energy crisis—have increased by a factor of a thousand, our data handling capabilities by a factor of ten thousand, our weaponry power by a factor of a million and our communications speed by a factor of ten million. However, in sectors dominated by social invention and labor-intensive approaches (such as education or politics), we see no comparable hundred-fold increases in the last hundred years—not even ten-fold

> **"Eventually, 'training' may be almost completely done by machine, while 'educating' will be facilitated by people."**

or two-fold increases. As a result, we in education are receiving heavy criticism, economic cutbacks, and demands for increased productivity.

Society has paid dearly in hidden costs for the technological gains cited above; many of our problems today stem from side-effects of rapid, uncontrolled implementation of technological solutions in the last hundred years. Now, to maintain this high-technology society, education must move to technological approaches both for economic reasons and to provide the intensive, elaborate training and socialization needed to cope in such a setting. Hopefully, we can find a way of maximizing the benefits and minimizing the costs discussed earlier, by applying technology only where appropriate, with forethought, and with suitable controls.

Given that we are intelligent enough to use instructional technology wisely, what will be its long-term net effects? One eventual outcome may be that training ("limited range of right answer" learning) will be almost completely done by machine, while educating ("multiple right answer" learning) will be facilitated by people. This implies that subjects such as reading and basic math may be machine taught, while areas such as creative writing will continue to be conveyed by human instructors.

A second long-term effect may be that new definitions of intelligence will emerge. Historically, our definition of intelligence has changed based on our technological capabilities. For example, fifty years ago, having a near photographic memory was an important part of being intelligent because the kind of rapid data retrieval that we have now was not available; today, memory is less important to intelligence. Similarly, as machines are developed with instructional skills, different human capabilities will be seen as indicating intelligence.

To work with others using machines as intermediaries, new types of communications skills will be necessary; we may see innovative communications styles that will allow us to be person-oriented and affective even when sending messages via the computer or television. After all, this is what a good media personality is able to accomplish; we may study Johnny Carson to learn the way he communicates sociability, social presence, and affect over the air waves, how he compensates for the loss of direct contact that takes place when machines mediate communication.

A third outcome may be that everyone in society will have a better understanding of the strengths and weaknesses of technology because all of us will be interacting with technology day-to-day, learning from and programming machines. We may become more intelligent and sophisticated in using technology when we continuously see what it is and is not capable of accomplishing.

In education, long-term effects will include centralization of curriculum development and finances, but decentralization of the learning environment into homes and communities. New types of government regulations will be needed to allow educators to interface with public utilities such as the Bell System; Federal and state regulation problems will become very complex. Different types of people will be attracted to teaching as a profession; some people who now reject education as a career will find technology-interfaced teaching attractive because the role itself will be more challenging and interesting. New evaluation strategies will emerge in response to larger grading pools and altered definitions of learner effectiveness. One way of summarizing these changes is to say that a new model of teaching and learning will be needed, with corresponding changes in roles and relationships for teachers, parents, industries, media, administrators and government.

### Getting There From Here

To make such a transition to instructional technology as effective as possible, three things must be done. One immediate agenda is to begin planning now, so that reliance on technology can be confined to areas in which machines are efficient and effective. The focus of instructional technology should be on training rather than educating; on small-scale, low-investment applications wherever possible; and on high reliability to avoid maintenance problems.

A second short-range objective should be to organize a national network of educational decision-makers to lobby government for appropriate regulations and to lobby information technology manufacturers for useful and inexpensive products. Without organized pressure on industry, educators will be offered junk for sale, and expensive junk at that! In computers, purchase of the machines themselves represents only 10% of user costs; programs for running the computers will be 90% of educational expenditures, and manufacturers will attempt to get away with whatever they can to boost profits. This implies that educational agencies must themselves learn to differentiate between good and bad high-technology products, an expertise which we need to start developing now.

The third initiative we should assume is devising anticipatory social inventions to regulate the use of instructional technologies; to reduce the negative effects that they may produce, and increase the receptivity of teachers and administrators to machines as a means of reducing costs. To accomplish this, we need to reconceptualize the training that we give teachers and administrators, to develop alliances with media associations and computer associations, and to explore creative ways to raise capital so that we can invest in these technologies without being saddled with too heavy a debt.

Taken as a group, these three immediate agendas illustrate an approach pioneered by British economist E. F. Schumacher known as "appropriate technology." Schumacher's strategies for managing technology are designed to minimize the negative side effects so often associated with increasing reliance on machines. Education's chances of a bright future are much higher if we anticipate the challenges these new technologies may pose than if we wait and find ourselves in a reactive, crisis-oriented posture.

We are facing a period in education similar to the introduction of the printing press 500 years ago. Before that time, those people who could read (a small percentage of the population) used a few hand-copied manuscripts as their source of information; for the rest of the populace, recitors and actors conveyed ideas orally. In converting to the printing press, people faced problems similar to those discussed here: a loss of the human factor, new skills required and valued abilities suddenly made obsolete, career shifts, massive needs for capital investment, etc. But, although decades passed before books were used to their full educative potential, the shift to the printed word for information dissemination ultimately did result in progress, increased learning, and exciting new frontiers for education.

Recent technological advances pose a similar opportunity for us. The traditional teacher is in a position analogous to that of clerks after the end of WW II, when the computer was developed. Suddenly, many fewer clerks were needed—but new, more interesting jobs were available for skilled personnel. We can be similar to monks copying manuscripts by hand while the printing press makes us obsolete, or we can be in the forefront by simultaneously developing instructional technology and retaining traditional educational approaches were appropriate.

One closing thought: it is easy to be psychologically hypnotized by the stability of the present. We are constantly tempted to be conservative and say, "I'll tinker around with innovations, but be sure to hedge my bets and put 95% of my energies into a traditional approach to my work. In this manner, no matter what happens, I can look as if I was prepared." This is a very understandable trait, but—as the energy crisis illustrates—it is easy to be trapped by it.

My university is built on a flood plain in Houston, near the Johnson Space Center. The major classroom building is twenty feet above sea level, and the entire exterior of this building (which contains eleven and a half acres of floor space) is glass. When I arrived, I asked the provost what would happen to the glass if a hurricane were to come, what wind speed the windows were rated for. She replied, "Don't worry, these windows are the best of their kind and are rated for 90 mph winds." When the next hurricane does come—this summer, in two years, or in twenty years—every pane of glass on the entire exterior of the building will blow off in 200 mph winds; and the roof of the Houston Astrodome, which is rated for 135 mph winds, will sail across the city like a gigantic frisbee and impale itself into the oil company skyscrapers! However, we choose to live as if this will never happen, because we are seduced by the relative stability of the present.

The best example of all is San Francisco. The largest single natural disaster in American history will come when the San Andreas fault finally shifts. There are elementary schools built on the fault line, dams and nuclear power plants within a few miles of the fault; the loss of life will be enormous. We know this disaster will come, but we are quite capable of indefinitely hiding our heads in the sand rather than dealing with the situation.

There is a Chinese saying: "Too late to dig well when house on fire." Hopefully, today's educators can rise above being hpynotized by present issues to look ahead.

\* \* \*

Christopher J. Dede is Associate Professor of Education and Future Studies at the University of Houston at Clear Lake City, Texas, and president of the Education Section of the World Future Society. He is currently in Washington at the National Institute of Education, 1200 19th Street, NW, Washington, D.C. 20208.

---

This article was adapted from a speech originally presented at the Summer Institute of Chief State School Officers held July 1979 in the state of Vermont U.S.A.

# Images of the Future: Some Questions for Study

by Gary D. Wooddell

Educating for the future implies training students in how to envision or "image" alternative future events. The limited research undertaken to date suggests that much more needs to be learned about how individual and collective images of the future affect attitudes and actions in the present.

Modern futures studies, and futures education, is based on a number of assumptions about man's relationship to his environment (including social milieu) and is also based on a particular view of the interactions between the time-concepts of past, present, and future. The result is a view which identifies man as an active agent, individually and collectively, in the construction and management of desirable future states. The interaction of time frames suggests, moreover, that consideration of such future states may play a significant role in present actions. The noted Dutch futurist Fred Polak, in his book *The Image of the Future*, introduced the terminology in the early 1950s. Since that time the concept of envisioning possible future states has become central to the study of futures. Harman states, "Someone has a vision of the future . . . and *as a result* certain events are taking place in the present."[1] Bertrand de Jouvenel adds, "Our actions properly so called seek to validate appealing images and invalidate repugnant ones."[2] As a final example, James Dator offers, "I believe that one of the major things shaping the future in reality is what people presently image the future as being."[3]

Thus, today much is written concerning the effects of future images, both individual and societal; yet little research has been conducted in this area. It would appear that research into the "imaging" of futures would contribute significantly to both futures studies and futures education. Polak suggested the same view over two decades ago:

> The relationship between conceptions of the time-dimension, the future, and the idealistic ethical objectives of mankind for that future, has been a neglected one and offers a fruitful field for research.[4]

In the 1960s, John McHale saw a similar need, "Important, but comparatively neglected, areas of futures thinking [include] the psycho-symbolic aspects of the future—the ways in which viable images of future life styles and social forms are previsioned . . ."[5]

But it is still unclear what it is about an "image of the future" that warrants attention. First, the term "image" needs clarifying. As used by Polak, Kenneth Boulding[6] and others, the term is used in much the same way as the verb "imagine"—that is, to create a mental picture of an object or event. The emphasis in both cases is not on capturing reality, necessarily, but on the act of creation. Thus, an image of the future is not necessarily open to criticism in terms of accuracy or correctness. The image of the future may be, and often is, purely fictional. According to Polak, this does not reduce the power of the image.

Creating an image of the future—or "imaging"—is rather easily related to life, because of the accepted use of the term in American society. Even today there is talk of a person's image, or the image of an object. The claimed power of the image of the future is also suggested by more mundane examples. Advertising and propaganda deal exclusively with the process of creating images. The success of such ventures is often dependent on the "power" of the image to sell the product. A single example may prove sufficient: it is quite apparent from events of the past decade that the glamorous images of cigarette smoking are significantly more powerful than the scientific evidence of the harm of smoking; simply, more people are smoking. Thus, an image—a vision of reality—may well have sufficient power to negate an aspect of the reality situation.

> **"Man's action in the present may be seen as a reaction to an event which has not occurred, . . . a reaction to an *image* of that occurrence."**

The potential power of the image as used in futures studies has additional ramifications. Specifically, the image of the future is an individual or collective envisioning of a particular state of affairs. If, as de Jouvenel has suggested, man has some control over the development of future states, then it is apparent that man will attempt to take action to attain that state which is preferable. Thus, man's action in the present may be seen as a reaction to an event which has not occurred. It is a reaction to an *image* of that occurrence.

The result is that action is a factor of the interaction of the future with the present. Of course, any action taken will enhance or reduce the probability of a given future; in this way the present affects the future. The conclusion may be drawn that much present action (or action to be taken in the immediate future) has its roots in the future; thus, analysis of the various images which guide humanity may prove of value in our efforts to deal with social problems.

Two areas of research suggest themselves, both as central to futures studies and as significant to our understanding of sociological processes. The first area focuses on the development of images of the future in individuals, and the effects that varied images may have on the behavior of those individuals. Indeed, this issue appears to be central to all education. For if, as has been suggested, individual images influence present actions, education must concern itself with understanding both images and the imaging process. The second area of interest concerns the issue of societal images of the future. If, as Polak suggests, each culture has a dominant image of the future which is largely shared by its members, then one may question the role which such an image plays in the life of the society. It is these two questions for which research directions might be suggested which appear central to the basic premises of futures studies and futures education.

## Individual Images of the Future

For purposes of clarity the initial research area might be restated as a question: "What specific effects does an individual's image of the future have on his actions in the present?"

Specific research into the area of individual images of the future has been limited. This is partially due to the present state of futures education. Much of the writing done in this area has focused on encouraging further development of futures education. This writing tends to be didactic and proselytizing in nature, offering ideas and suggestions, especially for "practical" classroom activities. These endeavors are understandable as part of the growing process of the field. The result has been, however, a somewhat startling lack of research into the basic issues on which futures education is built. Certainly there is interest in the "parent" field of futures studies for theory and for research. Futures education has not been characterized by this same interest.

The limited research in the area of individual images of the future falls into two categories. The first involves those images which the individual holds concerning the future of the social structure, of the civilization, and of the human race. The second involves those images which reflect personal futures.

A number of researchers have attempted to examine the images of futures which individuals hold. To some degree these efforts usually are characterized by surveys in which subjects are asked to describe their conceptions of the future. This informal approach has been used extensively in the classroom (including efforts by the author). Such efforts, however, have only produced a number of isolated samples and little attempt has been made to examine the data more closely. This viewpoint expressed the consensus of the participants at the Futures of Education conference, St. Cloud, Minnesota, June 1978, which included Draper Kauffman, Chris Dede, Joel Barker, James Dator, Scott Erickson, and Penny Damlo, among others. Thus, it appears that a sizeable number of classroom teachers are collecting information about images of the future, but little effort is being made to generate findings from this data. There are, however, a few attempts at more general studies; two should prove sufficient to indicate the general nature of such endeavors.

In 1975 Marvin Adelson and Samuel Aroni reported on their efforts to examine the images of the future held by college students.[7] This may well have been the first systematic attempt since the work of Nathan Israeli in the 1930s,[8] although Hadley Cantril reported somewhat disjointed efforts from the 30s throughout the 60s.[9] The Adelson and Aroni study focused on the correlation of visual images (photographs) and verbal statements about the future. The subjects were members of the freshman class at the UCLA School of Architecture (thus, it may be assumed that their visual aptitudes were probably considerably higher than those of a random sample of the United States population).

The researchers' hypothesis was that each individual would be able to interpret the portrayed images and that he would demonstrate (internal) consistency in his interpretations. The results of the study were inconclusive. Some significant consistencies were noted, but in all, the researchers were not satisfied that there was sufficient evidence to state that visual portrayals were effective in examining individuals' images of the future. This study does, however, raise some interesting questions about the relationship of images of the future to imaging capacity, and non-verbal or linkages of verbal and non-verbal approaches.

A more recent study conducted by Catherine McKenzie Shane was reported in *Phi Delta Kappan*[10] and summarized in Harold G. Shane's latest book.[11] The purpose of this study was to examine the views of America's youth concerning the future. The study sample consisted of 95 high school students, "drawn from socioeconomic and ethnic groupings ranging from big-city private schools to rural public schools."[12] Additionally, the students were selected on the basis of their social maturity, verbal skills, and willingness to cooperate.

It should be apparent that a detailed analysis of the responses is not necessary (nor did the researcher attempt it). The study achieved exactly what it wanted to achieve—the sample ensured that. It is interesting that no students were invited from big-city *public* schools, just as it is interesting that only in a footnote is the fact disclosed that many of these students were representatives to a national conference for student council presidents, sponsored by the National Association of Secondary School Principals. The responses, even from the "ethnic" subjects, were typically middle class: general optimism, with concern for the problems which confront the nation and the world—a well-educated, cultured image of the future. As Harold Shane notes, their image was "more or less a reflection of a *present* lifestyle."[13]

One group of subjects did stand out, however: a group of "drop-ins" at an urban alternative school. As opposed to the clear views of the other subjects, these subjects "revealed limited imagination with respect to change and the future" and "fuzzy" vocational plans.[14] It would seem that this very inconsistency is more worthy of research than the images of all the others, for it raises the issues of why these individuals have such images (or lack of images) and why they are different from the others.

The Shane study points out two problems with much of the informal research into images of the future which is occurring. First, it is extremely easy for a researcher to get the results which he wishes to get, simply by manipulating the sample, the sampling process, or the questions. Second, some groups of individuals are more accessible than others. Upper middle class whites are generally more "socially mature" (in the middle class white view) and more verbal than are other groups. Additionally, older children express themselves more fluently than do younger ones, thus encouraging examination only of images of the older students. The result is that much of the data collected, even before analysis, is worthless because of intentional or unintentional bias on the part of the researcher. At the present time, therefore, there have been no significant studies on which we might base future efforts in research into the images of social futures held by individuals.

**"Vandalism, delinquency and much juvenile crime may more appropriately be attributed to an individual's image of personal futures than to his environment."**

The situation with regard to research into individual images of personal futures is little better. An informal study reported by Alvin Toffler[15] has indicated that individuals do make distinctions between their images of social futures and their images of personal futures. However, considering the status of research into images of social futures, this tells us very little. Toffler's book, *Learning for Tomorrow*, contains what is probably the foremost work to date on images of personal futures, yet that work does not even claim to be research.

Benjamin Singer describes what he terms the "future-focused role-image."[16] In many ways, Singer's concept is related to the psychological construct of "self-concept," which is the individual's picture of himself. This picture includes not only a physical representation of the body (which is of great importance according to child-development specialist Guy Lefrancois),[17] but also an opinion of the psychological, mental, and moral "self." The future-focused role-image is most simply this picture of the "self" projected into the future.

Here, again the present and the future interact. One's "self-concept" in the present usually has its reflections in one's image of a personal future, which in turn guides actions in the present—"usually" because the malleability of the future suggests the possibility of altering the "self" in some future. Thus, the 98-pound weakling may have a poor self-concept, but a positive image of his personal future, because he has plans for developing his physique. The different between self-concept and image of the personal future, then, is the time dimension. The self-concept is present- and past-bound. It is a function of the past and present experiences. The image of personal futures, of course, is a function of the "to be." Even though it exists in the present, its force comes from the future. This is the essence of Singer's article. He cites some peripheral research on Operation Head Start, but he has little other than the logic of his argument with which to be convincing. Even so, his work provides a number of starting points for further investigation. He suggests that educational performance may be related directly to the individual's ability to delay gratification, which, in turn, is a factor of his image of the future. Additionally, he suggests that "vandalism, delinquency, and much juvenile crime may be more appropriately attributed to the individual's image of personal futures than to his environment," citing the few individuals who manage to rise above the conditions of their early lives. Singer suggests that these individuals may have more positive images of what the future can be; he offers that most middle class children are instilled with such a view.

Pauline Bart and Alvin Poussaint offer further thought on this issue.[18] Bart suggests that females are socially conditioned to hold different images of personal futures than males. Poussaint elaborates on the racial differences in images of personal futures.

Another extremely important issue for further study is the effect of "significant others" on an individual's image of the future. Research has indicated that the opinions of others appear to have high correlations with an individual's self-concept.[19] Singer cites reports of Operation Head Start which indicate the high correlation between an individual's future-focused role-image and his parents' expectations and desires for their child's future.

In a more recent study, E. Paul Torrance and C.R. Reynolds describe several aspects of images of personal futures.[20] They employ written soliloquies and sociodrama as techniques to expose underlying images. Unfortunately, this study does not report findings on the images themselves, but instead reports only the correlation between certain images and self-perceived alienation, and also between images and cerebral functions (learning and thinking styles). The evidence is somewhat unclear due to the generalizations and assumptions which are not explained in the report of the study.

Finally, Edward Cornish reports on research by the sociologist Arthur Stinchcombe and other research in conjunction with Operation Head Start which points to the differences in images of the future among different age groupings.[21] Cornish concludes that younger children appear to have more optimistic images of the future (social and personal) and that pessimism sets in as children get older; his rationale for this observation is unclear (although informal observations seem to bear out this contention). In a description of the efforts of classroom teachers to implement futures education, Cornish reports that some teachers, such as Sister June Wilkerson and Joe Epping at Regina High School in Minneapolis, Minnesota, feel confident that they can "improve" students' images (make the images more optimistic) through educational experiences.

In summary, the research to date on individual images of social and personal futures has been sporadic and less than rigorous. However, these few attempts suggest a number of specific areas for study, and offer at least some little indication of what such study may find:

- individual images of social and personal futures are directly related to actions and behavior in the present;
- individual images of personal futures are not necessarily consistent with images of social futures;
- individual images of the future, especially future-oriented role-images (personal futures) are directly related to school performance;
- there is a significant correlation between a child's achievement and his parents' image of the future concerning the child;
- individual images of the future are malleable through apropriate intervention strategies;
- the following factors are significantly correlated with differential images of the future: socioeconomic status, ethnicity, and age.

Thus, the area of individual images of the future provides a number of specific directions for futures research.

## Collective Images of the Future

The second general research area concerning images of the future might be stated as follows:

> Do societies have identifiable collective images of the future and, if so, what role do such images play in the life of the society?

Polak, of course, maintains that societies, and cultures, do indeed have such guiding images. Jib Fowles, of the University of Houston at Clear Lake City, disagrees, arguing that societies are the combinations of complex interactions among individuals, and that any idea of "guiding image" is much too simple to explain how a society lives and changes.[22] Polak's historical analysis is very convincing, however. He traces references to such images back as far as the ancient Middle East (Egypt and Mesopotamia). He states,

> The kind of images that we discuss are shared public images of the cosmos, God, man, social institutions, the meaning of history, and others of similar scope. Again in all these images it is the time-dimension of the future that gives them their special force.[23]

Working from samples of art, literature, philosophy, and other artifacts of each culture, Polak generates a picture of each culture's image of the future, from ancient Egypt, to Hellas, to Christianity in medieval Europe, and finally to the modern Western world. His studies suggest, "The rise and fall of images of the future precedes or accompanies the rise and fall of cultures."[24] Thus Polak presents historical research from which he develops a theory of societal images—or cultural images—of the future. He suggests that the need for continued research is more than an academic endeavor:

> We need to understand our ailing visions in order to know what to reject and what to accept in them, but all our study is only a preliminary clearing of the decks for the urgent vision-work of creating tomorrow. Self-analysis is only meaningful if it liberates us to choose our own destiny.[25]

Willis Harman agrees. "Discovery of a suitable guiding image of the future," he writes, "is clearly our society's most crucial task."[26] Certainly, a primary benefit from such research might be the clarification of the value systems underlying many of our present conflicts. For if images of the future do indeed guide social action in the present, then present values may be seen as beliefs about the kinds of events which enhance or retard the probabilities of certain images.[27]

Research in this area has not been as intense as might be expected from the central role of the image in modern futurism. The reason is, of course, partially the size and complexity of the issue. A societal "image" is a very difficult concept with which to come to grips; its measurement hinges on how one defines "society" and "image," and neither of these terms has been examined in much detail. Additionally, selecting the image which appears to be dominant is extremely difficult, especially in a period of rapid change. The result is that analysis of societal images is certainly more manageable, and perhaps only possible, from the historical vantage point. In other words, societal images may require, because of their pervasive and dynamic character in a society, that they only be examined after the society or culture in which they exist has passed. Polak attempts to look at recent society's images, but this section of the book is much less convincing than the earlier historical accounts.

There is, however, the possibility that at least some indications of the societal guiding image might be garnered in the present. Numerous studies have attempted to analyze artifacts of present society for indications of images of the future.[28] Additionally, national polls and surveys are conducted frequently in an effort to pull together some information on dominant values and, thus, images. At best, however, the information from such efforts is only suggestive and has yet to add significantly to our understanding of societal images of the future.

Even so, these efforts do suggest some possible directions for additional research, based on the following tentative hypotheses about societal images of the future:

Futurist educator Gary Wooddell cautions that biases on the part of researchers tend to make the results achieved in earlier assessments of personal futures imaging among students appear highly questionable. For example, the fact that older children express themselves more fluently than do younger ones has led researchers to concentrate on the older students' images only.

- a society's dominant values are highly correlated with the guiding image of the future;
- artifacts of a culture/society (music, literature, mythology, philosophy, art, lifestyle, etc.) indicate that culture's image of the future;
- indications of a societal image may be seen in artifacts in the present;
- (as Polak states) the nature of a society's image of the future correlates highly with the condition of that society.

It is apparent that the concept of the "image of the future" is central to modern futurism. Further rigorous study, of both individual images and societal images, should prove valuable not only to futures studies and futures education, but to our understanding of the psychological and social implications of man's attraction to the future.

* * *

## NOTES

1. Willis W. Harman, *An Incomplete Guide to the Future* (San Francisco: San Francisco Book Company, 1976) p. 1.
2. Bertrand de Jouvenel, *The Art of Conjecture* (New York: Basic Books, 1967) p. 27.
3. James A. Dator, "Alternative Futures & the Futures of Law," a paper prepared for the Future of Law conference, Antioch College School of Law (Institute for Alternative Futures, January, 1978) p. 6.
4. Fred Polak, *The Image of the Future*, translated and abridged by Elise Boulding (New York: Elsevier Scientific Publishing Company, 1973) p. 10.
5. John McHale, *The Future of the Future* (New York: George Braziller, 1969) p. 15.
6. Kenneth Boulding, *The Image* (Ann Arbor: University of Michigan Press, 1956).

7. Marvin Adelson and Samuel Aroni, "Differential Images of the Future," in Harold A. Linstone and Murray Turoff, ed., *The Delphi Method: Techniques and Applications* (Reading, Mass.: Addison-Wesley, 1975).
8. See Nathan Israeli, "The Social Psychology of Time," *Journal of Abnormal and Social Psychology*, 27 (July, 1932) pp. 209-213; "Wishes Concerning Improbable Future Events: Reactions to the Future," *Journal of Applied Psychology*, 16, 5 (1932) pp. 584-588; and "Group Predictions of Future Events," *Journal of Social Psychology*, 4 (May, 1933) pp. 201-222.
9. See H. Cantril, "The Prediction of Social Events," *Journal of Abnormal and Social Psychology*, 33 (July, 1938) pp. 364-389; "A Study of Aspirations," *Scientific American*, 208 (February, 1963) pp. 41-45; and F.P. Kilpatrick and Cantril, "Self-Anchoring Scaling, a Measure of Individuals' Unique Reality Worlds," *Journal of Individual Psychology*, 16 (November, 1960) pp. 158-173.
10. Catherine Shane, "Coping, Caring, Communicating, Youth Looks at the Future," *Phi Delta Kappan* (September, 1976) pp. 117-121.
11. Harold G. Shane, *Curriculum Change Toward the 21st Century* (Washington: National Education Association, 1977).
12. H. Shane, p. 159.
13. H. Shane, p. 27.
14. Ibid.
15. Alvin Toffler, ed., *Learning for Tomorrow: The Role of the Future in Education* (New York: Vintage, 1974).
16. Benjamin D. Singer, "The Future-Focused Role-Image," in Toffler, pp. 19-32.
17. Guy R. Lefrancois, *Of Children: An Introduction to Child Development* (Belmont, Cal.: Wadsworth Publishing Company, 1973).
18. See Pauline B. Bart, "Why Women See the Future Differently from Men," and Alvin F. Poussaint, "The Black Child's Image of the Future" in Toffler, pp. 33-55, and 56-71.
19. See Lefrancois, p. 297.
20. E. Paul Torrance and C.R. Reynolds, "Images of the Future of Gifted Adolescents: Effects of Alienation and Specialized Cerebral Functioning," *The Gifted Child Quarterly*, 22 (Spring, 1978) pp. 40-54.
21. Edward Cornish, *The Study of the Future: An Introduction to the Art and Science of Understanding and Shaping Tomorrow's World* (Washington: World Future Society, 1977).
22. In a conversation with Jib at the Alternatives to Growth conference (Houston, Texas, October 1977).
23. Polak, p. 14.
24. Polak, p. 19.
25. Polak, p. 305.
26. Harman, p. 114.
27. For a detailed examination of the relationship between values and conceptions of the future, see Kurt Baier and Nicholas Rescher, eds., *Values and the Future: The Impact of Technological Change on American Values* (New York: Free Press, 1969).
28. See, for instance, I.H. Buchen, "Science Fiction Futures," *Intellect*, 103 (April, 1975) p. 459; and B.L. Cooper, "Images of the Future in Popular Music: Lyrical Comments on Tomorrow," *Social Education*, 39 (May, 1975) pp. 276-285, and "Exploring the Future through Contemporary Music," *Media and Methods*, 12 (April, 1976) pp. 32-34.

# Tomorrow in Brief

**Forecasts
Trends
Innovations
Ideas**

### New Help for the Blind: "Seeing" with Sound

A new device resembling a pocket flashlight may eventually replace the walking stick as an aid for the blind. Developed at a vocational school in the West German town of Furtwangen, the device emits ultrasonic waves that bounce off nearby objects, such as walls or curbs, and cause the device to vibrate with greater or lesser intensity depending on how close the objects are. A company in Freiburg, West Germany, plans to market the devices.

### Telephone as Medium of Future.

By 1990 there'll be a billion telephones in the world, nearly all of them direct dial, says Wilson Dizard, a Georgetown University specialist in international communications. The U.N. is now developing a world telephone which will have 17 digits so you can soon dial any phone in the world just like a local call.

"You can do almost anything through telephone—oral, print, visual," Dizard says. "The computer is very basic. Already in England they are taking the television and the telephone and hooking them into a computer so you can dial the data of your choice such as racing results or weather. The information comes up on your television set and the TV is converted into a computer terminal. It's a universal information system. We really haven't had a period like this since printing developed in the Renaissance. Computers are going to be the printing presses of the 21st century. We'd better get ready for them."

### Push-Button Translation:

A pocket computer that can translate between English and five other languages is now being marketed in the United States. When an English word or phrase is punched into the keyboard, the device flashes the appropriate words in French, German, Spanish, Portuguese, or Italian. The manufacturer, the Lexicon Corp. in Florida, plans future versions that will translate Russian, Chinese, and Japanese.

### Television is reaching into more homes all around the earth.

In the United States, where few people had television before 1950, some 98% of all households have TV, more than three quarters of them color sets. About half the homes have two TV sets, the National Geographic Society says.

But the tiny Mediterranean principality of Monaco surpasses the U.S. in sets per capita—648 per thousand inhabitants, compared to 632 in the U.S. Britain has 328, West Germany 311, France 272, Italy 229, and the U.S.S.R. 200.

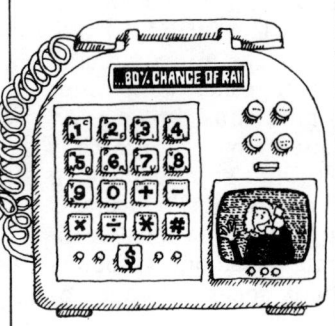

# Education and the Creation of the Future

by Scott W. Erickson

Introducing future studies into a school curriculum can do more than prepare students for a world of change—it can be a step toward actively changing the world.

## Purposes of Education

Certainly there are many purposes of education, on many different levels; but, examined from a general sociocultural perspective one can identify two primary and conflicting purposes. One can be termed a conservative function in which the purpose of schooling and education is to preserve, as far as possible, the existing culture. The second can be labeled a progressive function in which schooling and education is meant to help change the existing culture. The concept of the future is treated in quite different ways in each of these two opposing traditions.

**The Conservative Tradition.** The conservative tradition has been the dominant force in the history of American educational practice. Adherents of this position have taken two slightly different tracks, both of which have led to a conservative cultural impact.

The first of these is commonly referred to as *essentialism*. This position holds that schools should teach those things which are absolutely necessary for an individual to function in the culture. While one can argue about what is essential, this position generally advocates teaching the basic skills such as reading, writing and arithmetic. Knowledge is packaged in discreet subject matter areas and is imparted to students by highly trained specialists who can impart sure if not certain understanding of this -ology or that -ology. Specialization is the rule and the fact is prized. It is of these specialists that it is said that they know more and more about less and less until they know everything about nothing. Essentialists generally treat the future only in terms of scientific predictability, which most often effectively precludes thinking about the future of social matters. Essentialist educators are rarely sympathetic to the introduction of future studies courses into school curricula.

The second conservative position is often referred to as *perennialism*. This position holds that some knowledge does not lose its value even though conditions may change. Schools should teach those things which are always of value to human beings, which are represented in the works of the great masters of history. A sound liberal education based on the great books of history will prepare students for any future developments. While this argument has merit, it assumes that the future will not be radically different from the past and that the old virtues will remain useful. The results, in a sense, are schools that produce people, as Alvin Toffler says, tooled for survival in a system that will be dead before they are.[1] Perennialists do not ignore the future, but their activities can too often be characterized by the construction of elaborate plans of how to cope with catastrophes which are already upon us.

**The Progressive Tradition.** The progressive tradition calls for change in education and schooling to allow for changes in society as a whole. It is possible to identify two wings of this position as well.

The first of the two major wings of this position to appear began with the work of John Dewey and is often referred to as *experimentalism*.[2] This position holds that knowledge can be based only on our experience and thus our educational activities should be based on the results of that experience. Education becomes one experiment after another. Keep what works and go on to further experimentation until something better is discovered. No one educational model results from experimentalism but rather a set of innovations. During most of this century no school or university was without its innovation or special program. But they did not always succeed. One reason is because of conservative opposition, but another problem is with the experimentalists themselves. Many experimentalists design innovations intended to correct problems they experienced in their own student days. Actually, this of course is very clever and is one of the few things that allows education to remain only one generation behind the times. The future studies activity inspired by experimentalism consists largely of extrapolating past trends into the future and using them as the basis of planning. On this basis experimentalists often welcome the addition of future studies to the curriculum.

The other major wing of the progressive tradition is commonly referred to as *reconstructionism*. Reconstructionists are more impatient with the rate of change than are experimentalists. George Counts sounded the battle cry of this position in 1932 when he asked *Dare the School Build a New Social Order*. Students should not be prepared for the future or even taught to plan for it only, the schools themselves should help reconstruct society according to a vivid and attractive image of the future. Some see a danger in this notion. If schools can be used to create a future that one likes, it may be possible for someone else to use schools to create a future that one would not like. Reconstructionists counter with the argument that while schools certainly help preserve culture, they also help change it whether one likes it or not. Therefore schools should help create the future according to a conscious plan adopted in an agreed upon fashion rather than according to unconscious social norms. In the past, little of American education has been based on this position. One reason is that in earlier years it was equated with the kind of central national planning practiced by some of the socialist countries that are not always friendly toward the United States. Still, the reconstructionists have convincingly argued that education should move from the ideas of preparing and planning for the future to helping to create the future and that the curricula of schools and universities need to be adjusted accordingly. Perhaps more than others, reconstructionists welcome the introduction of future studies into the school curriculum.[3]

## Education in a New World

Educational futurists have come from philosophical backgrounds that could be described as perennialist, experimentalist or reconstructionist, but more and more the reconstructionist position is becoming the most influential of these various traditions in future studies. Recent research indicates that educators are coming to agree that education must address concerns such as the accelerating rate of change, the issues surrounding growth, third and fourth world pressure for equity in a new economic order and the prospects of world peace.[4] On these and many other issues, modern educational leaders are moving toward positions long held by reconstructionists.

If we keep going is this direction much of the focus of education needs to be changed, a process already begun in many places. Most of the schools are still basically essentialist and the public seems to support the idea that teaching the basics is a good thing. But we find that moving to a futures creation mode does not require us to give up the basics. In trying to create a desired future, students and faculty quickly learn that reading, writing, arithmetic and many other skills are necessary. But they need not be taught in isolation and only in abstract terms. They can be taught as part of a process with a purpose people can relate to. This makes education more exciting and more useful. But what might such an approach be?

Many different approaches have been suggested.[5] To fully succeed in interpreting future studies into a school's curriculum with the goal of using it to help create the future would require a whole systems approach.

Planning a whole systems approach to education is greatly facilitated by the development of modern general systems theory. It provides a framework within which to build a specific proposal for education. The proposal suggested here argues that for future studies to have a genuine impact on education, the introduction of futures courses should be followed by innovations that would lead to something like the following.

Instead of concentrating on discreet subject matter areas, educational offerings should be designed to develop an understanding of several broad areas of concern. This is not to suggest that students simply be subjected to a series of liberal arts requirements, but that, to take the fullest advantage of the introduction of future studies, all course offerings should attempt to address themselves to what could be termed the new ABCs.

## The New ABCs

The new ABC's are: an all-time approach to the curriculum; a consideration of the biosphere in all curricular matters; and the fostering of a cosmocentric orientation toward curriculum construction.

**An All-time Approach.** The introduction of future studies into the schools requires that educators reconsider their temporal orientation. The addition of future studies obviously adds the future time dimension to one's thinking, but the addition of the future should be accompanied by the recovery of the past. In all our educational endeavors we need to look both forward and backward in time. Too much of our education concentrates only on the present and it would benefit greatly by adding insights from the dimension of the future and recovering insights from the dimension of the past.

It is troubling that much of our academic activity has become ahistorical. In some cases we seem to have lost our sense of history. In a sense this is tragic; not because the names of old kings and queens are important in themselves, nor because history may repeat itself and we can be forewarned, but because an understanding of historic change reveals part of the wonder of the human animal and highlights the sometimes bizarre, sometimes wonderful and sometimes surprising variations that are possible in human affairs. In many ways an understanding of history is a handmaiden to foresight into the future. In a forecasting or future studies activity one should look as far back as one plans to look forward.

**Biosphere.** Education should instill an understanding of the workings of the biosphere. We all need to comprehend the range of factors which influence life in all its forms. It is better that this concern not be isolated into separate departments, but be studied and discussed as a part of all curricular areas.

In this area in particular it is important to show that everything is connected to everything else. A holistic approach here is much more appropriate than more isolated environmental studies, biological studies or studies of human behavior. Such integrated approaches are certainly possible, as is demonstrated by the Chinese discipline of Kung-Fu. This regimen is a holistic approach to intellectual, physical and emotional development in all life. This suggestion would require more integration and synthesis than is common in the United States, but it is also a process that has already begun and which will probably increase our chances of coming to understand the interdependence of all life forms with each other and the natural world. While biospheric considerations are common to all curriculum areas, their recognition is certainly facilitated by future studies.

**A Cosmocentric Perspective.** The introduction of future studies into a curriculum is often accompanied by the call for a global approach to the study of human problems.[6] This idea is criticized by some who argue that if humans cannot learn how to get along with each other in a small village or city how can one expect matters to be improved by the introduction of a larger perspective? In response, someone using a systems approach might suggest that situations are often improved by the introduction of information or concepts from outside the closed confines of the immediate problem.

One example of the closed versus open approach is in energy. Energy problems in our villages and cities take on different meanings when examined from a national, global, or cosmic perspective. Energy reserves are often measured in world terms. But this is no longer sufficient. Energy planning for the future is incomplete without taking into consideration solar energy sources. Yet, in many of our studies of the future the earth is assumed to be a closed system. It is true that not even the global perspective is commonly accepted as a metaphor for planning, but it may be time to begin the switch from a basically closed geocentric system approach to an open, cosmocentric system approach.[7]

Of course, at this time there is no one unified approach to the study of the future. And not all the various approaches to the study of the future follow the criteria of the New ABC's listed above. But in the process of futurizing a curriculum, it is useful to start with one general introductory course.

### Future Studies in the Classroom

There is still a great deal of disagreement about what is the most appropriate content for a future studies class. One approach which is useful for a general introductory course is an alternative futures curriculum which compares several different images of the future and critiques each one. Three widely held images of the future today are commonly referred to as the low technology,[8] the intermediate technology[9] and the high technology approach.[10] Table 1 summarizes the different assumptions made by each of these images of the future.

The answers that each of the three images of the future supplies in each of these basic areas provides the foundation for its propelling image of the future.

### Table 1

| Assumptions | Low | Intermediate | High |
| --- | --- | --- | --- |
| Abundance | Not enough | Sufficient | More than enough |
| Growth | None | Organic | Forever |
| Nature | Nature knows best | Change but be gentle | Humans can do better |
| Population | Too much | Improperly concentrated | Room for more |
| Technology | Bad | Must be ecological | Good |
| Work | To survive | Is the joy of life | To gain leisure |

Each of these positions assumes a different kind of past; perceives a different kind of present; and plans for a different kind of future.

**Abundance.** On the question of abundance the low-technology position assumes that there is not enough of anything to long provide the kind of life to which individuals are now accustomed. Spokesmen for the low-technology position argue that we are running out of natural resources, food and other vital items for the survival of society. For them this is true at the present time and will be even more so in the future.

Intermediate-technology advocates argue that there is a sufficient amount of everything that society needs as long as it is utilized wisely and not wasted. They argue that this has always been true and as long as our appetites do not grow too large it will continue to be so in the future.

High-technology advocates argue that there is more than enough of all essential materials. Whenever we run low on one resource, another is developed to take its place. They agree that we certainly should not waste things on purpose but believe a certain amount of unavoidable waste should not get in the way of progress.

---

## "In a forecasting or future studies activity one should look as far back as one plans to look forward."

---

**Growth.** The low-technology position holds that growth in population and industrial development is not desirable. Since we live in a finite world we must learn to live within the limits that are imposed by nature.

Intermediate-technology advocates argue that some growth should take place but in an organic fashion; that we must continue to grow, but that each portion of our society should grow in proper relation to each of the others.

The high-technology position holds that growth can continue forever. This does not mean that unlimited growth can occur in a finite time or place but that times and places change and that for society to prosper and mature it must continue to grow in all areas.

**Nature.** Those who hold the low-technology position argue that nature knows best. When humans deal with other life forms and the physical environment they must come to recognize that trying to change the natural laws will lead only to disaster. In dealing with nature humans must realize that nature bats last.

The intermediate-technology position holds that human beings can change nature and even improve on it slightly; but that this must be done gently and with no violence. The forces of nature are more powerful than humans and a violent confrontation with nature will lead to the end of humanity. But by working in harmony with nature beneficial changes can be brought about.

High-technology advocates believe that humans can vastly improve upon nature, and argue that the progress of civilization itself can be equated with the taming, altering and improving of what nature gave to human beings in the beginning.

**Population.** The low-technologists suggest that there are already too many people on the earth and that population growth must be stopped. Some even argue that life on earth would be more pleasant if the population of the world could be reduced.

Intermediate-technologists believe that the world is not really overpopulated, but that the population is simply improperly concentrated. Some areas of the world are insanely congested while others are severely underpopulated. They agree there is a limit to the number of people who can comfortably live on the planet but they believe this number should be based on proper concentrations in specific areas rather than simply on the world-wide aggregate.

High-technologists maintain there is room for many more people on earth. By applying our advances in technology to improving natural conditions many more people can live quite comfortably on the same amount of land. But the great promise for accommodating population growth, they believe, lies in expanding the number of places where people can live to include under the ground, under the sea and out in space.

**Technology.** Low-technology advocates argue that advancing high technology cannot be trusted because for every problem that it solves many more problems are created. Everyone would be better off, they believe, living a simpler life based on a simpler technology.

Intermediate-technologists hold that for technology to be useful it must be ecological. Certainly we should not abandon our tools but if they do violence to nature, they should not be used. We should use only that technology which we can control and introduce advanced technology only when we understand what the consequences will be.

High-technologists are technological optimists. For them technology is good. Civilization is always confronted with problems and opportunities; technology is simply a means for solving the problems and taking advantage of the opportunities. When new problems arise technology can often supply the answer. In fact, technological progress is what allows more and more people to live better and better.

**Work.** Low-technologists suggest that people must work to survive. That was true in the past, is true today, and will be true in the future.

Intermediate-technologists suggest that the joy of work is the joy of life. They suggest that much of life's fulfillment comes from a job well-done. It is difficult for a person to feel good about himself if he does not have meaningful work. Therefore, work should be designed to be interesting and meaningful for the individual worker.

Scott W. Erickson proposes a new set of ABCs for education: an All-time approach, Biosphere awareness, and Cosmocentric orientation.

High-technologists argue that we work to gain leisure time. Any device which can save labor is good because it frees individuals from dehumanizing labor so that they can devote themselves to higher pursuits. A human being's true end is the creative use of leisure time which can allow individuals to develop to higher levels in whatever they choose to do.

Since there is so little agreement about which of these three images of the future is the most desirable or realistic, students need to be familiar with each of them. Another reason for including all three in the curriculum is that they do not address themselves to the new ABC's, outlined above, with equal clarity and force. In fact, none of the three positions demonstrate a sensitivity to all three of the ABC's. The following table demonstrates this point.

### Table 2

|  | Low | Intermediate | High |
|---|---|---|---|
| All time | No | Yes | Yes |
| Biosphere | Yes | Yes | No |
| Cosmocentric | No | No | Yes |

The low-technology position allows for the least amount of alternatives, in its interpretation of the past, in its evaluation of the present circumstances and in its image of the future. The intermediate and high technology positions have a firmer sense of historic change and a less authoritarian image of possible futures.

The low and intermediate technology positions gave the public an understanding of the holistic nature of the biosphere. It may be that there would *be* no future studies at this time if it were not for the work that the low and intermediate technologists have done in this area. It is unfortunate that some high technologists still do not recognize the importance of biospheric considerations.

The low and intermediate technology positions hold a closed system, geocentric orientation. Almost alone, the high technologists argue that even our most serious Earth-based problems can best be solved by assuming an open system, cosmocentric orientation.

Each of these positions has produced a different image of the future, each with its own limitations and strengths. The New ABCs can slowly be brought into the curriculum by teaching each of these general approaches to the study of the future. This in turn can help schools become institutions able to help create a desirable future.[11]

Of the many purposes of education, the one suggested by the educational philosophy of reconstructionism is increasingly being accepted as the one which can help schools become partners in efforts to create desirable futures. The introduction of future studies into the school curriculum can help this process along. Even though this effort should often begin with one introductory future studies course, the initial efforts should be supplemented with general futurizing of the entire curriculum to allow schools to help create the future.

## NOTES

[1] In Richard W. Hostrop, ed., *Foundations of Futurology in Education* (Homewood, Ill.: ETC Publications, 1973), p. v.

[2] John Dewey, *Democracy and Education* (New York: Free Press, 1966).

[3] See George S. Counts, *Dare the School Build a New Social Order?* (New York: John Day, 1932); William H. Kilpatrick, *A Reconstructed Theory of the Educative Process* (New York: Teachers College Press, 1931); Van Cleve Morris, *Philosophy and the American School* (Boston: Houghton-Mifflin Co., 1961); Nobuo Shimahara, *Educational Reconstruction: Promise and Challenge* (Columbus, Ohio: Charles E. Merrill, 1973); and G. Max Wingo, *The Philosophy of American Education* (Boston: D.C. Heath, 1965).

[4] Harold G. Shane, "America's Educational Futures: 1976-2001," THE FUTURIST, Vol. X, No. 5 (October 1976), pp. 252-257.

[5] James Stirewalt, "The Future as an Academic Subject," WORLD FUTURE SOCIETY BULLETIN, Vol. XI, No. 1 (January-February 1977), pp. 16-20 and Vol. XI, No. 2 (March-April 1977), pp. 9-14.

[6] See Barbara Ward and Rene Dubos, *Only One Earth* (New York: W.W. Norton, 1972) and Jan Tinbergen, Ed., *RIO: Reshaping the International Order* (New York: Dutton, 1976).

[7] Arthur M. Harkins, "Humanism in Space," *Futurics*, Vol. 1, No. 3 (Winter 1977), pp. 79-88.

[8] See Jay W. Forrester, *World Dynamics* (Cambridge, Mass.: Wright-Allen Press, 1973) and Donella Meadows, *et. al,* *Limits to Growth* (New York: New American Library, 1972).

[9] See Mihajlo Mesarovic and Eduard Pestel, *Mankind at the Turning Point* (New York: Dutton, 1974) and E.F. Schumacher, *Small Is Beautiful* (New York: Harper, 1973).

[10] See Gerard K. O'Neill, *The High Frontier: Human Colonies in Space* (New York: William Morrow, 1977) and G. Harry Stine, *The Third Industrial Revolution* (New York: Putnam, 1975).

[11] See Theodore Brameld, *The Climactic Decades:* Mandate to Education (New York: Praeger, 1970) and Theodore Brameld, *The Teacher as World Citizen: A Scenario of the 21st Century* (Palm Springs, Cal.: ETC Publications, 1976).

Scott W. Erickson is the president of Future Systems in Minneapolis, Minnesota. This article is adapted from a speech delivered at a conference sponsored by the Future Studies Program Board of the University of Northern Iowa, October 14, 1977. The author's address is: Scott W. Erickson, President, Future Systems, P.O. Box 14067, Minneapolis, Minnesota 55414.

# Educational Predictions: Past, Present, and Future

**by Betty Dillon and Ralph Wright**

Examining past predictions to determine their accuracy offers a useful method for identifying potential problem areas in present-day forecasts. Here a group of 69 school administrators assess the accuracy of 42 predictions made between 1900 and 1940 regarding the future of American education, and offer a few predictions of their own on developments likely to occur between now and the year 2000 in such areas as teaching methods, curriculum, administration, special education, and school/community relations.

Educators, like people in all fields of human endeavor, have suffered from limited or ineffective predictions upon which to make decisions. The most notable example of this failure is the present oversupply of teachers which came so unexpectedly but which might very easily have been predicted and planned for.

Recently, a group of approximately 120 school administrators from across the United States and Canada was invited to serve as a panel of experts to determine the degree to which predictions about education made 20, 30, or even 40 years ago had proven accurate. In addition, the administrators were invited to make their own predictions about what schools might be like in the year 2000.

These administrators were part of a study leave program funded by the Danforth Foundation and organized by the National Academy of School Executives Branch of the American Association of School Administrators. The Danforth/NASE program covered the period from 1974-77, with approximately forty administrators being eligible to participate for a two-month period each year. Each of the three groups made contacts with or direct visits to many school districts or school-related institutions in more than thirty states, the District of Columbia, and Canada. As a result, they were in a unique position to broadly review and report on the state of current education in relation to items selected from earlier predictions.

Among those who participated in the Danforth/NASE program, and who were requested to assist with this project, 69 responded to a survey developed by the authors based on a literature review identifying past predictions of what education would be like in the 1970s. Of this number, 29 were superintendents, 21 held other central office positions, six were in institutions of higher education (including one college president), seven were principals, and others responding were state department officials, a Bureau of Corrections officer, and a NASE staff member.

## Selection of Predictive Statements

A search of the literature revealed a relatively limited number of predictive articles relating to education. Thirteen sources were selected from which to draw predictive statements for the survey, covering a period from 1931 to 1955. (An article by H.G. Wells, written in 1901, was also included because of its relevance.) They came from such diverse sources as the *Ladies Home Journal* and *The Nation's Schools*. A list of the publications from which items were drawn will be found in Appendix I.

The authors selected 52 items which might reasonably be found and noted accurately—either by their presence or absence—by the panel of judges, and organized them under six headings: Organization and Administration; Teachers and Teaching Methodology; Curriculum; Special Education/Guidance Services/Student Services; Physical Facilities, Materials, and Equipment; School and Community.

Some of the predictions were uncannily accurate, such as a 1939 prediction that "the population of the United States will begin to decrease" and that such a decrease "will probably lead to a decrease in the number of teachers in the elementary schools."[1] Others were amusing by their inaccuracy, such as the one which predicted that electrical energy would be so inexpensive that it would not be metered.

Respondents were asked to rate each item on a five point scale. The responses were tabulated and scored using the following numerical values:

a. Not True       −1
b.       +1
c. Somewhat True   +2
d.       +3
e. Very True     +4

Total scores for individual items ranged from 45 to 259. In comparing the responses to different items, it may be helpful to note that if all 69 respondents had rated an item as "Very True," it would have received a total score of 276. A score of 138 would have been obtained if all respondents had indicated that an item was "Somewhat True." Thirty-five of the items scored at or above this figure, and 17 scored below it.

The composite scores for each of the items under each heading are reproduced in the accompanying chart (Figure 1). There are, of course, many limitations to the interpretation of these numerical scores, but they do provide a means of comparing the validity of the questionnaire items.

The following is a summary of the areas of agreement and disagreement with predictions as revealed by the survey.

---

## FIGURE 1

### Organization & Administration

| | Statement | Total Score | Rank Order |
|---|---|---|---|
| 1. | All-year educational programs will be considered. School buildings will be open days and evenings all the year round. | 150 | 8 |
| 2. | Society will demand that educational agencies assume increased responsibility for youth until the age of 19 or until youth is absorbed in adult activities. Education will be more effectively free to all young people for a period of 14 years with provisions for scholarships or remunerative employment to provide needs, including food and clothing where necessary. | 142 | 10 |
| 3. | The competition between the school and other governmental agencies for funds for the more adequate support of services will become more intense. | 247 | 2 |
| 4. | How to provide more education for less money is a problem which will concern school authorities. | 259 | 1 |
| 5. | The school will more frequently be involved in bitter conflicts between state, national and local pressure groups. | 220 | 3 |
| 6. | Control of schools by state governments will increase, especially in matters of finance, curriculum, school buildings, and teacher welfare. The state will pay an increasingly large part of the expenses of the school. | 202 | 4 |
| 7. | All expenditures for public education will be viewed with strong suspicion by taxpayers. | 196 | 5 |
| 8. | Teachers and children will plan their own use of time. | 128 | 11 |
| 9. | Research studies will be continued and more effectively utilized for the improvement of school programs and pupil ability. | 150 | 9 |
| 10. | Administrators will be overburdened with no time to think. | 190 | 6 |
| 11. | Future elementary schools will include nursery and kindergarten divisions, as well as primary and intermediate areas. | 189 | 7 |
| 12. | No crowded classes will be found. Twenty-five pupils will be a maximum number for any teacher, and that number will be lessened in nursery school and kindergarten. | 67 | 13 |
| 13. | Elementary schools will be child-community-centered, and no child will spend more than half an hour getting to and from school. | 93 | 12 |
| 14. | There can be no placement of subject matter in the elementary school nor will pupils be penalized for the lack of ability in academic skills. The ugly emphasis upon marks, promotions, and lines of demarcation between school grades will vanish. | 45 | 14 |

### Teachers and Teaching Methodology

|   |   | Total Score | Rank Order |
|---|---|---|---|
| 1. | It is very likely that 25 or 30 years hence (1964-69) the population of the U.S. will begin to decrease and this decrease will probably lead to a decrease in the number of teachers in the elementary schools. The diminution in attendance in the high schools will not be so noticeable. | 169 | 4 |
| 2. | Teaching will become an increasingly respected profession. | 62 | 8 |
| 3. | Specialists will be available for consultation when teachers need help. | 174 | 2 |
| 4. | Elementary schools will be staffed by people who have been selected because they have chosen to make work with children a permanent profession. They will be emotionally, spiritually, and physically well adjusted in democratic living and will know how to help each child. | 125 | 7 |
| 5. | Tenure and other security measures will be assured . . . provided teachers engage in continuous in-service improvement. | 172 | 3 |
| 6. | Courses in professional training will give a thorough grounding in understanding child growth and development. Certification will be given only to those who complete academic requirements and who prove themselves ready for it. | 137 | 5 |
| 7. | Diagnostic instruments will be used for spotting students' shortcomings. | 184 | 1 |
| 8. | The teacher will teach and confine his moral training, beyond enforcing truth and discipline, to the exhibition of a capable person doing his duty as well as it can be done. | 135 | 6 |

### Curriculum

|   |   | Total Score | Rank Order |
|---|---|---|---|
| 1. | School citizenship will be emphasized, with attention to honesty, cooperativeness, good sportsmanship, tolerance, and civic mindedness. | 132 | 10 |
| 2. | The elementary school will become a children's society which will seek for itself acceptable standards of behavior. The mores of this society will be so clear to all concerned that individuals who deviate will stand out sharply. There will be permissiveness wherein mistakes are not crucial, and children have support in their unhappiness. | 84 | 15 |
| 3. | Minority interest groups in economic, occupational, patriotic, political, and religious fields will increase efforts to modify schools in terms of such minority viewpoints. | 211 | 2 |
| 4. | The school reinforces the idea of the value of all work by eliminating from the school program and records everything that implies a hierarchy of educational values such as "academic," "non-academic," etc. | 86 | 14 |
| 5. | Children will be better able to read and write and do arithmetic. | 116 | 12 |
| 6. | Curriculum revision will be in the direction of practical, utilitarian courses. | 144 | 8 |
| 7. | Specialization will lead to specialized schools and a population in which everyone has at least a high school education. | 141 | 9 |
| 8. | The study of science will take an increasingly important place in the curriculum. | 129 | 11 |
| 9. | Schools will present an even greater number of courses that will appeal to the varied interests and abilities of children. | 219 | 1 |
| 10. | The mathematics departments of our secondary schools will provide appropriate courses for the neglected groups of students whose needs cannot possibly be met in traditional courses. | 148 | 7 |
| 11. | Instructional programs will be more concerned by community problems, such as poverty, housing, safety, sanitation & health. | 163 | 6 |
| 12. | There will be more orientation toward consumption, including intelligent use of radio, newspapers, and magazines, as well as food, clothing, etc. | 170 | 5 |
| 13. | Schools will be patterned after technical schools, training students in specific vocations from typing to foundry casting (apprenticeships). | 92 | 13 |
| 14. | Work experiences for youth will count as credit toward certification. | 198 | 3 |
| 15. | School-work programs include opportunities in industry, business, professional offices, the school itself, community social agencies, and the homes. The school provides coordinators, and the general oversight of the whole program is vested in a coordinator of life-work education. | 183 | 4 |

### Special Education, Guidance Services, and Student Services

| | Total Score | Rank Order |
|---|---|---|
| 1. There will be ungraded classes with teachers trained to aid the handicapped with civic and vocational instruction to fit their mental capacity. | 177 | 6 |
| 2. Maladjustments and personal difficulties are detected and dealt with before students graduate. | 142 | 8 |
| 3. Extensive programs of guidance will be provided for all youth, including those out of school. | 117 | 9 |
| 4. Children at the extremes of the intelligence scales will be much better cared for in the schools of the next half century. Greater provision will be made for the very bright and for those of duller mental qualities. | 178 | 5 |
| 5. Guidance, especially vocational guidance, will be of great concern. The school uses a variety of means, such as orientation courses, aptitude tests, and observations of student interests, to encourage the development of special interests and aptitudes. | 181 | 4 |
| 6. Schools in the future are likely to give more attention to what we call the personality of the child. The new demands placed on the school will cause the extra-curricular activities to be expanded. | 168 | 7 |
| 7. The problem of discipline will be a major one. | 224 | 1 |
| 8. Greater care will be taken to preserve the health of pupils and to remedy their physical defects. | 198 | 2 |
| 9. Care will be taken to diminish the number of drop-outs. | 197 | 3 |

### Physical Facilities, Materials and Equipment

| | Total Score | Rank Order |
|---|---|---|
| 1. As schools have made use of radio, filmstrips, moving pictures, public address systems, tape recorders, and soon television, they will make use of any other machines or gadgets that the genius of man may devise which will help pupils to do more effective work. Materials and equipment will be more adequate, e.g. classroom reading materials, aquaria and living plants, and more emphasis on producing rather than accumulating audio-visual material. | 213 | 1 |
| 2. There will be a large demand for books both in the central library and in classroom libraries. | 212 | 2 |
| 3. Adequate supplies of every kind will be available. Taxpayers will supplement all economic deficiencies affecting best education for all children. | 106 | 3 |

### School and Community

| | Total Score | Rank Order |
|---|---|---|
| 1. Schools will develop a marked degree of cooperation with other agencies engaged in educational work, such as libraries, recreational facilities, health services, guidance clinics, etc. | 169 | 2 |
| 2. Schools will have to face charges of radical elements that the schools and teachers are extremely conservative, and of conservative elements that these same schools and teachers are extremely radical. | 176 | 1 |
| 3. Teachers will acquire more expertise in the interpretation of the school to its community. | 123 | 3 |

---

### Organization & Administration

Finances have clearly become the number one problem of administrators, who seek to provide more education for less money as the schools do indeed compete with other agencies for the tax dollar in an atmosphere of suspicion and bitter conflict between national, state, and local pressure groups. State governments *are* increasing their controls over schools.

Schools are asked to assume increased responsibility for students from nursery school or kindergarten through adulthood.

Predictions that teachers and children would plan their own use of time with classes of no more than twenty-five pupils were not found to be generally true. Neither was it found that "the emphasis on marks, promotions, and lines of demarcation between school grades" had vanished. Achievement in academic areas is still viewed as important. The dominance of the community elementary school has been weakened by bussing for integration purposes and by the closing of schools due to the declining birth rates.

Persons filling out the questionnaire were asked to add any statements which they felt were important in describing education in 1976 but which were missing from the list of predictive statements in each area. Civil rights issues, desegregation, bilingual education, and affirmative action were mentioned as new areas of major concern. It was also noted that state and federal governments exercise increasing control and frequently mandate programs without adequate funding. Educational units are becoming larger and there are fewer administrators.

A trend toward specialization in administration was pointed out and several stated that the business management function is now frequently separated from the function of educational leadership. A new style of leadership is demanded as negotiations and contracts are more common; teacher advisory groups, parents, and the public are more involved in decision making; and there is a general emphasis on the "politics of education." One superintendent stated, "Administrators need a law degree to survive."

The short tenure of superintendents was noted, and one wrote, "The financial situation causes redefinition of role and the re-establishment of priorities, the first being survival." Another stated, "Administrators are demeaned and suspect, which is a national syndrome."

Despite the awareness of such problems, the general tone of the responses was optimistic.

## Teachers and Teaching Methodology

The respondents confirmed that diagnostic instruments are used for spotting students' shortcomings and specialists are often available for consultation when teachers need help.

Teachers generally have tenure and other security measures, but the predicted decline in enrollments and consequent decrease in teaching positions have become realities.

The respondents were not so confident that predictions about the adequacy of teacher preparation and classroom performance had been fulfilled. The lowest rating in this section was given to the statement, "Teaching will become an increasingly respected profession."

Comments indicated that teachers are better trained than in the past, they are more specialized, and they do a better job of meeting individual needs of students. Mention was made of team teaching, use of criterion-referenced tests, behavioral objectives, and alternative educational programs. "Methods and expectations have been adapted to accommodate low achieving students," but "in general, high ability students must find their own challenges."

"Teachers need better training in teaching the basics of reading and math" and more staff development opportunities and incentives are needed for "experienced senior teachers."

A number of comments related to negotiations. "Negotiation has greatly altered the image of the teacher." "Teachers are more militant." "Focus on child is lost in teacher power struggle." "Unionism, negotiated contracts, strikes, teacher layoffs, no jobs for new teachers."

## Curriculum

The most striking feature of the present curriculum was found, in fact, to be its diversity. Some of this has been brought about by minority interest groups wanting their viewpoints represented. School-work experience programs for credit, with the school providing coordinator-supervisors of opportunities in the community, are also now widespread.

There is current emphasis on intelligent consumption of commodities, and instructional programs are also concerned with community problems. Curriculum revision tends to be in the direction of practical utilitarian courses, including provisions for students whose needs cannot be met in traditional programs, making it possible for nearly everyone to obtain a high school diploma.

School citizenship, science, and the basic skills are *not* felt to be receiving undue emphasis. On the other hand, there is no perceived trend toward extreme permissiveness or elimination of the hierarchy of educational values.

Comments related to the cross-currents present in current curriculum movements. "A highly fragmented high school curriculum results from attempts to meet all interests." "More emphasis is being given to vocational and career education." "Back to Basics" movement at all levels." "Special disadvantaged programs of many kinds." "More time is spent in how to learn and unlearn." "There is a lack of K-12 articulation." One respondent noted, "Adults, uneasy with change, search for earlier times and quieter tones."

## Special Education, Guidance Services, Student Services

Discipline is recognized as a major problem by administrators as well as by other groups who have been surveyed.

Schools take great care to preserve the health of pupils, to remedy their physical defects, and to diminish the number of drop-outs.

Guidance services are extensive and encourage the development of special interests and aptitudes. Greater provision has been made for those at the extremes of intelligence scales. Many special interests are accommodated by extensive extra-curricular activity programs.

In many schools there are ungraded classes to aid the handicapped with civic and vocational training to fit their mental capacity.

To some extent maladjustments and personal difficulties are detected and dealt with before students graduate.

Predictions that extensive guidance services will be provided for out-of-school youth have not been widely achieved.

There has been a substantial growth in Special Education as a result of "education for all" legislation mandating programs and the provision of state and federal funding. One superintendent was concerned that "state requirements for special education will exceed the ability of schools to finance them."

The trend to provide guidance services continues in elementary as well as secondary schools despite "role controversies." In some systems guidance services are having difficulty holding the gains made under the 1958 National Defense Education Act.

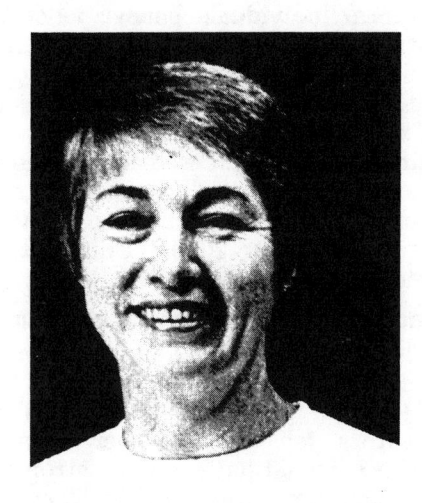

Betty Dillon and Ralph Wright report that many school administrators see their role changing from that of leader to mediator in the future as teachers unionize and the community demands a greater voice in local education policy.

## Physical Facilities, Materials and Equipment

There seems to be general consensus that schools do adapt modern technology to educational use, but books continue to be the primary source of information.

Respondents did not agree that "adequate supplies of every kind" are available.

Administrators surveyed pointed out that modern schools are designed to meet the needs of students and are planned for multi-media teaching. "Open space schools" and "carpeted classrooms" are mentioned. "Costs are skyrocketing."

"Programs of remodeling or replacement are slowed down or stalled by financial problems." "Tighter budgets leave problems of maintenance and updating of equipment."

In some communities there are problems of "excess space and school closures." "Closure of schools has cost many superintendents a job."

"Learning Resource Centers are commonplace, using both print and non-print materials." There is "community criticism from ethnic, sexist, or moralistic viewpoints." "Computers enhance services to students."

## School and Community

Respondents generally agreed that schools face conflicting charges by both radical and conservative elements. They note that schools are developing a high degree of cooperation with other agencies engaged in education-related work.

The respondents were not nearly so confident that "teachers will acquire more expertise in interpretation of the school to its community."

"The school and community are merging" summarizes many of the statements of the respondents. Typical comments were, "Schools are more community-centered." "The school has become a community center. The community is more involved in school affairs and demands a part in developing policies and procedures." "Parent and community involvement in decision-making includes student and faculty personnel matters."

Some statements were not so positive. "Pressure groups have power to disrupt the schools." "Issue of civil rights vs. neighborhood control." "Communities increasingly resist the local financing requirement." "School boards need more expertise in school-community relationships." "The tax revolt and accountability have led to community involvement." "Neighborhood school concept disappearing." "Larger schools result in loss of community feeling with school at its center."

"School administrators have had to be responsible for and handle most public relations activities of the schools."

## Conclusion

Although fragmentary records have been kept of past predictions and their outcomes, and the art of predicting is not very sophisticated even today, it is interesting to note that many of the selected statements were quite correct. It may be that such concerns as fiscal pressures and confusion about who should be responsible for the schools will always be with us and could be predicted perennially, but there appears to have been some sensitive forecasting in items related to minority demands, variety of course offerings, work experience, and concern for discipline. One could hardly find a more "on target" way to express the current situation than that found in one of the 1942 sources which forecast that "schools will have to face charges of radical elements that the schools and teachers are extremely conservative, and conservative elements that the same school and teachers are extremely radical."[2]

## Predictions for the Year 2000

Finally, those educators involved in the survey were asked to make their own predictions about what schools and schooling would be like in the year 2000. Perhaps significantly, several of those responding to the survey failed to complete the predictive section. The responses of those who did might best be classified as conservative but optimistic. Following is a summary of their predictions in each of the categories identified.

## Organization and Administration

The current emphasis on efficient management, better business practices, and accountability through such processes as "management by objectives" will continue. Associated with this will be a change in role for the chief administrator. There will be fewer administrators, and they will acquire better skills for working collaboratively with a variety of groups to include: the administrative team, teachers (who will acquire progressively more control through the negotiation process), and parents.

Typical comments: "It will be more difficult to act in a leadership role. Rather, the administrator will find himself a mediator." "The superintendent will head an administrator-teacher team and run the school through negotiation." A more specific description of the anticipated sophistication of the administrative role was "organizational diagnostician whose responsibility will be to better coordinate and evaluate personnel and procure needed resources."

A concomitant of the changing role of the administrator was reflected in several predictions that administrator preparation courses would include more behavioral science, organizational development, and interpersonal skills. Several of those polled anticipate some form of demonstrated competency check for administrators.

Governing units will become larger, in the opinion of several respondents, with the state more frequently becoming the central unit. Perhaps in concert with this, a number of those surveyed indicated that they believe the role of the present board of education will change. One said, "Unless school boards change themselves or their governance structure, they will die of their inability to function." One educator suggested that board members might even be selected for their special expertise, such as in child development. Another predicted that boards of education would become less and less effective as teacher unions become more powerful— and objective supporters of quality education might not choose to be involved as board members.

Several individuals believe federal funding will continue to increase, with accompanying direction from outside the immediate locality. This seems to be in opposition to several comments that local control would become stronger.

Since educators are well-acquainted with historian Arnold Toynbee's "rally-rout-rally" notion,[3] it is not surprising that one individual surveyed predicted that by the year 2000, "Education will have returned to the days of 'The Little Red Schoolhouse'."

## Teachers and Teaching Methodology

The changing role of administrators and boards of education particularly as related to teachers was reflected in the comments in this section. Many educators felt that teacher organizations, and teachers, would have a much stronger voice in the year 2000 than they do now. They anticipate that teachers will be strongly involved in decision-making at all levels, particularly in matters which affect them directly, such as inservice training.

Many of the respondents anticipate a much more professional, competent teaching staff to have emerged by the turn of the century. They expect that teachers will be capable of effectively diagnosing and dealing with even severe learning problems. They expect instructional staff members to have a variety of alternatives from which to choose, and they expect classes to be "more stringent, academic, scholarly, but tempered by humanistic treatment of children." Many references were made to requirements of demonstrated competency for teaching assignments, and the necessity for prolonged preservice training to prepare incoming staff members for the more scientific approach to teaching and learning which will be required.

The most commonly mentioned methodology change foreseen was a vastly expanded and refined use of the computer and related technology for the storage and retrieval of information needed to plan for individual learning needs. Throughout the predictions, the word "individual" or "individualized" was repeated many times.

Two very contrasting points of view were expressed in two comments, one of which was: "Teaching methodologies of 1976 will still be used in 2000." The other suggests that "teachers will be replaced by mechanical, chemical means of learning."

## Curriculum

The single most commonly mentioned item in this category was a form of the "school without walls" concept. This was expressed through many comments about work-study; credit for field work; education in the community; and relevant, practical "hands-on" experiences. The idea was further expanded in the section on facilities where many administrators mentioned the change in school facilities which will result from holding school in other than the traditional manner.

It was evident that these educators still expect the basic skills to be very important in the year 2000, but in an individualized format and with a differentiated curriculum, some of which will be self-taught or mediated. One focus appeared to be unique—that of "survival skills needed for an alien environment." Areas of emphasis listed, which are other than the traditional basics, were: consumerism, ecology, conservation, technology, evaluation of media, job retraining, inter-personal relationships.

### Special Education

"Clearly the most active area for the next quarter century." Again, the group indicated that there will be a much more sophisticated means of diagnosing learning needs at the turn of the century, and meeting those needs. One said, "All children with special needs will receive adequate attention (very comprehensive). Schools will accept their responsibility for every human being regardless of potential or lack of it for learning." The group expects the present move toward integration or "mainstreaming" to continue except where there are extenuating circumstances.

The one area mentioned by nearly every respondent was the area of the gifted. Almost universally, they feel that this will be an area of strong emphasis throughout the next 20 years. Many comments were made about a continued proliferation of services for more and more specific learning problems as they are identified.

One respondent optimistically predicted an end to the need for special provisions for the abnormal or retarded. He said, "Genetics and activities performed by the medical team attending the birth will take care of most of these problems at or before birth."

### Guidance Services

There was a reasonable consensus that guidance services as they are now delivered by counselors will not exist in the year 2000 or that their function will have changed. "Guidance services as we know them will disappear—emphasis will shift to individualized services, provided by all community members through a community service bureau. In-school guidance will be provided by teachers or other members of the instructional team."

It was predicted that guidance services will be sophisticated, and individualized. Teachers will be the major counselors, supported by a vast array of resources from within the entire community. These consultative services will assist with behavior difficulties, classroom management, specific learning diagnosis and prescription, and will draw on a coalition of community agencies, private consultants, or research organizations for help with problems which are beyond the scope of the school.

### Student Services

Student information systems will become more comprehensive and useful in terms of placement, matching of appropriate learning environments and/or matching of teachers and students. More and more specialized personnel will be added. There will be individual tailoring of educational programs to fit all students—college bound, non-college bound, etc., by determining what students need to know or be able to do to accomplish their goals.

### Physical Facilities, Materials, and Equipment

In the year 2000, much more learning will take place in areas other than formal "school buildings" than it does today, say those surveyed. Particularly, learning will take place in the community and at home—with computer, TV, and other electronic assistance. One respondent suggested "There may be no central learning place for many, other than an office to which to report occasionally." Another makes the projection that "Fifty percent of the students will have education offered in non-traditional facilities located apart from larger schools."

Even where school buildings are designated for that purpose, the respondents predict the facilities will be somewhat different. "Large elaborate plants will become superfluous." "Beyond elementary level, school will be much more community-based, with fewer of the 'palace-factory' type institutions." "There will be less space per classroom, more space for group meetings, libraries; less open space, less carpeted areas, less air-conditioning, more solar heat, less 'fancy' buildings with 'vandalism-prone' areas."

Flexibility appears to be a commonly projected need. "Schools will not be permanent structures, as we know them today. Rather, there will be a small permanent facility and satellites which can meet the needs of peak populations and be moved to serve new needs." Several mentioned a campus-like approach with several module buildings which could be moved as needed and divided or united to accommodate changing group sizes and needs.

One individual chose to predict that the American yen for "bigger and better" will not have been phased out by 2000, however. "Facilities, materials, and equipment will continue to improve because American people equate up-to-date facilities and equipment with effective learning more frequently than they do good teaching."

### School and Community

Predictions in this area centered around the development of a strong cooperative relationship between the school and community. A majority of the comments dealt not only with today's K-12 target population, the need for community input, and use of the community as a resource, but also with use of the school by the *total* population, from "three to ninety years old." Several spoke of making the school a year-round, 24-hour facility. One implied that a "community educator" might replace the current school administrator in meeting the needs of a much broader audience. Another proposed that "local school councils" might replace many of the functions of district school boards.

## Conclusion

At least in part, schools today in the United States are similar to what they were predicted to be in some publications of 20, 30 and even 40 years ago. Many educators in this study say that schools have not changed materially over that period of time and that they are not likely to change very much in the future. Others say that if the schools do not change, they will be unable to survive—and that current unrest and dissatisfaction is evidence of their dysfunctional nature.

No one has yet resolved to the satisfaction of all the philosophical question of whether the task of schools is to maintain the societal status quo or to improve it. Perhaps they are to do some of both. At any rate, 69 thoughtful educators, chosen for their acknowledged leadership, have shared their observations through this study, clearly indicating their quiet optimism—tempered with realism. They do not anticipate radical change, but they continue to expect emphasis on maximum achievement for each student, in a flexible environment which is responsive to individual needs and the needs of society.

They do foresee many of their roles changing to acquire a more collaborative management style, and although the scene may be somewhat disquieting to preview, their comments indicate that these particular administrators view the future with neither alarm nor pessimism. In the words of one superintendent, "All in all, you couldn't ask for a better vocation. The times are exciting and interesting." No doubt that will still be true in 2000.

* * *

## NOTES

1. "Future Trends in Education," *The Elementary School Journal*, 1939, 4, p. 96.
2. What is Ahead in Education?, *The Phi Delta Kappan*, 1942, 24, (5) pp. 219-220.
3. R.F. Butts, "Arnold J. Toynbee's Philosophy of History," *Educational Theory*, Winter, 1972, pp. 3-25.

Betty Dillon is Director of Staff Development for the Lincoln, Nebraska, public school system.
Ralph Wright is the Director of Secondary Education in Rochester, Minnesota.

* * *

## Sources of Predictions Cited In Questionnaire

Dale, Edgar. "Schools Look Ahead." *The Texas Outlook*, 1944 28 (9), 19-20.

Dove, C.J. "This is my idea of Tomorrow's School." *The Nation's Schools*, 1943, 31 (5), 44.

Edmonson, J.B. "What is Ahead in Education?." *The Phi Delta Kappan*, 1942, 24 (5), 219-220.

French, W. "Characteristics of a Secondary School Meeting the Needs of Youth." *The National Society for the Study of Education Yearbook*, 52 (Part 1), 1953.

Goldberg, H. "Motion Pictures in Schools." *Ladies Home Journal*, 1931, 48, 31, 135.

McHale, K. (ed.), "Future Possibilities in Liberal Arts Education: Some Expert Opinions." *The National Society for the Study of Education Yearbook*, 31 (Part 2), 1932.

Nesbitt, M. "The Elementary School of Tomorrow." *Educational Leadership*, 1955, 12 (4), 217-226.

Ogburn, W. "Future Trends in Education." *The Elementary School Journal*, 1939, 4, 95-105.

Pelton, F.M. "Predictions on the Future of Inventions and Changing Social Customs, and Their Effect on Education," *The Clearing House*, 1938, 13(3), 131-134.

Percival, W.P. "A Guide to Trends in Education." *The Dalhousie Review*, 1955, 34, 363-367.

Tow, S. *The Prospect Before Us.* London: Marston & Co., Inc., 1948.

Wells, H.G. *Anticipations of the Reaction of Mechanical and Scientific Progress Upon Human Life and Thought.* New York: Harper & Bros., 1901.

Wrightstone, J.W., & Meister, M. *Looking Ahead in Education.* Boston: Ginn & Co., 1945.

# Looking at the Future in Education

**by Dwight W. Allen and Jake Plante**

Recent public school studies in Paterson, New Jersey and New Haven, Connecticut indicate that students in school today have a greater interest in studying the future than in any other academic subject—yet teachers are generally ill-equipped to meet this dominant need. Few educators seem to have examined how children's conceptualization of the future affects their intellectual and emotional development.

The formal study of the future is regarded by most public school educators to be of minor importance to the elementary and secondary curriculum—at most an interesting sidelight or change of pace from the so-called basics. Yet the experience of many educators has provided more than a little empirical evidence to support the view that future time perspective and images of the future are vital factors of personality and behavioral development.

Two recent educational studies in Paterson, New Jersey and New Haven, Connecticut underscore the value of future-oriented curriculum and indicate that there is a much broader basis for studying the future than simply preparing students for a changing world. In addition to the knowledge gained from an intentional study of emerging issues and possibilities, "the future" may be the *most desired* subject of students in public schools today. In addition, a strong relationship appears to exist between students' attitudes about the future and their levels of self-esteem and social responsibility. This three-fold combination of academic learning value, student interest and major psychological concomitants suggests that an opportunity exists in education to infuse new life into our public schools, particularly those in our urban areas—by developing a curriculum to study the future.

## Interest in Studying the Future

A comprehensive educational testing program was conducted recently in the Paterson, New Jersey School System.[1] A major purpose of the program was to determine the degree to which various academic subjects were considered by students to be important content areas. The Paterson Public School System is urban, multi-racial and ranks lowest in the State on 10th grade student reading achievement scores. In many ways, Paterson is a perfect example of the urban school environment which demands change.

The study sample included over 2,000 students from 34 intermediate schools (grades 5-8) and 400 students from two high schools (grades 9-12). Out of a total of 20 academic subjects tested, "the future" was judged by both age groups to be the *most important* subject for them to study.

A breakdown of the results shows that 75% of the intermediate students stated that studying the future was "very important," 17% felt it was "important," 6% said it was "somewhat important," and only 2% felt it was "not important at all." Figures for high school students were nearly identical: 77%, 16%, 6%, and 1% respectively. The next highest ranked subjects were math with "very important" ratings of 74% by middle schoolers and 69% by high schoolers and reading with 65% and 63% respectively. Singularly high ratings were given to subjects of "health" by intermediate school students and "English" by high school students. Not even sex education could outrank students' anked interest in the future! Sex education's "very important" ratings placed it sixth among intermediate school students with 56% and fifth among high school students with 44%. Other lower rated subjects included science, social studies, art, music, physical education, foreign languages, language arts, and city problems. Finally, the top ratings remained unchanged when analyzed on the combined basis of "very important" and "important" scores (as well as on the basis of factors of sex, age and ethnic background).

The findings in Paterson were in many ways surprising. First, it had not been predicted that "the future" would be among the top five or so subjects, let alone the highest rated subject. Secondly, future studies received a consistently high rating among both intermediate and high school students. And, most importantly perhaps, the high ratings suggest that in a school system such as Paterson where many students may need added motivation to increase their learning, as well as the development of a broad interest in education, there is a subject which does appeal to a vast majority of students. In other words, studying the future appears to produce a genuine "spark" of intellectual curiosity among students in Paterson that could lead to higher aspirations and greater academic achievement.

## Emerging Issues

Will Rogers once remarked that "things ain't the way they used to be and probably never was." Because history, like all things, changes with time and is subject to interpretation, our knowledge of it should be used as a reference for decision-making rather than as a script. To the degree that we need to understand the historical antecedents of issues and events, we must also anticipate their widespread effects over an extended period of time. A good decision, then, involves a thorough consideration of both the past and the future.

Results of the Paterson School Survey suggest that many students have a strong natural desire to learn more about the future. They may be interested in the prospects for medicine and health care,

---

### "Not even sex education could outrank students' naked interest in the future!"

---

energy, transportation, work, marriage, and the family. Or, they may want to understand more about the various tools for studying the future, for example: trend forecasting, impact assessment, and needs analysis. As it is, many public schools concentrate heavily on the historical aspects of current subjects without providing an even balance of future-oriented inquiry. Students spend their time, for example, learning the American chronology of Washington crossing the Delaware, the War between the States and Roosevelt's "New Deal" to end the Great Depression. And invariably, the school term ends somewhere between World War II and Watergate leaving students to figure out for themselves what it all means for the future. Is it any wonder why many students cannot conceive of the future as something other than the past?

One possible solution to the greater need many children have to investigate the future is to offer a specific course on emerging issues. However, the ultimate goal is not to give equal time to emerging issues but to integrate knowledge about the past, the present and the future. And this goal can be accomplished in many ways—through an appropriate study of history, current affairs, the future, science, math or any other field of study.

Why isn't there more educational emphasis on emerging issues today when the rapidity of change is outpacing students' ability to adjust to it? Many educators shy away from the presentation of emerging issues because they may seem too complex, too value-laden or because the evaluation of future-oriented thinking may appear too difficult. In addition, few educators have the proper resources to prepare an effective curriculum on the future. This situation is being addressed, in part, through the development of new future-oriented pre-service and in-service teacher training programs and the greater availability of such programs. These training programs are intended to reduce some of the inadequacies related to teaching the future in school and to provide teachers with the methods and materials needed to develop effective presentations of emerging issues. As a result, these teachers are better equipped to help students understand and explore the possibilities for the future as well as the possibilities for today.

## The Psychology of Anticipation

It is often stated that the primary purpose of future-oriented curricula is to prepare students for their future lives. However, because of our preoccupation with the "objective future" or what "it" is we think students should be preparing for, we have until recently been remiss in our examination of future cognition and its relationship to personality and behavior. By turning the mirror of time around, images of the future can offer us major new insights into the here and now. Therefore, another important reason for teaching the future is to help students understand how their views about tomorrow affect their present feelings and attitudes.

For many years, images of the future were not judged to be a legitimate area for educational and psychological research. Not until 1960, when Melvin Wallace and Albert Rabin published a comprehensive review and analysis of literature in the field of time perspective, did the investigation of future attitudes gain general acceptance among educators.[2] Today, there is a growing body of research to indicate that individual attitudes about the future are closely related to social and psychological development. Significant variations in future time perspective have been found on the basis of sociological factors such as: age, sex, socio-economic status, ethnic background and criminal delinquency, as well as major aspects of mental health.[3]

Major improvements have been made in the measurement of future time perspective. For instance, we now know that time perspective embodies several major dimensions: the extension of the time horizon; the dominance of the past, the present or the future; the integration of these time periods; and the degree of optimism or pessimism.

Also, images of the future can be analyzed according to factors such as: quantity, complexity, realism, novelty and diversity. There remains little question today that the issue of "future orientation or the lack of it" is greatly oversimplified.

Of special interest is another dimension of future time perspective called the "active and reactive" domain. It is defined as the degree to which someone is future-dominant and believes that human effort and personal decision-making can have a decisive effect on the course of events, many of which are possible (active), versus the degree to which a person is present-dominant and believes that the future will be determined primarily by factors of fate and chance (reactive). In a recently completed study involving over 400 public high school students from urban and suburban schools from New Haven, Connecticut and Westfield, Massachusetts, significant relationships were discovered between an active orientation toward the future and higher levels of both self-esteem and social responsibility.[4] These relationships were also found when urban and suburban test scores were analyzed separately. In addition, suburban students were discovered to be significantly more active oriented than their urban counterparts. The findings suggest that increased active orientation toward the future can help to reinforce and strengthen self-esteem as well as responsible behavior toward others. They also suggest that many students, particularly those in our urban schools, seriously underestimate the degree to which they can influence future events. It is apparent, therefore, that many students could derive great benefit from an educational program designed to expand their knowledge of emerging issues, develop open attitudes about future possibilities and increase their sense of choice, and of control over events in their environment.

**Shaping the Future**

Conceptualization of the future is an integral part of the psychological profile. John Kennedy illustrated this once when, following trouble with his back, he remarked that he could stand any kind and any amount of pain, provided he knew that it would end. As Kennedy implied, the power of our image of the future may be of far greater importance than we suspect. Indeed, our images of the future may influence our present experience even when objective conditions in our environment do not warrant such experience.

The purpose of teaching the future is to diagnose where students are, where they want to be, and then provide them with the tools to get there. Also, teachers must help to make future possibilities *more real* for students.[5] Because the value of information about the future is equivalent to its applicability to our present set of circumstances and choices, images of the future must possess realism and they must be realizable. For instance, if a youngster wanted to become a doctor it would be important first to explore how the health profession and the role of the doctor are likely to change in the years ahead including their relationship to other areas of society. Secondly, he or she would need to identify a model, thereby confirming its integrity as a future possibility (perhaps by means of a field trip to the hospital). Finally, it would be necessary to develop a step-by-step understanding of how this goal can be realized. The youngster then has an appropriate idea of where to begin—with a specialized reading, volunteer service or whatever. By establishing a link between where a child is and where he or she hopes to be, hopes and expectations which are based on emotional responses can be transformed into a useful blueprint for personal choice and planning.

Teachers who seek to interest their students in the future should at the same time seek to awaken students to their abilities to play an active role in their changing environment. In the process of learning how their actions produce effects, positive or otherwise, students can become more conscious of the relationships between thought, behavior and consequence as well as how they can make greater use of their energies. They can also acquire a better understanding of "outside forces" which exert in-

---

## "The purpose of teaching the future is to diagnose where students are, where they want to be, and then provide them with the tools to get there."

---

fluence over them and their range of choices. Indeed, only by learning what these forces are and how they affect them will students become aware of their own abilities to shape events.

It is important to recognize that who we are, what we do, and what happens to us are, in many ways that we may not understand, our choice. Isabel Hickey wrote that "character is destiny—we change our destiny by changing our attitudes and patterns of behavior."[6] In other words, we change our future by changing who we are today. Moreover, by clarifying our choices, we will increase our ability to influence the future, not simply survive it.

An illustration of how the *raison d'etre* of education is becoming increasingly defensive is found in the popular idiom of the seventies, "coping"—that is, adjusting oneself to a stressful situation or turbulent environment. The term might be used to describe the situation of someone, for instance, who is attempting to control a car at high speed following the blow out of a tire. The aim is to make the best out of a bad situation.

In reference to the future, coping implies that events are unforeseeable, uncontrollable and more successfully dealt with by a strategy of caution and reaction. Creativity and risk-taking are minimized. In contrast, a major objective of future studies is to help students to see that, however complex, the future is understandable and can be influenced.

Thus, there are times when students might do better to heed the old Latin aphorism, "*audentes fortuna juvat,*" or "fortune favors the bold."[7] The inability of some students to understand this is likely to reinforce a negative cycle of self-fulfilling prophecy in their lives. Consequently, schools today must reaffirm their commitment to helping students gain greater mastery over their present lives by understanding their past and anticipating their future, not simply coping with their present environment.

There are several important influences which an intentional study of the future can have on greater learning and personal development:

**Responsibility.** Awareness of the future is essential to the development of ethical and responsible behavior. As John Platt remarked, "Morality depends upon foresight." Even though individuals may accept social norms of helping and fellowship, their behavior may not be consistent unless they are aware of the consequences of their actions. The unwillingness or inability of some people to think ahead and anticipate the effects of their behavior may also help to explain why major discrepencies often exist between their words and deeds or intended and actual behaviors.

Exploring the possibilities for the future allows students to see how they can influence the future, thereby helping them to take greater responsibility for their actions which contribute to making the future. Also, in learning to examine the long-term impact and side-effects of social occurrences, students learn to examine their own actions more closely, resulting in greater sensitivity to those around them and the development of more positive social relationships.

**An Open Mind.** When students first begin to study the future they often do so with strong preconceptions or "present baggage." A systematic investigation of alternatives and options for the future can show students how to "leave their baggage behind" and to develop a more open view of future possibilities as well as present ones.

An open attitude about the future is essential to the development of a strong imagination, a diverse set of interests and a willingness to experiment with new ideas—important qualities of good planning and forecasting. There are many famous examples in history of how people failed to see what was about to happen because there was, in the words of Arthur C. Clarke, "a failure of nerve or imagination."[8] For example, famed surgeon Alfred Velpeau wrote in 1839 that "the abolishment of pain in surgery is a chimera. It is absurd to go on seeking it today. 'Knife and pain' are two words in surgery that must forever be associated in the consciousness of the patient."[9] Or Vannevar Bush, who as president of the Carnegie Institution of Washington in 1945 told President Truman that "the (atomic) bomb will never go off, and I speak as an expert in explosives."[10]

Students who learn to work with the concept of an open future should also gain greater appreciation of the need for self-motivation. It has been said that there are two types of students—those who are self-starters and those who aren't. In light of the need for more students to become self-starters, an open view of the future enables students to see the ways in which greater personal initiative can make important differences in the outcome of events.

**Optimism and Aspirations.** As the old saying goes, "the good guys don't always win." It is necessary therefore that students obtain greater insight into the major problems as well as the major opportunities of our time. A hard look at possible undesirable events is an essential part of objective future analysis. However, while there may be 1,001 ways for society to destroy itself, it is paradoxical that students will generally depart from a class on emerging issues with a more optimistic social outlook than when they began. The reason for increased optimism is that greater information and knowledge about the future helps people to overcome the tyranny of the unknown. If they know the obstacles that face them, they will have greater confidence and self-assurance. Moreover, a future studies class often serves as something of a support group for the future.

It should be noted that increased optimism can be a sign of greater realism and not that one is hiding from problems and issues. Indeed, research has shown that greater optimism is related to a broader and more integrated view of the future, more extensive planning and higher academic achievement[11]—characteristics which involve a good sense of the practical.

How many students today do not aspire very high because they labor under a present-bound fatalism regarding society's chances for success in the coming years? How many children perform below their natural abilities because they lack a broad, positive set of personal images for the future? It is clear that increased knowledge of emerging issues can help students to build a more hopeful social outlook, raise their aspirations to meet their real potential, and assume greater command of their lives.

**Concept Building.** A study of the future can also introduce students to many universal concepts which have relevance to their own personal experience. For example, concerning the role of cooperation, today's trend toward more complex social interrelationships tends to negate the notion of society as a "zero-sum game" in which those who benefit do so in direct proportion to the losses of others. There is a growing awareness that all parts

> "Research has shown that greater optimism is related to a broader and more integrated view of the future, more extensive planning and higher academic achievement."

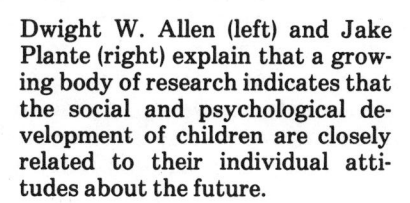

Dwight W. Allen (left) and Jake Plante (right) explain that a growing body of research indicates that the social and psychological development of children are closely related to their individual attitudes about the future.

of society, like those in any living organism, must function cooperatively in order for each to grow. Furthermore, the psychology of scarcity is less prevalent today because we are discovering vital new ways to do "more with less."[12] We are beginning to realize, therefore, that many of today's shortages are artificial and that our resources are unlimited if we use them wisely and prudently.

As a society, we are limited more by a conceptual scarcity than an economic one. Our need for new conceptual growth is illustrated in the following comparison: travelling by car offers a number of distinct advantages to walking. A Volkswagen, priced at $4,000 provides the same basic service, however, as a $40,000 Mercedes. Therefore, the more significant factor is the $4,000 difference between walking and driving, not the $36,000 for a more luxurious ride. Yet, how many people think that in order to make driving worthwhile they need a Mercedes? Consequently, education must deal more powerfully with conceptual growth and the real choices and opportunities we have for development. Schools must become more than a source of information, they must become a source of wisdom. As T.S. Eliot asked, "Where is the wisdom we have lost in knowledge? Where is the knowledge we have lost in information?"[13]

**Appreciation of Diversity and Differences** Finally, exploring the many possibilities for the future enables students to develop a better understanding of multi-cultural and multi-racial perspectives as well as a deeper appreciation of basic individual differences. Cultural stereotypes, which result from a tendency to extrapolate personal relationships into future ones, are broken down in the process of exploring future occupations, demography and other subjects. Studying human differences and diversity in a future-oriented context can be a nonthreatening and highly creative means for helping students to eliminate prejudices they may feel toward others simply because they are different. While learning about the favorable aspects of difference and diversity, students also learn how to cultivate and choose from among today's growing number of lifestyles, fashions and products. This involves an examination of the tremendous "information and sensory overload" in our society and how to select information which has a truly fundamental and lasting (i.e., future) value.

Because of changes which are likely to occur in the years ahead, students studying the future learn to handle surprise and incongruity better. Respect is given to the humble notion that events can not always be anticipated. For example, it has been reported that the Alaskan pipeline has unexpectedly produced increased breeding of caribou due to warmer temperatures near the pipeline. In addition, because no possibility is inevitable, students learn to work amidst ambiguity thereby increasing the likelihood of serendipity or accidental discovery. The result, finally, is a set of more flexible and versatile thinking skills which help students to succeed in uncovering third and fourth alternatives to seemingly dichotomous "either-or" situations as well as in anticipating broader consequences and side-effects.

## Futurizing Education

Children born this year will be in the college graduating class of the year 2000. It is evident that many significant changes will occur between now and the end of the century—changes more dramatic perhaps than those which have occurred in the 21 years since Sputnik launched us into the space age. We must therefore begin to anticipate the effects which these changes will have on the ability of schools to provide effective instructional programs.

Today, the most prominent issue in education is the concern with low achievement scores in the 3R's and what can be done to raise them. From local communities to the Federal government, there is insistence that public education get "back to the basics." For some, this means a fundamental return to the past. For others, it means that basic skills such as reading and writing must receive renewed and considerably greater emphasis in the classroom.

From a future-oriented standpoint, reading and writing are and will continue to be essential social skills. However, it is also important to remember that many school children appear to lack vital decision-making skills such as the ability to think of alternatives, set realistic goals, plan a work schedule and anticipate problems. These deficiencies appear linked to the growing symptoms of the times: a faster rate of change and lack of cultural signposts. Yet the fact remains that individuals are forced to make more general and major life decisions now than ever before. Consequently, it is imperative that we design educational programs to help students to acquire more proficient decision-making skills.

In addition to program development, educators and parents alike must become more sensitive to how conceptualization of the future affects a child's attitudes and emotions. There are too many confused "turned-off" students in school today who want and need greater direction and hope for tomorrow. Since one important way this can be accomplished in a school environment is through a stronger interest in a subject, the students of Paterson, New Jersey may be telling us something very important. Indeed, they may be far ahead of their professional mentors!

In its many variations, a formal study of the future is a way for students to obtain a better understanding of emerging issues and their expected short and long-term effects. In turn, it serves as a "window" on the present enabling students to clarify their personal values, to establish a realistic set of goals and to chart a course of study that they are able to understand for both its present and future value.

How is "the future" introduced into the classroom? There are two basic approaches: 1) by incorporating a study of the future into existing school subjects, or 2) by developing specific instruction on the future. Both approaches are valid, though each has its own characteristic strengths and weaknesses. For instance, an independent study of the future tends to be a more effective means of learning process-oriented skills such as brainstorming, cross-impact analysis and forecasting but generally provides a less detailed analysis of any one issue.

## The Future of the Future

The vision for education is severely limited today. As a result, many schools are selling their students' futures short. Their curriculum is unable to reach and stimulate children, whose low expectations and underutilized potential blocks further interest in learning as well as their ability to grow in new ways. However important, "back to the basics" movements may close off our options for helping students to build richer and more spirited dreams. Therefore, a new vision for education is needed that will help us direct learning toward the important frontiers of the future. Indeed, because of the rapid pace of change, our survival as a society demands it.

As educators, we must begin to develop new curriculums in the area of emerging issues. These new resources will help us to evaluate more effectively the ways in which future-oriented thinking affects the social and psychological development of children. Along with curriculum, new methods are needed to test time perspective and foresight ability—all of which need to be incorporated more readily into the learning programs of our elementary and secondary schools. There must also be greater emphasis on creating educational environments which encourage experimentation with information and theories about the future as well as institutional changes that allow students greater flexibility in designing their educational program both in school and in the field.

We are now beginning to understand the pervasive psychological power of images of the future and their importance for learning and achievement. Conceptualization of the future has been proven to be an important indicator of present experience as well as an important predictor of emotional and behavioral development. Most notably perhaps, an open and active view of future possibilities is related to higher self-esteem and greater social responsibility. And, as the findings in Paterson show, there is hope indeed! We do not have to accept the inevitability of school not working for a large majority of students today, especially those in our cities. On the contrary, because students have a broad interest in the future, a curriculum to study the future may well provide combined pre-school opportunities in education to help students learn where they are, dream large dreams of where they want to go and address in an immediate and practical way how to get there.

## Notes

[1] *The 1978 Paterson School Survey*, 1978, Paterson, New Jersey.
[2] Melvin Wallace and Albert Rabin, "Temporal Experience," *Psychological Bulletin*, Vol. 57, 1960: 213-36.
[3] Ibid.
[4] Jake Plante, "A Study of Future Time Perspective and its Relationship to the Self-Esteem and Social Responsibility of High School Students," Doctoral Dissertation, 1977.
[5] Jock McClellan, "What is a Futurist," *Futures Information Interchange Newsletter*, Vol. 3, No. 4, 1975: 1-6.
[6] Isabel M. Hickey, *Astrology: A Cosmic Science* (Bridgeport: Altieri Press, 1970), p. 5.
[7] Max Gunther, *The Luck Factor* (New York: MacMillan Publishing Company, 1977), p. 141.
[8] Arthur C. Clarke, *Profiles of the Future* (New York: Harper and Row Publishers, Inc., 1973), pp. 1-21.
[9] Joseph Martino, "Blunders of Negative Forecasting," *THE FUTURIST*, December, 1968, p. 121.
[10] Martino, *FUTURIST*, p. 121.
[11] John E. Teahan, "Future Time Perspective, Optimism, and Academic Achievement," *Journal of Abnormal and Social Psychology*, Vol. 57, 1958: 379-80.
[12] Hugh Kenner, *Bucky: A Guided Tour of Buckminster Fuller* (New York: William Morrow and Company, Inc., 1973), p. 18.
[13] T.S. Eliot, "The Rock," I, 1934.

\* \* \*

Dwight W. Allen is University Professor of Urban Education at Old Dominion University and Norfolk State College, Norfolk, Virginia. Jake Plante is Senior Energy Planner for Franklin County, Massachusetts.

# Educational Futures: A Reconstructionist Approach

### by Jim Bowman, Chris Dede and Fred Kierstead

Three futurist educators offer their assessment of today's educational process, and suggest one way to revamp outmoded systems to bring them nearer the goal of participatory, life-long learning for all.

Today has become tomorrow... but "tomorrow" has become uncertain, confounding, nearly incomprehensible. With a rush of events that has shaken our faith in governments, friends, enemies, gods, and, ultimately in ourselves, the advent of the future has caught humanity completely unprepared. It has left us guessing rather than choosing. We find ourselves sitting in on a high-stakes game of progressive poker and we do not understand the rules of the house.

America today is witnessing the end of the industrial era and the beginning of a new and uncertain age. Many Americans feel great anxiety about the future, and find that the very foundations of our traditional value system have been eroded. Participatory government has become a matter of minimizing unavoidable loss. The work ethic has become a job ethic, and unemployment continues to rise. Neverending economic expansion no longer seems a realistic goal as the limits to growth become increasingly clear through ecological deterioration, the worldwide population explosion, inflation, energy shortages, depletion of natural resources, and an increase in mental illness. Threatening information has increased at an exponential rate. Problems appear to be multiplying just as the gross national product used to multiply. As a result, society is experiencing increasing racial tension, crime, drug abuse, alienation, and suicide.

Traditionally, the American educational system has served as a rear-view mirror reflecting the established values and objectives of an earlier time. But today, the schools function more as a kaleidoscope—magnifying and distorting multiple expressions of our contemporary crisis-culture. Criticism of education is rampant in the literature of the profession today, but there is little consensus about what is *wanted* from the schools.

When the Russians launched a satellite in 1957, the consensus in America was most evident. Powerfull social forces called upon educators to produce engineers, nuclear scientists, physicists and technicians. At the present time, however, educators are being asked to satisfy far more ambiguous demands couched in such terms as "performance-based education," "competency-based teacher training," and "accountability." How much easier it would be for educators if they were all being told one message such as: "Produce more engineers!" or "Go back to basics!"

Industrial era education has reached a developmental breaking point. We are witnessing the end of "transmissive" schooling, in which a teacher passed along known information and students, seated *en masse*, consumed finite units of knowledge and later competed against each other in regurgitative exercises. Spectatorism, consumption and competition in the classroom are all external reinforcement mechanisms whose effectiveness has been largely based on their parallels to the job market. These mechanisms embodied the industrial,, middle-class ethos of deferred gratification. But as traditional employment patterns have changed, with many job opportunities becoming less available or less appealing, the concept of schooling for deferred gratification has become a dangerous by-product of a system which is obsolete.

The school curriculum—in a word—is history. We have generally interpreted education as history, and believed that the future would be an extrapolation of the past. We assume that if we do a good job today, tomorrow will take care of itself. We are already living on borrowed time.

Certainly every area of activity demands some grounding in "history." One cannot become a writer, scientist or technician without acquiring a store of prerequisite background knowledge (in language, chemistry, etc.) and useful information generally accepted as fact. It is reasonable to assume that in the future such information will be transmitted primarily over closed circuit or public television.

Jim Bowman and Fred Kierstead (left and right, front) discuss Future Program plans with Chris Dede (left behind Bowman) and two colleagues at the University of Houston at Clear Lake City: Cal Cannon, Dean of Human Sciences, and Josephine Sobrino, Program Director in Professional Education.

Photo: Frank Grazzaffi, UH/CLC

American society has entered the age of communications. Lectures on every level and in every field will probably be taped and made available to all interested individuals. We already have the technology to make some 1000 different television programs available to home viewers at any given time. *Sesame Street* is perhaps only the beginning of a revolution at all stages of learning.

Teachers often complain that they are tired of "spoonfeeding" students. Students often reciprocate by complaining about boring lectures. Yet, at the same time, both teachers and students bemoan the loss of interpersonal relationships and the creation of impersonal, mechanistic education. Most taxpayers have already opted for education via the most economical means.

If the primary function of education continues to be transmissive in nature, some teachers will become script writers for the media. Discipline problems, like yellow buses, will disappear. The school itself, as we know it, will disappear.

The telecommunications media may answer the need for transmission of information, but many educational theorists have long proclaimed that education should involve much more than transmission alone. The American philosopher John Dewey, for example, argued that education should be a participatory, social experience.[1] George S. Counts, himself a distinguished educator and author, extended Dewey's work with his own perception of educational institutions as reconstructive sources of societal change.[2] We believe that these needs do exist, and that American education will begin to implement a pragmatic/reconstructive philosophy in the 1980s.

If the primary function of education becomes reconstructive in nature, traditional schools will be superseded by problem-analysis centers where both students and teachers will be active participants in planning and implementing alternative societal futures.

We can imagine a future with multiple educational experiences available to people of all ages. It is possible that state-supported public institutions will be very involved in designing transmissive education through the media. This will be integrated with problem analysis centers. We may evolve a public education system composed of priority centers, community analysis centers, societal analysis centers and international analysis centers.

All centers would be attended on a voluntary basis. They would be available at all hours for individuals of all ages. The priority center would serve the needs of children from birth to approximately age seven, but might also be attended by interested parents. In the future, early childhood education will be as important as college education was during the industrial era.

After sufficient preparation in basics (which might—or might not—be reading, writing and mathematics), individuals could choose to attend community, societal or international problem analysis centers. For example, a person might begin to analyze the problem of crime at the Community Analysis Center, and later increase his or her perspective on crime in a national context by participating at the Societal Analysis Center. This same individual might then return to the Community Analysis Center or go to the International Analysis Center for still further insights into the nature and context of one or more problems. In fact, since most problems are interdisciplinary, an individual's "curriculum" may look like a cross-impact problem matrix and not at all like the traditional "menu" of academic subjects.

The present paralysis in education—with competing goals, competing interest groups, competing scapegoats—is blocking any concerted effort to work toward shared visions. Yet, achieving significant changes in our present educational system will require a massive, concerted effort by many individuals and organizations. It is our hope that the first conference of the World Future Society's Education Section, to be held in Houston, October 20-22, 1978, may provide an opportunity to share and analyze our visions of education in and for the future.

**NOTES**

[1] See for example Dewey's arguments in *Democracy and Education* (New York: The Free Press, 1916).

[2] George S. Counts, *Dare the School Build a New Social Order?* (New York: John Day, 1932).

# RECOMMENDED READINGS
## A SELECTIVE BIBLIOGRAPHY

### World Future Society Publications

Cornish, Edward, ed. *The Future: A Guide to Information Sources.* Revised 2nd edition. Washington, D.C.: World Future Society, 1979. 722 pages. Paperback. $25.00. The revised and expanded second edition of this indispensable guide to the futures field contains even more information than the highly-praised first edition of 1977.

Cornish, Edward, ed. *1999: The World of Tomorrow.* Washington, D.C.: World Future Society, 1978. 160 pages. Paperback. $4.95. This first anthology of articles from THE FUTURIST is divided into four sections: "The Future as History," "The Future as Progress," "The Future as Challenge," and "The Future as Invention."

Cornish, Edward. *The Study of the Future: An Introduction to the Art and Science of Understanding and Shaping Tomorrow's World.* Washington, D.C.: World Future Society, 1977. 320 pages. Paperback. $9.50. A general introduction to futurism and future studies. Chapters discuss the history of the futurist movement, ways to introduce future-oriented thinking into organizations, the philosophical assumptions underlying studies of the future, methods of forecasting, current thinking about what may happen as a result of the current revolutionary changes in human society, etc. The volume also includes detailed descriptions of the lives and thinking of certain prominent futurists and an annotated guide to further reading.

Didsbury, Howard F., ed. *Student Handbook for The Study of the Future.* Washington, D.C.: World Future Society, 1979. 180 pages. Paperback. $5.95. This supplement to *The Study of the Future* is designed to help students develop a basic understanding of the field of futuristics. Much of the material has been "classroom-tested" by students in futures courses at Kean College of New Jersey.

Didsbury, Howard F., ed. *Instructor's Manual for The Study of the Future.* Washington, D.C.: World Future Society, 1979. 24 pages. Paperback. $2.00. A brief complementary volume to the *Student Handbook for The Study of the Future,* containing course outlines, research suggestions, teaching aids, bibliographical additions, and more.

Jennings, Lane, and Sally Cornish, eds. *Education and the Future.* Washington, D.C.: World Future Society, 1980. 120 pages. Paperback. $4.95. Contains selections from THE FUTURIST and the *World Future Society Bulletin* on the future of education. Packed with ideas for the classroom.

Kierstead, Fred, Jim Bowman, and Christopher Dede, eds. *Educational Futures: Sourcebook I.* Washington, D.C.: World Future Society, 1979. 254 pages. Paperback. $5.95. This book contains selected papers from the first conference of the Education Section of the World Future Society, held in Houston, Texas, in October, 1978.

Martin, Marie. *Films on the Future.* Washington, D.C.: World Future Society, 1977. 70 pages. Paperback. $3.00. This is the third revised and expanded version of the film guide first produced in 1971. The films are grouped by major subject areas (Education, Technology, etc.). A brief description of each film is supplemented by information about length, source, and rental costs.

### Other Publications of Interest to Futurist Educators

Armbruster, Frank E. *Our Children's Crippled Future: How American Education Has Failed.* New York: Quadrangle, 1977. 320 pages. Hardbound. $15.00.

Bowman, Jim, Fred Kierstead, Chris Dede, and John Pulliam. *The Far Side of the Future.* Houston, Texas: Educational Futures, 1978. 154 pages. Paperback. $5.95.

Brameld, Theodore. *The Teacher as World Citizen: A Scenario of the 21st Century.* Palm Springs, CA: ETC Publications, 1976. 83 pages. Paperback. $3.95.

Ciba Foundation Symposium 36. *The Future as an Academic Discipline.* New York: Elsevier, 1975. 224 pages. Paperback. $13.50.

Dunstan, Maryjane, and Patricia W. Garlan. *Worlds in the Making.* Englewood Cliffs, NJ: Prentice-Hall, 1970. 370 pages. Paperback. $8.95.

Frymier, Jack R. *A School for Tomorrow.* Berkeley, CA: McCutchan, 1973. 307 pages. Hardbound. $13.65.

Glines, Don E. *Educational Futures I, II, III, and IV.* New York: Anvil Press, 1978-79. Set of four paperbacks. $26.00.

Gross, Ronald. *The Lifelong Learner.* New York: Simon and Schuster, 1977. 190 pages. Paperback. $3.95.

Henley, Stephen P., and James R. Yates. *Futurism in Education: Methodologies.* Berkeley, CA: McCutchan, 1974. 510 pages. Hardbound. $16.00.

Hollister, Bernard C., and Deane C. Thompson. *Grokking the Future: Science Fiction in the Classroom.* NP: Pflaum/Standard, 1973. 168 pages. Paperback. $5.50.

Hostrop, Richard W., ed. *Education . . . Beyond Tomorrow.* Palm Springs, CA: ETC Publications, 1975. 324 pages. Hardbound. $12.95.

Hostrup, Richard W., ed. *Foundations of Futurology in Education.* Palm Springs, CA: ETC Publications, 1973. 248 pages. Hardbound. $10.00.

Kauffman, Draper L., Jr. *Futurism and Future Studies: Developments in Classroom Instruction.* Washington, D.C.: National Education Association, 1976. 60 pages. Paperback. $3.50.

Kauffman, Draper L., Jr. *Teaching the Future: A Guide to Future-Oriented Education.* Palm Springs, CA: ETC Publications, 1976. 298 pages. Paperback. $7.95.

Nelson, Doreen G. *City Building Education Program: Architectural Consultant Edition.* NP: Center for City Building Educational Programs, 1975. 111 pages. Paperback. $11.95.

Newitt, Jane, ed. *Future Trends in Education Policy.* Lexington, MA: Lexington Books, D.C. Heath & Co., 1979. 142 pages. Hardbound. $15.95.

Rubin, Louis. *Educational Reform for a Changing Society.* Boston, MA: Allyn and Bacon, 1978. 215 pages. Hardbound. $16.95.

Rubin, Louis, ed. *The Future of Education: Perspectives on Tomorrow's Schooling.* Boston, MA: Allyn and Bacon, 1975. 213 pages. Hardbound. $14.95.

Rust, Val D. *Alternatives in Education: Theoretical and Historical Perspectives.* Beverly Hills, CA: SAGE Publications, 1977. 238 pages. Paperback. $8.95.

Shane, Harold G. *Curriculum Change Toward the 21st Century.* Washington, D.C.: National Education Association, 1977. 184 pages. Paperback. $6.00.

Shane, Harold G. *The Educational Significance of the Future.* Bloomington, IN: Phi Delta Kappa Educational Foundation, 1973. 115 pages. Paperback. $4.55.

Sullivan, Edward A. *The Future: Human Ecology and Education.* Palm Springs, CA: ETC Publications, 1975. 154 pages. Hardbound. $8.95.

Toffler, Alvin, ed. *Learning for Tomorrow: The Role of the Future in Education.* New York: Vintage. 423 pages. Paperback. $2.95.

Wagschal, Peter H., ed. *Learning Tomorrows: Commentaries on the Future of Education.* New York: Praeger, 1979. 164 pages. Hardbound. $19.95.